EAT IT
ANYWAY

EAT IT
ANYWAY

FIGHT THE
FOOD FADS,
BEAT ANXIETY
AND EAT
IN PEACE

Eve Simmons & Laura Dennison

FOR KATH AND TEENA, WHO BROUGHT ME BACK TO LIFE – EVE

TO GRANDAD GEORDIE, WHO SADLY PASSED AWAY BEFORE HE GOT TO SEE THIS BOOK PUBLISHED – LAURA

An Hachette UK Company
www.hachette.co.uk

First published in Great Britain in 2019 by Mitchell Beazley,
an imprint of Octopus Publishing Group Ltd, Carmelite House,
50 Victoria Embankment, London EC4Y 0DZ
www.octopusbooks.co.uk

Text copyright © Eve Simmons & Laura Dennison 2019
Design and layout copyright © Octopus Publishing Group 2019

Distributed in the US by Hachette Book Group, 1290 Avenue of the Americas,
4th and 5th Floors, New York, NY 10104

Distributed in Canada by Canadian Manda Group, 664 Annette St, Toronto,
Ontario, Canada M6S 2C8

ISBN 978-1-78472-580-8

A CIP catalogue record for this book is available from the British Library.

Printed and bound in Great Britain.

10 9 8 7 6 5 4 3

Editorial Director: Eleanor Maxfield
Senior Designer: Jaz Bahra
Designer: Geoff Fennell
Senior Editor: Leanne Bryan
Copy Editor: Clare Sayer
Illustrator: Laura Dennison
Cover Photography: Kay Lockett
Production Manager: Caroline Alberti

DISCLAIMER

All reasonable care has been taken in the preparation of this book but the
information and advice contained in this book are intended as a general
guide. This book is not intended to replace treatment by a qualified practitioner.
Neither the authors nor the publishers can be held responsible for claims arising
from the inappropriate use of any remedy or dietary regime. Do not attempt
self-diagnosis or self-treatment for serious or long-term conditions before
consulting a medical professional or qualified practitioner. Do not begin any
dietary regime or undertake any self-treatment while taking other prescribed
drugs or receiving therapy without first seeking professional guidance.
Always seek medical advice if any symptoms persist.

CONTENTS

CONTENTS

INTRODUCTION

The definition of "healthy eating" has been chewed up, spat out and redigested enough times to make Joe Public give up and seek out their nearest branch of McDonald's. Our mindless obsession with eating "right" is such that we're now more concerned about what our Instagram followers think of a poorly lit picture of our dinner than we are of that food's effect on our own palate. Or, indeed, our happiness. We seem to be living in a time where we no longer eat with our hearts, emotions or heritage – but with our waistlines (and our followers) in mind.

We're taking a bet that the reason you were drawn to this book in the first place is because you've already got a shelf full of health, food and diet books that you've underlined, dog-eared and studied time and time again in a quest for "becoming the best you"...are we right? All with the philosophy that by shovelling a few more overpriced avocados into your day, your gut will reduce in size, your skin will clear up and all your problems will melt away along with the cellulite marring your thighs. Might we also assume that you're a little bored, like us, with the current conversation around food, especially the one aimed at women? It might comfort you to learn, then, that we too have felt the same way. We are prepared to offer you an alternative to those platefuls of vegetables that inundate your Instagram feeds. A book so matter-of-fact and concerned with how you can repair your fragile love affair with food, it could quite possibly change your life.

Want to know a secret that the health and diet world doesn't want you to know about? You can't tell how healthy a person is just by looking at their size. Want to know another? There is no such thing as "bad" or "naughty" food. Okay, okay, here's one more, just for luck: gaining weight or being fat might not actually be the worst thing in the entire world, as society would have you believe.

Enter...us! Two journalists who crashed into the culinary world with a website called Not Plant Based, aimed at those who felt neglected by the food and health industry and who were seeking some sort of salvation. Not Plant Based grew in popularity (much to our surprise) by pioneering a fresh method of "dieting", which involves only one simple, golden rule: eat what you like, and don't worry about it. It's a way of eating that is delicious, free of "guilt" and requires a hell of a lot less money spent in health food shops. A lifestyle in which your mental health is paramount and the only expectations are the ones you may – or may not – assign to yourself. It's a diet where gluten is not the bloat-inducing devil, but instead a treasured ingredient critical to the spongy deliciousness of so many of our beloved recipes. A meal plan that involves plenty of dairy – which, by the way, is your bones' best friend – a helping of protective fat and, of course, a bag full of sugar. Best of all, our approach comes recommended by dietitians, as demonstrated by the medical professionals who offer their scientific support.

While we've never claimed to be experts within the field of nutrition ourselves, during our years of research and through speaking to numerous dietitians, doctors, specialist researchers and psychologists, we've absorbed a wealth of extensive knowledge that is sourced from the very best minds. They all tell us that good physical health begins with good mental health. Feeling good about yourself, being confident in your size and caring less about your eating behaviours are the only #goals we encourage; we believe this can be achieved by taking the "everything in moderation" approach. Engaging with your body and respecting your physical and emotional self is key. As survivors of eating disorders, we have a deep understanding of dangerous deprivation and have spent a shameful amount of time worrying, obsessing and criticizing ourselves over our food choices, before finally reaching the conclusion that there really was – and is – nothing to worry about. We're here to argue that good mental health is to food is what gluten is to bread, what cheese is to wine, what ice cream is to jelly: crucial.

The pages of *Eat It Anyway* will line your stomach in preparation for the millions of meals that await you. With help from scientists, psychologists and dietary experts, we fight the food fads and educate you away from redundant worries – all to enable you to eat in peace.

If you're already a fan of our website, you can expect the same (humble brag) quality content with extra servings of *je ne sais quoi* peppered throughout to enhance your desire for non-bullshit advice about food. Some of the nation's best-loved cooks will lend a floury hand too, providing you with an extensive menu of extra-special recipes to try out. How could you resist attempting the Hairy Bikers' Chicken and Wild Mushroom Pie? Or a slice of

Ruby Tandoh's favourite loaf of bread? Even if you're not a culinary goddess, we at least plan to make you hungry enough to open that drawer full of takeaway menus.

In a world where access to specialist treatment for serious mental health conditions, such as eating disorders, is limited, we hope this book can go some way to fill that gaping hole. Having both witnessed the destructive and agonizing storm that eating disorders bring down upon families, friends and individuals of all ages, we are all too aware of the desperate need to climb out of it. While we can't promise to drag you fully out of that darkness, we aren't afraid to jump in there with you. In our experience, that helps – if only a little.

The essence of this book partly lies with our unwavering commitment to brutal honesty, but mostly because we are irritated. Irritated by the abundance of wellness advocates and "health coaches" who, with their mindful eating guides and hyperbolic Instagram captions, suggest that the resolution for eating disorders is to practise self-love mantras in front of the mirror and spend ten minutes fingering a chocolate bar. So throughout the pages of this book you'll find plenty of pithy, witty jibes at the clean eating brigade, laughing in the face of their lacklustre cauliflower pizzas. But seriously though, the reason we make jokes is because the gritty reality of the consequences of their actions on our lives and the lives of those who love us are too painful to face without the buffer of humour. If you think about it, it's not funny at all really. Regular bone density scans (because half of all women with anorexia will develop osteoporosis) are not funny. Being confined to a hospital room while your boyfriend celebrates his 24th birthday with your circle of friends is not funny. Infertility at the age of 26 is not funny. Waking every morning at 4am to the violent wretches of the patient in the room next to you is not funny. A collection of sore, purple bruises on an arm plagued by daily blood tests is not funny. And being haunted by a terror that, if you're not careful, it may well play out all over again, is definitely not funny. That, my friends, is the brutal, putrid, life-destroying reality of eating disorders. If having a selection of medical professionals informing you of the risk of imminent heart attack can't make you reach for the cereal box, a self-love e-zine probably isn't going to either. We don't mean to come across as dismissive. Of course body positivity and worldwide acceptance of diverse bodies is crucial for a harmonious society and good mental health, but they aren't the answer to eating disorders.

For most, eating disorders are nothing to do with body image. Nor are they about food, exercise or "willpower". By their very definition, eating disorders are serious, clinical, mental illnesses, which arise as a result of an unresolved emotional vulnerability or trauma. They can occur at any time, and to anyone. Fussy eater or not. There are various theories, and increasing evidence suggests a powerful genetic predisposition, leading to the three-pronged factor theory: first, there may be a genetic or biological vulnerability; next comes a environmental "trauma" – abuse, death of a loved one or perhaps just a constant feeling of difference at school. Finally, there's an all-important trigger that delivers the fuel for the combination of messiness to combust and eventually, at a significant point in time, catch alight. Said trigger could be anything from a relationship breakdown, a few nasty Facebook comments, or, of course, a foray into fad diets. The eating disorder then acts as a mightily efficient way to bypass complicated and painful emotions and presents a golden opportunity to seize control. Only, you're not in control of course, and prising that practised "protective" regime from your nerve-wracked hands is increasingly impossible. Until it is possible.

We've met girls who survived off cough sweets for their entire university education; others whose battles rage on ten years after their single, unforgivably unhelpful, GP appointment. Women who have been unwell with anorexia since the age of 13 – and who are now aged 65. All too often we neglect to see this condition for what it truly is: a serious illness that ultimately kills. When a collection of kind doctors informed Eve that if she failed to eat appropriately and gain a modest amount of weight she would be forced to live – for the foreseeable future – in a psychiatric hospital, she spent the night before the proposed admission date in an "over my dead body" mindset. She sought to make one last-ditch attempt to keep on the (semi) sane side of the hospital. Yet, she still rejected an extra scoop of ice cream – and wasn't yet full. She wanted to do anything necessary to keep out of hospital, but simply couldn't.

By contrast, we have also met women (and men) who have lived their entire lives uncomfortable in bigger bodies and who are trying to heal emotional wounds by overfilling their stomachs. We've seen people lose their teeth to bulimia and their souls to the pain of not feeling "good enough" at their eating disorder.

While the carb-shunning bloggers and the self-appointed nutritionopaths may not have caused either of our eating disorders, they certainly didn't help. Our life-threatening conditions went disguised, unnoticed and rejected by those in a position to help. They granted our disordered thoughts the permission to grow and multiply, reinforcing the habitual, restrictive pathways that eating disorder treatment will help you to break. Worst of all, the very behaviours that were destroying our health were justified to the outside world *because* they were "healthy".

There's a profound lack of substantial and reliable nutritional information in the world of food and (sharp inhale) "wellness". It's an unfortunate truth that the next generation of dieters will rely largely on the filtered Instagram stories of self-professed "personal trainers" for their nutritional guidance, rather than dietetic experts. To eat with our animal instincts is not considered as important as the UK's leading dietitians argue it to be. Isn't that dreadful? Like, just really, really sad?

What a terrible shame it is that the simple, cheap ingredients we've bought at the local supermarket for generations are being vilified – especially given that, when you look at the facts, there really is nothing for most people to be afraid of.

After decades of Atkins, Cambridge, South Beach, Dukan and now Plant-Based, and with little change to our nation's levels of obesity, you'd think that we'd have got the message by now. Despite experts preaching the same sensible message: "eat a balanced diet in moderation", each and every fad diet or "health" trend picks up as much steam as the last – and has us reading their books, replicating their dinner plates and buying their "energy balls". Isn't it about time you saved your money for things that you actually enjoy?

Since starting our website back in 2016, we've had countless conversations with some of the best medical professionals, dietitians and doctors there are, and as a result we've finally cracked the secret to your edible harmony. Surprisingly, it's got nothing to do with the food you're eating. We've concluded that central to all mealtimes should be unapologetic pleasure, rather than elitist superfoods. In fact, it transpires that there's actually no need to intellectualize every mouthful or compensate for the previous night's four-course dinner with a half-marathon the next day. Not only does a comforting plate of buttery pasta make you happy on a miserable day, but a good, hearty portion of carbohydrates is actually GOOD for you.

Any dietetic expert will tell you that the brain is your second stomach. The contextual cues regarding our food choices are endless, and distinguishing the emotional and intellectual from the purely physical is pretty impossible. Added to the internal "what do I want to eat?" battle is the endless flow of marketing, advertising and social media messages congratulating us on that perfectly photographed bowl of granola and shunning us for chowing down on a couple of slices of toast.

The recent onslaught of restrictive, faddy diets disguised as "healthy lifestyles" has unfortunately promoted the notion that a daily portion of chia seeds washed down with a blended green concoction will catapult you to superhero levels of health. However, Ursula Philpot, dietitian and senior lecturer at Leeds Beckett University, finds this "one size fits all" approach worrying. She uses the example of the now-glorified vegetable kale. "Watercress is actually more nutrient-dense than kale, but people are buying kale because it's seen as something magical due to its great PR."

Isn't it about time you enjoyed a chunk of the filthiest chocolate mud cake imaginable? Like, actually, really enjoyed it, without the inevitable guilt gates immediately flooding open? Isn't it about time you put your mental health first and attributed your worth to YOU and not the number of calories you consume on any given day? It's been a while, huh?

Our own turbulent relationships with both food and anxiety and our learning of countless others who tell a similar story led us to realize just what is possible when food exists without fear. Laura's called time on her six-year-long fight with bulimia since recognizing that anxiety, depression and feelings of inadequacy were at the root of her food fixations.

As for Eve, she's tackled her anxieties head-on – and, as it turns out, the only thing she was truly scared of was herself. Four years on and nothing seems quite as scary any more – least of all food.

Forget the picky eating, ditch the [enter trendy name here] diet and sod the "shoulds" and "should nots". Life's too short to skip dessert or opt for courgetti. Instead, grab your spoon, because within the pages of *Eat It Anyway*, nothing is off the table.

LAURA'S STORY

Growing up I don't remember gold stars being handed out in exchange for good behaviour in my house, but I do remember KitKats in abundance. I remember mashed potato thick with lumps, mixed together with strips of Cheddar cheese and Heinz tomato spaghetti straight from the tin. I remember squashed sandwiches with real butter and Billy Bear shaped ham slices. My childhood in Dudley – a large town in the UK's Midlands known for pioneering an undesirable accent – and my fondness for carbs and gluten has given me an unbreakable love for junk food that I think will last until my dying days. No oatmeal in the nursing home for me thanks, just bring me mac 'n' cheese...with extra cheese, please. Oh, and a beer.

When I really think about it, every tummy-warming memory I have garnered throughout my life is in some way linked to food. I couldn't tell you what my cousin's wedding dress looked like, but I could tell you that there was a help-yourself pick-and-mix stand near the bar. I couldn't tell you what happened on my best friend's

21st birthday night out – perhaps in part due to the amount of vodka lemonades I'd necked – but I could tell you that I had cheesy chips with barbecue sauce afterward – and that it was fucking good.

Although I was a melancholic and worried child – the sort to fret about global warming every time I cleaned my teeth – I grew up unable to identify this aggressive angst as anything other than "complaining" or "moaning", when in reality I have always suffered with episodes of extreme anxiety and mild depression. I remember going to see a counsellor in college, after I'd spent weeks in tears and days unable to get out of bed, only for her to tell me that my "depression" wasn't actually depression. Imagine that: a counsellor with no real medical background telling me that my mental health concerns were false, instead of referring me to a specialist. A couple of weeks after my last session with this woman was when I went on my first diet – being the incredibly vulnerable young duck that I was.

Food makes me happy. It's the one thing I have always been able to turn to whenever I have felt lacking in love or attention, and it's also how I celebrated when those needs were fully met. Food has held my hand when boys I fancied didn't fancy me back, it was the salve to heal the wounds left behind when I didn't get into my first choice of university and it was a constant when my family life was struggling. Unfortunately, this great, edible love of mine soon became my Achilles heel.

I was 16 when a man first made a comment about my weight, and that comment was that I had put on weight. I was a five-foot-seven, athletic teenager, and even though I'd never bought a piece of clothing beyond a size 10, I had no reason to doubt this man when he cautioned me, given the big watery wisdom in his eyes. I went home, stripped down to my underwear, pushed out my new-found gut and let the realization that I was fat (I wasn't) sink in and infect my brain. My heart crashed to the floor with a mighty thud along with all my goals, dreams and self-esteem. Not only did

I have to worry about boys and acne, but now I had to worry about calories and the number on the scales too.

I tackled my first diet the way I tackle most things, head-on and with both enthusiasm and naivety. I was totally uneducated about food and began restricting the amount I ate over a month until I lost a significant amount of weight. Coupled with a gruelling workout schedule, I became exhausted, grey and unhappy – but most importantly to me at that time, thin. I yearned for an alternative to going hungry all the time, and one day experimented with making myself sick. To my surprise and regret, I was pretty good at it. Now I could eat everything at my disposal and just empty it all down the toilet! Can you imagine my delight?

Little did I know that bulimia would evolve into a monster far greater and far more aggressive than anything I had ever experienced before. I hurtled out of control, losing friends, not leaving my room and spending all my free time and money on food so that I could throw it up again – sometimes I would perform this routine up to six times a day. I'd make myself sick and dabble with laxatives in an effort to break away from the bingeing I'd do when my body grew tired of starvation. Bulimia switched from something "I'd just try to see if it worked" to something that was completely ruining my life at a time when I should have been having fun and growing up stupidly. Because of this you can excuse me for wanting to punch the nearest wall when I see jokes thrown about on Twitter about bulimia being the "cheater's diet".

Memories of my happy childhood are now clouded by flashbacks to sessions spent staring into the pit of the toilet with my swollen cheek squished against the white plastic. Each time, I wouldn't stop until I'd thrown up so much that I could gargle the bile. I'm fully aware that this isn't a very nice image, which is why I kept schtum about my problem until the age of 21, when I finally plucked up the courage to tell my parents.

I managed to kick the bulimia over time, but this only exposed a previously masked binge eating disorder, which added an additional 2 stone to my frame since I was unable to purge the evidence. Each time I thought I'd destroyed the last fucking Horcrux, my eating disorder would once again rise from the ashes unscathed. I was unable to return to a "normal" way of eating after having bulimia for such a long time, and because I couldn't stop myself from eating, my body turned bloated and sore under the burden of having to regularly digest such enormous quantities of food. At this stage in my recovery, I think was at one of the lowest points in my life. I was miserable, and in my mind veering toward the most ugly thing I could think of at the time – being fat.

Recovering from a binge eating disorder left me vulnerable to yo-yo dieting again. In a bid to avoid adding fuel to my dormant eating disorder, I tried veganism, as I had seen on social media countless before and after photos of people who had shed tons of weight by turning to this "lifestyle". At this time losing weight was still the thing that I believed would "cure me". Don't get me wrong; I think veganism is a brilliant thing to do if done for ethical and environmental reasons, but I was simply using veganism as a way to keep my body small, and it became a dangerous shield for further disordered eating without the fear of anyone questioning me about it. My veganism lasted six months, even though I realized it wasn't for me a month in. Although I was fearful about being ostracized from a fairly "cultish" group, I'm proud to be able to fly the flag for others who have tried it and found that it didn't work for them either. When you have an eating disorder, veganism – or any other kind of restrictive diet – can be a dangerous thing.

Much like my attitude to my food choices today, when it came to weight management methods in my late teens, nothing was left unsampled. Carb-free, vegetarian, vegan, fat-free, Dukan, fasting, Atkins, "the alkaline way" – you name the diet, I tried it. As I dove fork-first into the brutal world of dieting, there began a new wave of remarketed diets known as "lifestyles". I'd buy all the books from all the unqualified bloggers with large Instagram followings, highlighting every other sentence, convinced that because these "meal plans" and "healthy recipes" weren't labelled as "diets", my obsessing over their food rules was totally normally. Of course I now realize that this was not the case, and I was simply using their "methods" as a way to disguise my eating disorder. But nothing worked – at least nothing helped me lose weight and keep it off, something that I never needed to do in the first place.

To enjoy food without receiving a pounding from an enormous meteorite of guilt feels foreign to me, but that is how I now eat through my life. After six years of juggling multiple eating disorders and fad diets, this new freedom is taking some getting used to.

I never thought that I would get to the point in my life where I could eat two bowlfuls of chicken mayo pasta for lunch and not think twice about it or feel the need to compensate with a run later – but I just did (I'm writing this right now with oily-mayo fingertips). I never thought that I could wake up in the morning content with not weighing myself. I never thought I could put on around 2 stone (I don't know exactly how much because I don't weigh myself any more) and feel happy with myself, knowing that my mind is brilliant and that my non-existent thigh gap does not detract from my worth. Most of all, I cannot begin to tell you how proud I am of myself for turning such a negative experience into a weapon to help others who are currently going through the same shit I did. In the world of eating disorders, there are few who are willing to openly talk about their struggles with bulimia, binge eating and laxative abuse, but I am pleased to be one of those to do so, because it's important for me to be the voice I wish the younger me had had.

My eating disorder story swills around my head often, and when I have the chance to think about the huge chunks of my youth

I lost to it, I can't help but feel crushed. As my friends were learning how to socialize, roll joints and strawpedo bottles of Lambrini, I was learning the calorie count of every item in the nearest vending machine. Although I do indulge in regret at times, the thing that makes me even more upset is the thought of others experiencing the same mental health issues that I did in secret, without any help, and imprisoned by the same embarrassment I had felt.

If you had told me, before beginning Not Plant Based, that I'd be co-writing a book telling people how they can eat everything after living with bulimia and binge eating disorder, I'd have laughed in your face. Never throughout my years with an eating disorder did I think I would be able to enjoy food the way I can now, the way I used to as a child: selfishly and unashamedly. I can't wait for this book to help you do the same.

Since I never received any professional treatment for my eating disorder, my recovery began with our website, Not Plant Based – a small germ planted in the big, wide online. During my research in the build-up to its launch in September 2016, I watched a BBC documentary called *Clean Eating's Dirty Secrets*, in which the presenter Grace Victory (who you'll meet later in the book) debunked 2016's healthy eating trends, namely "clean eating", and explained how they could potentially be harmful to those who followed them. One of the people she interviewed was Not Plant Based's other half Eve; I got in touch with her and, well, here we are.

I often wonder whether, had I met Eve sooner and been lucky enough to have the support of someone who was going through the same shit as me during my teens, or had access to a book like this one, there would even be a story of mine to write.

EVE'S STORY

From the burger juice that dribbled down my chin on my first date with my boyfriend, to the Tupperware of chicken soup that Mum forced upon me every time I went back to university, food is the staple, vital ingredient within the recipe of my life. Each cherished memory kick-starts a craving; every moment of joy has an aftertaste. Food was always a friend, a confidante and an endless pleasure source (not in a weird way).

When acute anxiety struck at the age of 15, I worried about the onset of schizophrenia; my potential propensity to commit murder; whether or not life was in fact one big, never-ending dream; whether I was human in body but frog in spirit (you get the idea)... but NEVER food.

"I could never be anorexic," I used to chime, "I just love food too much."

Well, that was before the world discovered Facebook. And Instagram. And wellness bloggers. As it turns out, all it took was one demanding job in the fashion industry, bidding farewell to my family home and an avid interest in "health" blogs to undo an entire lifetime of carefree eating. I went from five-course tasting menus (with wine pairings) to drinking stock cubes in hot water for lunch in a matter of months. As my weight plummeted to near-fatal levels and I averaged a panic attack a week at dinner times, the self-inflicted "diet" I'd been experimenting with morphed into something a whole lot more complicated. Mostly because, no matter what the doctors told me, I couldn't stop. Well, until I was locked up in a mental hospital and forced to consume my required amount of calories every day, or else, that is.

What I wasn't aware of at the time was the detrimental effect of starvation on the brain – never mind the body. If you're unfortunate enough to go without carbohydrates for months on end, the brain is starved of essential sugars, making it perpetually exhausted. Bread was off limits from the minute I decided to go "healthy". This proved to be a particularly idiotic move considering that according to NHS guidelines starchy foods such as potatoes, bread, rice, pasta and cereals should make up just over a third of the food you eat. Apparently, the golden rule of eating "healthily" is, in short, that there are no rules and, as the old saying goes, a little bit of what you fancy really does do you good. The main dietitian-recommended diet, I've learned, involves eating plenty of starchy foods, vegetables, fruits, nuts, fish, lean meat and plant oils. So, the fashionista who thought she was being clever surviving off measly bowls of chopped-up fruit and veg was, in hindsight, pretty bloody stupid.

Not that I would have been receptive to anything other than the toned tummies of my trusted Instagrammers in my time of desperate need. The "wellness" warriors were the source of all my answers and, what's more, they were the only ones who truly understood my desire to "eat right". I owed them everything. They were the ones who showed me that I COULD eat pizza after all, providing the base was made from cauliflower. Sweet treats weren't off limits either; who needs sugar for sweetness and butter for moisture when sweet potatoes and half a banana do the trick just fine? I always wondered why no one ever ate my (rancid) sweet potato brownies.

Before you could even say "unrefined sugar", I was deemed unfit to care for myself by a team of medical professionals and was threatened with a section order under the Mental Health Act, unless I volunteered to be admitted as an inpatient to the eating disorders unit of a London psychiatric hospital. Suddenly, I had no choice but to eat the sustenance from which I was pathologically abstaining. Largely because there was a six-foot-four ex-prison guard sitting opposite me, glaring into my soul every breakfast, lunch and dinner. Can you guess what my prescribed diet consisted of? Protein, carbohydrates, fats, fruits and vegetables – in intricately calculated, balanced proportions. And not a chia seed in sight.

Within four weeks, my bones miraculously stopped clicking every time I got out of bed. I finished reading an entire book for the first time in months. I was able to engage in meaningful conversations with my friends and family without zoning out into oblivion every seven seconds. Bath time was an indulgent luxury again – for too long it had been a painful obstacle course where it was almost impossible to bathe for longer than five minutes without bruising several of my bones. Finally, I could discard the four layers, two scarves and fur coat I'd worn every day – in September. I had energy to walk up more than one flight of stairs; play with a friend's dog; run up to my boyfriend when he came to visit me in hospital. I COULD DO A PROPER POO.

As my body's cravings for nourishment reduced, so too did my mind's. No longer was my brain consumed with thoughts of calories, fat, weight and what I would give for a big, fat tub of strawberry cheesecake ice cream. My body was getting what it wanted and, as far as my mind was concerned, there were now more important things to think about. A fuck-off, kick-ass surprise 60th birthday party for Mum, for example. Because, isn't that what life's all about?

I'm regretful that it took a hospital admission to a psychiatric ward to propel me to tackle the anxious disposition head-on. The eventual catastrophe followed years of pretending that the constant undercurrent of panic was part and parcel of being an adolescent... and then a student...and then a twenty-something.

The root of this anxiety, I now know, was death. Well, insecurity, a lack of confidence – and death. Said death came courtesy of my dad, four days before my 13th birthday. He'd been ill – to varying degrees – with cancer since I was seven years old. Although my wonderful parents had gone above and beyond to hide the 5am ambulances and chemotherapy drugs from my brother and me, much of my childhood was accompanied by a sense of uncertainty, the feeling of not being like other families and – at times – sheer terror. For an uncomplicated child, there's not much more terrifying than the death of one of your parents. So imagine, then, at a time when new parts of your body are randomly growing, that the very thing that you fear most in the world happens. If you think it's a case of, "it made me stronger!" and "the worst has happened and nothing will be as scary", you'd be wrong. It makes you fucking petrified of just about everything.

My dad dying didn't cause my eating disorder, by the way. From death day to eating disorder day I went through almost ten years of totally carefree eating, my food choices led entirely by either my desires, my social surroundings or both. Sure, the repercussions of watching a parent die after years of a relentless illness have left my coping strategies patchy, and I was perhaps dialled up a notch on my vulnerability scale, but I'm sure there are plenty of half-orphans (yep, it's a thing) out there who *haven't* developed an eating disorder. Perhaps, instead, it was being a shy child who never quite found her safety in friendship groups throughout secondary school that left me with damaging levels of insecurity. Maybe the sudden immersion as an adult into a world of lollipop-head models and perpetual dieter colleagues kick-started something that was sort of there all along. The most likely truth is, of course, that it was no single one of these factors that resulted in my starvation, but a combination of all three – and many more. What it wasn't, however, was the fault of food, or anything to do with my capacity to enjoy eating. Nor, I believe, was it really related to what I saw in the mirror. It's a seemingly counterintuitive phenomenon that I'm not alone in experiencing. As eating disorders psychologist Kimberley Wilson says: "For many women, eating disorders aren't anything to do with a desire to be thin but rather, somewhere along the way they have internalized a feeling of unworthiness, not being good enough, or not fitting in." The most heartbreaking part of my illness was that it needn't have gone that far. Just as easily as I did develop an eating disorder, I could quite easily have not. The pervasive toxicity that is diet culture and thinness was catapulted onto my radar at exactly the "right" time. I was confused, vulnerable, impressionable and desperate to belong. The challenge of thinness offered a convenient – and seemingly glamorous – distraction. Who has brain space to assess your entrenched terror of rejection from a new job or relationship when you're almost blind with hunger?

Yet, through clinging to this coping mechanism, I've disrupted the sanctity of a harmonious relationship with food quite possibly for the rest of my life. All for the sake of an (entirely unnecessary) diet. And having been on both sides of the road, let me assure you; being skinny is SO not worth it.

Now, four years on, and having finally stripped back all the paintwork and confronted my childhood terrors once and for all, nothing seems quite as frightening any more. My brain is grateful for the breathing space and now regularly rewards me with experiences of genuine enjoyment – as opposed to its previous status: permanent panic.

Ever since, I have pledged to dedicate my journalistic skills to informing whoever wants to listen (and a few who don't) about the menace that is inaccurate, unhelpful health food information, in a bid to protect fellow worriers. My crusade was further strengthened by the stories of other silent but incredible sufferers I met along the way, one of whom was Laura. We talked for hours about gluten-free garbage, therapy and posh food bloggers (who will remain nameless) over Pret cappuccinos. The rest, as they say, is history.

Since then, as part of Not Plant Based, I've travelled the length and breadth of the Twittersphere on a mission to do the best I can to beat this beastly mental illness. From calling out the anxiety-provoking #nutribollocks, to finding – and telling – inspiring stories of recovery, to hosting the UK's very first Supper Club Support Group for Anxious Eaters. Along the way have been several revelations that have changed the course of my food-related thoughts forever. Conversations with just about every sufficiently qualified dietary expert that I came across arrived at the same fundamental "rule" for a healthy diet:

Eat whatever you want and don't worry about it. It works (and tastes) much better than cauliflower pizza – trust me.

"The Mini Fast! How skipping breakfast could make you slim!"

BREAKFAST

BUSTING BREKKIE MYTHS WITH THE HELP OF AN EXPERT

You have to feel sorry for the morning meal; it gets a lot of stick. For years, bloggers, magazines and shouty tabloids haven't been able to make up their minds as to whether breakfast is good for you or, indeed, the devil itself. Rumours about whether you should skip it altogether, swap it for warm water and a slice of lemon (yuck) or eat as much as you can within 30 minutes of waking have got everyone's heads muddled with conflicting advice. To tell you the truth, we at Not Plant Based are sick to death of the morning headaches when confronted with all the bonkers information out there, so we've decided to straighten out the big, fat breakfast lie once and for all.

Even before writing this chapter, we suspected that the truth about breakfast may lie somewhere between trusting your own body and eating whatever and whenever the hell you want in the morning...not the half a grapefruit that a health blogger told you to eat. Turns out we were right.

One of the big breakfast myths flying around picks on the scary stuff: carbs. Some cranks on the internet have moulded a carb-based rule out of thin air: "If you're going to eat carbs, eat them for breakfast so you have all day to work them off." Sounds, legit, right?

Wrong. There is no evidence to suggest that eating more carbohydrates at certain times of day will affect your weight. It is, in fact, total energy intake over a week that makes the real difference to body weight. If you choose to restrict carbs at a meal, the resulting calorie deficit could help you lose weight, but it will not necessarily be down to which meal you skip them at.

When you think of carbs at breakfast, what comes to mind? Toast with lashings of butter? An almond croissant? A toasted teacake? Or is it cereal, a food product that hasn't been able to escape "health" marketing over the years? Ever heard of the Special K diet? Where you can drop a dress size in two weeks by swapping two of your meals for a 30-g portion of Special K? Of course you have, you cereal (oops) dieter, you. If you have ever considered embarking on this diet, please be aware that 30g is a tiny portion to sustain an adult. Dietitian Ursula Philpot explains that manufacturers can only put one portion size on their packaging, so this leads to portion suggestions that are not useful or helpful for most people (30g is a portion for five-year-olds). It's a suggested portion size left over from when Brits ate cereal as part of a buffet style breakfast, to be followed by eggs, toast, bacon. Then, 30g is fine, but not as a stand-alone adult portion. If you look at cereal packaging from countries who mainly eat just cereal for breakfast (for example the Swiss) they will be 60g+.

If you can't stomach carbs in the morning, what should you be eating for breakfast? How about the "you should only have fats, proteins and veg for breakfast" rule? Should we all instead be eating spinach, avocado and eggs once the sun rises? Firstly...who is making up these rules? That's what we want to know. The truth is, as we said before, that it's overall calories across the week that counts, not having specific macros at specific times.

An even scarier breakfast rule that we've come across recently is "training fasting". This is where you do your cardio for the day, before you have eaten anything, which seems daft considering the scientific need for energy to create energy. Although training fasting has become very popular recently, no doubt thanks to the internet, unless you prefer not to eat prior to exercise, there is little advantage in doing so. For most people, having a bit of fuel on board usually means you can train harder and better. Eating adequate carbs and protein after exercising is also key to altering body composition, as is overall training and calories across a week. Skipping breakfast and then training will often create a huge energy deficit and low blood sugar levels that then catch up with you later in the form of unplanned eating or overeating.

It feels like breakfast has taken a worse beating by wellness and the internet than any other meal throughout the day. We've been led to believe that if we don't start our day in the "right way", by not eating the healthiest breakfast possible, we are destined for 12 hours of torture and a lifetime of steady weight gain and unhappiness.

Of course, this book is here to tell you that this is not the case.

Whether you love eating Cheerios for breakfast or struggle to eat as soon as you wake up, that's fine because everyone is different. For some "the most important meal of the day" *is* breakfast, but for others it's lunch, and for the rest it could be dinner. Research shows that growing children perform much better with breakfast inside them, but with us adults it's individual. Some people prefer not to eat until lunchtime, and provided they are fit and well that is absolutely no problem.

RECOVERING FROM AN EATING DISORDER?

Eve explains why you shouldn't skip breakfast.

Hands up if you've ever settled for an "on-the-go" banana, citing unfathomable levels of busyness as the reason for your calorie deficit? For the average, happy eater this inevitable morning mishap merely leads to an extra tummy growl at around 11am, and perhaps the purchase of a multipack of cereal bars in case the worst should happen again...

For us disordered eaters, however, going meal-less is so much more of a thing. Even now, almost four years into recovery, when I skip breakfast the cracks in the window expand into a narrow gap: still tight, but large enough for the whimpers of anorexia to seep through. I don't mean that every time I'm too busy for breakfast I am suddenly overwhelmed by an urge to ram laxatives down my throat or drown my sad, lunchtime salad with overflowing tears. It's just a little bit harder to *not* think about food. It's exactly this preoccupation that eating disorder recovery kindly mutes, allowing space for other, more important thoughts such as, "Am I too old to wear a velour crop top?" and "how long can I stay in bed before I have to empty the washing machine?".

Eating disorder or no eating disorder, in the age of super-speedy electric unicycles and "raw till 4" diets, skipping breakfast, once in a while, is unavoidable. Yet if you struggle with your relationship with food, it's imperative – for your mental health – that you *ignore* all the circulating nutrition nonsense that is 90 per cent likely to be untrue or inaccurate. Instead, stick to what scientists and psychologists *do* know as facts: breakfast is nourishing, delicious and – if your friendship with food is patchy – pretty invaluable.

According to Ursula, establishing a regular eating pattern – including breakfast – is fundamental for successful recovery. If you are a low weight, regular eating is particularly key because if you go for long periods without eating, the body may begin to use up your reserves, which can cause more weight loss or compromise organ function. But even for those who aren't in the process of regaining lost body weight, the psychological role of breakfast is still crucial – especially if your hunger and fullness signals have gone a bit higgledy-piggledy. "Breakfast is really important for reinstating hunger signals and stopping people feeling overfull," says Ursula. "The aim is to minimize risks of restricting, bingeing and overeating, and by eating three regular meals a day you're giving yourself the best chance."

Consultant psychologist Kimberley Wilson, who specializes in disordered eating, sees breakfast as an essential part of the puzzle for people who are "coming back to food", explaining that it's about rigidity and structure. "Breakfast and the regularity of mealtimes can be a framework on which to hang your anxiety around food. You know there is a meal coming, you know what it consists of – therefore you know what is coming and, in theory, as time goes on you'll be less frightened. It takes some of the fretting and deliberation out of how to eat." Kimberley's suggestions certainly ring true for me. After surviving all morning on a meagre handful of blueberries for the best part of three years, the predictability of my trusted bowl of Weetabix was an achievable breakfast ritual. After eating the same bowl – with exactly the same amount of full-fat milk and banana slices – every morning for eight weeks, the sting of breakfast diminished and eventually I was able to make the progression to porridge.

"If you've had chronic eating disorders," Kimberley explains, "your trust in your body becomes completely eroded. So skipping breakfast can mean you are hungry, but aren't able to detect those signals. Often people don't believe they can trust their body so it's easier to stick to a regular pattern." Kimberley points to the example of a client who, although she has regained her weight and is now at the end of her treatment, panics desperately about skipping breakfast for fear that old habits may strike. I feel you, girl. But Kimberley says there is a way in which it is possible to be overcome with life's busy pressures and still focus on recovery.

"For just three days see what it's like to trust your satiety and hunger signals. The goal is to think, food is food and to trust your body without needing people to schedule your meals for you. If at any point you notice the petulant bastard in your brain sticking his/her oar in, the following day – have breakfast.

"As for the rest of the population, is breakfast a good way of preventing disordered eating patterns? And does it reduce your risk of succumbing to an unhealthy, unbalanced diet? In theory, yes. "For most people," Ursula explains, "skipping breakfast is going to make you hungrier throughout the day. Short-term energy stores will be run down overnight, so they need replenishing in the morning. If you don't replace them, you'll get hungry."

While there are people with chronic health problems who may be advised to skimp on breakfast, for most, a morning meal is the most healthful habit to adhere to post-slumber. And the majority of cultures worldwide begin their day with something to eat.

"We do have to value our own nutritional needs," says Kimberley, "but there is no need to skew one way or the other, it's about what is best for you. And if you have gone eight hours without food, then yes, breakfast is a good idea."

So, don't be weird; have breakfast. Taste it. Enjoy it. And, if you're feeling hard enough, try eating something *other* than a bowl of goddam Weetabix.

WHY NOT TO WEIGH YOURSELF EVERY MORNING

Laura uses her own previous obsession with weighing herself to try to convince you to frisbee your scales into the nearest bin.

Are you a once-a-weeker? A beginning of every day-er? Perhaps you're even partial to stepping on the scales a couple of times a day – once as soon as you wake and once before bedtime. Maybe after every meal? After every piece of toast? Or maybe you don't even bother at all, content instead with remaining firmly in the "numbers don't matter" camp.

Me? I was a self-confessed once-a-dayer back in my eating disorder days and, like most people, I'd always check in bright and early – as most scale-addicts do – before eating or drinking, stripping right down to my birthday suit. I was comforted by the sound of the scales clattering against the tiled bathroom floor and the physical lightness I felt as I watched the numbers decrease each day. I used to jot my weight on my bedroom wall in long, black columns of permanent marker. When I developed a penchant for binge eating later on in my eating disorder, I'd also have to write down the huge leaps up on the scales, sometimes 4–5lb a day. Devastated, I'd start a new column; soon enough my bedroom walls were pinstriped with a disorientating art exhibit of my poor mental health.

In late 2016 I took a giant step into the arena of self-help and destroyed my bathroom scales, sending them crashing into the abyss that is the communal bin outside my old block of flats (although I regretted my theatrical display as immediately as the glass shattered). Shit. How would I be able to maintain a stable weight now? How would I be able to tell if I'm getting a little chubby? I'll have to buy some new ones, I thought.

Weighing yourself exposes a complexity of issues, tricks and emotional breakdowns that extend far beyond stepping on to a white piece of plastic or a slab of glass. The existential dread many of us associate with the task seems to add yet more unneeded blows to our already vulnerable selves. It's a wonder we even bother...

Hang about, why do we even bother? Why was my immediate thought when I destroyed my scales that I couldn't function without them? Are we chasing after nothing more than a glorified number that has no actual significance to our health and how we feel? Are we chasing a holy grail that, in reality, is just a plastic party cup filled only with disappointment?

In short, yes.

Ultimately the aim should be not to weigh yourself at all. There's just no need to, unless you are someone who has been advised to lose weight for health reasons or, at the other end of the spectrum, someone in recovery for an eating disorder who is trying to gain weight (in both instances you should be monitored by a medical professional, of course).

To understand why weighing yourself is truly futile, it helps to get a little science-y. The human body, assuming you have one, tends to fluctuate naturally and healthily within a 2-kg band (around 4–5lb). As you know, we aren't scientists or qualified dietitians, so we'll allow Ursula to explain this bit...

WEIGHT IS MADE UP OF THREE DIFFERENT AREAS:
1. **FLESH WEIGHT,** which contains the likes of our bones, muscles and blood; these don't tend to change a lot.
2. **BODY FAT,** which changes over time but doesn't increase or decrease particularly rapidly.
3. **WATER AND SUGAR STORES.** Now these are the guys who are responsible for the short-term changes to your weight. So, if you gain a few pounds overnight and want to curl up in a ball and have a little cry, just consider that it is probably down to simple fluid changes within the body. Fluid changes that

could be altered by a whole manner of factors, including how hydrated you are, your calorie intake, how many carbs you've eaten and also your activity levels.

Feel better now? Good.

A better and more heartening gauge of whether you have put on weight or lost it is to ask yourself, "Do your clothes fit?" And more importantly, "how do you feel?" The latter question is the best indicator for how well you are nourishing your body. If you're worried about undereating, you should look out for the effects of starvation, which include a preoccupation with food, feeling cold, feeling anxious and feeling exhausted. Of course, if you are recovering from anorexia or an eating disorder and are required to regain lost weight, medical professionals will keep a strict eye on your weight. Regular weigh-ins are an essential part of your recovery and a close monitoring could quite possibly save your life.

If you're overeating, you're probably deep down already aware that you're doing it, and occasional overeating isn't the worst thing anyway. If you feel that, yes, those extra five Yorkshire puddings every Sunday, however delicious, have caused you to put on a little weight and if you're not happy with that, it's initially a good idea to ride out that feeling for a few days. This is because perceived weight gain is often to do with how you feel emotionally rather than any actual change. If after those few days you're still convinced of a change in your weight but you're also the sort to get fixated by the number on the scales, it might be useful to ask somebody else to check it for you. Ask somebody that you trust, tell them your weight band (those 2kg, remember?) and they can then check the scale without you even having to look.

What about measuring your body with a measuring tape? A lot of "healthy eating" blogs and publications have reinforced the idea that this is a better way to keep our health and bodies in check, but, actually, this can be just as much a slippery slope as weighing yourself. Anything to do with body checking and numbers can contribute to disordered eating and a disordered relationship with your body. The more body checking you do, the more miserable you tend to become.

Although I am still tempted to step back on the scales every once in a while, I now accept that my fixation on the numbers was an unhealthy way for me to interpret my own body and health. If ever I do spot a tempting set of scales, say in a friend's house, I may step on them and realize I've put on a few pounds...but the difference is that now I'll shrug and go eat a doughnut, because there's more to life. At one point weighing myself was a potential "trigger" for me to slip back into a pattern of destructive eating in order to achieve a pointless "goal weight", but now that I've allowed the dust to settle on my obsession, I feel more comfortable living my life unaware of how much I weigh.

At the time of writing this book and since starting our website, I have put on weight, yet I feel the best that I have in a very long time. This has made me realize that happiness and health are not altogether determined by the number on the scale but, more importantly, they are to do with caring for your mental health. To put on a little weight, to have a little cellulite and that wobble when you walk, isn't actually all that bad for your health.

I hope that, after reading this, you might follow my lead by tossing those scales in the bin and packing your measuring tape back into the sewing kit. Make yourself a brew and save the numbers for the sudoku in this morning's paper.

HOW TO SWAP YOUR CYBER BREAKFAST FOR ACTUAL FOOD

Have you ever had a cyber breakfast? Perhaps you had one this morning. A cyber breakfast – a term coined by us – is when you skip eating actual food and instead devour your Facebook, Twitter or Instagram feed as you run late for work. If you're anything like us – not that we enjoy admitting it – one of the first things you'll do when you wake up is check Instagram for the posts you've missed, the notifications on your latest selfie, or just to stalk that model who makes you feel really shit about yourself...are we right? Nothing like starting your day off with a healthy helping of self-doubt, eh?

Social media is a weird one, because there are lots of ways in which it can be used as a platform for good; what with fundraising, giving introverts a voice they never had in the real world and creating brands geared toward achieving real, positive change (cough cough, Not Plant Based). It can also be great for making cyber pals, like one of ours, Michael Zee, who runs the Instagram account @SymmetryBreakfast, which as you'd predict posts the perfectly symmetrical breakfasts he makes for himself and his partner Mark. He has been a big fan of Not Plant Based (for which we are extremely grateful) from the beginning. Michael has managed to create a beautiful and positive brand, using the fickle social media platform, and it's the perfect place to start when looking for inspiration for how to swap your cyber breakfast for actual real food. Since you're already on the web, take a look at his account and ogle American pancakes with thick-cut bacon, maple syrup, a wedge of orange; Palestinian za'atar, dried mint and sweet paprika with walnut sourdough toast; Parmesan Dutch puff with roasted heritage tomatoes, basil and plenty of black pepper; or Shanghai pork wontons in a delicious soup with crispy youtiao.

However, not every average Joe has time to make such edible masterpieces each morning – and Michael himself admits that his breakfasts haven't always been so glorious. "Growing up I remember eating a lot of Weetabix, but after I went to university breakfast became coffee and hand-rolled cigarettes." Nowadays, however, his morning meal is surely enough to get you nice and hungry for real-life food.

We, more than most, realize that social media can also be a consuming pit of despair, if overused or used in an inappropriate way, which is why we are more than keen to give you some social media relief in the morning.

Even though @SymmetryBreakfast has close to a million Instagram followers, that doesn't necessarily mean that Michael is immune to the shittier effects of social media either. "I've always believed and even said in my book that 'comparison is the death of joy', but I take my own advice with a pinch of salt. I am also deeply competitive, and it's incredibly hard not to look at some of my peers or other accounts with a large following and think 'I need to be doing that, or producing new content or merchandise or one of these cool partnerships'."

Since this digital world business is all relatively new to us, the studies into how social media negatively affects our mental health are few. But ask most people with an Instagram account and they will tell you how low it can make you feel. It's estimated, at the time of writing, that around 40 per cent of the world's population use social media and spend an average of two hours of their day using it – but we're guessing more. Think about it: immersing yourself for two hours a day (probably more) within a world that is superlative and expensive and glamorous when you feel you aren't any of those things is going to make you feel like you are worthless.

A study, published in the journal *Computers in Human Behavior*, found that people who use seven or more social media platforms were more than three times as likely to have high levels of general anxiety symptoms as those who use only up to two. A different study conducted in 2016 involving 1,700 people found a threefold risk of depression and anxiety among people who used the most social media platforms. Reasons for this included cyberbullying, feeling like time spent on social media is a waste and having a distorted view of other people's lives – Instagram is particularly awful for this last point.

Michael has advice for distancing yourself from social media in the mornings. "Start with the device you're using because it's the root of all your woes. I have switched off all notifications that don't come directly from a human being. You are addicted to your device telling you things. Stop it. My homepage only has apps that are directly linked with productivity or serve a function: Mail, Messages, Spotify, Calendar and McDonald's delivery. Everything else is on the second page or after."

Instagram and many other internet holes have been used to promote pro-ana content and stupid, stupid diet culture for years, which has made us anxious eaters feel like we are no good at the size we are right now. For someone with disordered eating (or an eating disorder) social media presents a cobweb-fine line between getting well and getting worse, and with unregulated support, the likelihood is that most of the time the latter will happen.

If you're a breakfast skipper but a social media fiend, our advice to you would be to use your time on social media to inspire your morning plate. Instagram has opened our square eyes to cuisines and cultural dishes we never would have been able to experience otherwise, and now all it takes is a simple google to get the recipe.

Michael explains: "Food on Instagram is definitely an eye-opener for thinking about where to go travelling. I've loved and cooked Mexican food at home for many years and we've finally decided to visit. I'm sure my current knowledge is only the tip of the iceberg, but making a mole or being given some cricket salt as a gift is what gives me the inspiration to research further and make something happen.

"I try to talk about a lot of positives in the world, different cultures, traditions, stories and recipes in a way that everyone can feel included. When @SymmetryBreakfast was in its infancy, I knew I wanted to make something that everyone could see a bit of themselves in; I think that's partially its success and why I have a truly global following."

Try setting aside at least 20 minutes a morning to feed yourself well – providing you're not one of those people that feels sick at the thought of eating in the morning. Treat this routine as self-care, and treat yourself to breakfasts outside the boring realms of Cheerios. Take a leaf out of Michael's book.

BRUNCH WITH CHEF DAN DOHERTY, FORMERLY OF DUCK & WAFFLE

We're all about making the most out of our meals and so the idea of combining two breakfast favourites – yogurt and eggs – is a compelling one that Dan has thankfully introduced us to.

TURKISH EGGS WITH YOGURT, CHORIZO, BUTTER AND MINT

I fell in love with this dish having first eaten it at Kopapa in Covent Garden. It was such a surprise to me, I couldn't imagine it working at all but, when I ate that first bite, it all made sense. That was the dish that inspired me to make this version. I use chorizo to infuse the butter and leave the meat in for a bit of texture. I recommend you serve it with toast, and lots of it, to mop up all those juices.

Serves 2

80g chorizo sausage, skinned and diced
50g butter
100g Greek yogurt
2 tablespoons white wine vinegar
4 eggs
bread, for toasting
sea salt flakes and freshly ground black pepper
4–5 fresh mint leaves, thinly sliced, to garnish

In a frying pan, lightly sauté the chorizo for a few minutes over a medium heat until it releases its natural oil. Add the butter and allow to melt and bubble together for 2–3 minutes, then turn off the heat and set aside.

Put the yogurt into a saucepan and gently warm through. Don't let it boil or it'll curdle and split – you want it to be warm, not hot.

To poach the eggs, bring a saucepan of water to the boil and add the white wine vinegar. Meanwhile, break the eggs into individual cups or ramekins. When the water is boiling use a spoon to create a whirlpool in the water. Slide the eggs one by one into the middle of the whirlpool. After 3 minutes, the eggs should be firm on the outside yet soft in the middle. Remove them from the pan and put them on a plate lined with kitchen paper to drain. Now is the time to toast your bread.

Divide the warm yogurt between 2 bowls and spoon the eggs on top. Using a spoon, lift the chorizo out of the frying pan and scatter it around each bowl, then divide all the butter from the pan between them. It looks like a lot of fat, but trust me – this is what it's all about.

Season with salt and pepper and sprinkle over the mint. Break into the eggs with the toast and allow all the components to just fall into one another.

"Dairy has been linked to a myriad of conditions including eczema, asthma and weight gain. And certain scientists have even linked it to breast and prostate cancer and diabetes."

– Daily Express

DAIRY

DON'T BE AFRAID TO MILK IT

Eve calls upon the dietetic experts and health gurus to uncover what the real deal is with the white stuff. Why do some of us drink milk at breakfast and do we even need it?

I've always pitied my friends who don't like the taste of milk. As far as I'm concerned, there's no better morning nourishment than a squeaky-clean bowl – fresh out the dishwasher – filled to the brim with crunchy cereal (it doesn't matter which one), drenched by one almighty splash of ice-cold milk. Usually semi-skimmed and occasionally accompanied by a handful of raisins.

As I entered my teens and my dairy palette matured, I discovered the simple delight of a tomato and Brie sandwich, which soon became my go-to lunch choice when the vending machine was out of roast chicken salad. Pretty soon into adolescence, my core friendship group consisted of 65 per cent of the Greek population of north London and so began a love affair with salty, gooey, barbecued halloumi. Oh, and then there was ice cream. As a conflicted, overdramatic teenager, I often wondered whether Ben & Jerry's was created with the sole purpose of providing communal merriment for my group of hormonal girlfriends. We were strategic about it, mind you. You had to get the flavour right. As hard as we tried to finish it, a tub of Phish Food always ended up half eaten, half neglected, usually resulting in a marshmallowy milk that eventually made it back into the freezer and stayed there until my older brother came home drunk and unearthed it.

When I was first struck by food anxiety, dairy was one of the first food groups on my "hit list". A plethora of websites (ever-reliable, of course) then informed me that cow's milk was pretty awful for your gut anyway and that it contained the "must-be-avoided-at-all-costs" ingredient: fat. Decision made. Needless to say, four years later, I'm still on a strict prescription of daily calcium tablets to account for the vital nutrients I starved my body of. And that's after the nurses spent six weeks feeding me mugs of full-fat milk to keep the old body functioning.

According to the NHS website, milk and dairy products are great sources of protein and calcium and are an important part of a young child's diet. Anything from yogurt to cheese, soured cream and soya milk (fortified with calcium) counts toward your intake of dairy, providing vital protein and calcium for cell renewal and bodily repair – as well as easing the absorption of other nutrients.

The breakfast debate has never been so heated – what with Instagram #breakfastgoals providing endless options for your morning meal. Is cereal still a "thing"? Should you chuck everything in a blender? Do you serve it in a glass jar or in vintage china? What the hell is a bloody chia seed? Well, according to historical evidence, there's a reason why milk and cereal have evolved as breakfast champions. Essentially, the aim of breakfast has always been to set you up until your next meal and keep you from feeling hungry during the morning's activities. As grains satisfy hunger for longer – and historically were pretty cheap – grain-based breakfasts have been typical since day dot. The first cold breakfast cereal, developed in the 1860s by an American vegetarian, was made from oatmeal and soaked in milk overnight. This cold, slushy gruel was later developed into granola-type cereals, with the addition of tastier ingredients such as flour and cornmeal[1]. Current thinking remains pretty much the same. According to the NHS, a healthy breakfast consists of whole grain or whole wheat cereals that are low in sugar and contain vital fibre and B vitamins. Both these are essential for your bodily functions and play a key part in reducing the risk of heart disease and type 2 diabetes.

Then came the discovery of vitamins in the 1910s and, with that, widespread milk mania. All of a sudden, Western civilization could ward off deficiency diseases such as scurvy, osteoporosis and hypertension with one simple ingredient: milk. Not only was the addition of milk a form of daily protection from illness, but workers found it kept them fuller for longer and it made the original oat nuggets a little easier on the old teeth.

Today, the Dairy Council of California recommends a big splash of the stuff – cold or hot – for the 8g of protein and nine essential vitamins and minerals packed into every cup[2]. The NHS advises much the same, and that we should seize the opportunity to add a nice pouring of calcium to our diet at breakfast time. The scientific arguments for milk in the morning are hotly debated and are probably down to historical tradition more than anything else. "It was, and still is, an easy way to consume a lot of nutrients in one go," Sarah Leyland, consultant osteoporosis nurse for the National

Osteoporosis Society, explains. Said nutrients include a few grams of protein; a generous helping of potassium; as well as vitamin D, vitamin A, several B vitamins, magnesium and, of course, calcium. We've all seen enough "Got Milk" ads to be well aware of the link between milk and calcium – but what actually is calcium?

Lifelong biology enthusiast Dr Robert Recker has found his professional home as head of the Osteoporosis Research Center at Creighton University, Omaha, Nebraska. He's spent the majority of his 40 years as a practising scientist in bone health and, most notably, investigating dietary and lifestyle choices that affect our bone health. "Calcium is a heavy metal, and has many roles in human physiology," Dr Recker says. "A prominent role is to precipitate onto collagen in bone to make bone as strong, pound-for-pound, as steel." Yep, thanks to calcium, our bones are literally as strong as steel. But it's not just about bones. "Low levels of serum-ionized calcium can precipitate seizures in vertebrates, including humans. Accordingly, vertebrates have mechanisms to safeguard the serum levels of calcium to protect against this potentially fatal problem." In other words, if our calcium levels drop too low, human beings could fall victim to life-threatening seizures.

We can't avoid losing a large percentage of calcium through excretion (pooing and peeing), but it's when this isn't replaced via diet that we may run into trouble. As Dr Recker plainly puts it: if we do not replace those losses, we cannot survive. And although it is possible to source calcium from vegetables such as kale, broccoli and spinach, the quantity – and quality – doesn't compare to the animal-based stuff.

"Calcium intake is very difficult on a vegan diet," he says. "Most vegetables contain very little calcium and those that contain plentiful calcium (spinach, for instance) are chemically combined with compounds like oxalate, making an insoluble salt that cannot allow the calcium to be absorbed." Don't get me wrong – leafy veg and soya milks (especially those that are fortified with calcium) are great alternatives, if you NEED an alternative. Dairy is an easy and obvious way of getting the calcium we need.

Of course, the journey to good health involves more than just a diet of dairy. It's exactly this mantra that's most important to senior nurse Sarah. As adults, our bodies require about 700mg of calcium per day (a typical glass of milk contains 125mg). As you get older, you're more at risk of hip fracture if you lack calcium in your diet. Yet, it's your overall, yearly platter that determines a body's ability to use nutrients effectively. "More and more, the research tells us that it is all about balance," Sarah says. "Nature has its way of saying you need to have things in balance. It's not about eliminating anything. As long as you're getting a broad range, you'll be fine." As for the school of thought that cow's milk = bad/acidic/gut devils, Sarah exposes such ideas for exactly what they are: myths.

What about the excess nasty chemicals in milk that some wellness bloggers warn against? Do they run wild in our bloodstream should the worse happen and we guzzle down more than the amount in two average-sized cappuccinos? Sarah and Dr Recker both agree that the body normally balances things out, excreting excess amounts in the urine. There's a reason why human beings – and most animals for that matter – are nourished with milk from almost the second they enter the universe. Be it tradition, evolution or science, the truth is, it really does work.

"Nature has made animal mother's milk essential in providing proper nutrition for infants," Dr Recker says. "Human evolution has been included in this. Thus, both cow's milk and human mother's milk are designed by nature to supply the nutrients for infants. All of the elements are there for nutrition: protein, sugar, trace elements, most vitamins, and so on."

Now, I enjoy a soya latte as much as the next person, mainly because the milk transforms into a gloriously nutty froth, providing an indulgent, sweet topping to a morning coffee. When it comes to breakfast, however, I will continue with my daily splash of cold milk, because my teeth, eyes, hair, muscles and bones are well and truly and utterly worth it.

WHY WE SHOULDN'T FEAR CHEESE

Laura justifies her own love of cheese and explains why you shouldn't feel bad if you can't always afford "good" cheese.

Sometimes – when I've nothing better to do – I think back to my restrictive days and fret over all the incredible meals that I missed out on in favour of my waistline. I bet if I sat down and really thought about it, I could calculate (near enough) to the gram how much cheese I missed out on over the years, given my current insistence on having it with almost everything I eat and my resistance of the stuff back when dieting was all I cared about.

Okay, I'm probably exaggerating a touch...but my point is that I really love cheese, and for someone who really loves cheese I missed out on a lot of opportunities to eat more cheese because of my eating disorder and the many thoughts circling around my head, telling me that the stuff was totally bad. I take it you have just read Eve's section on dairy, explaining why dairy (and therefore cheese) DOES have some nutritionally brilliant properties when, like everything, it is eaten in moderation. I am here to add to this, by explaining the positive mental benefits that routinely eating something you love can have, and how you anxious eaters should try to get more of the food you adore into your diet rather than run away from it. For me this is cheese...in all forms.

I've never come across a cheese I didn't like. Honest. From the milkiness of a wheel of Brie, freshly melted and stuffed with garlic cloves, to pungent Stilton spread on sweet rye crackers, to those plastic rounds of Babybel when I was a small human – cheese has been a dear friend to me throughout my life, indulging me with a rainbow of flavours to accompany the highs, lows and, well, the days when I just fancied some bloody cheese. Cheese to me represents joy, and each time I eat it I am reminded of how far I have come in my recovery. Eating cheese also symbolizes my rebellion against years of being unkind to my body. It's a salty middle finger to the eating disorder voice, once loud in my head, telling me that I wasn't deserving of any pleasure when it came to food. Years later, I believe that an important part of your recovery is to face your fears and for me (once upon a time) that was eating cheese. I'd been brainwashed into believing the advice that "plant-based" was the way forward and that dairy equalled certain weight gain. If you're still not convinced I'd suggest reading the first section of this chapter again.

Life is too short to deny yourself small indulgences. Of course we swear by "everything in moderation", but I also firmly believe that if you resist every urge to eat your particular "vice", over time you will just end up overeating anyway. Trust your body, because more often than not when you are craving something, there is a reason for it. If you allow yourself the freedom to eat intuitively you will eventually learn to relax into your meals and cheese-covered snacks without anxiety – and that's coming from a former binge eater.

When it comes to cheese, it's the processed kind that we tend to fear most – I know I certainly did. Cheese comes in eight classifications, including blue, hard, semi-hard, pasta filata, semi-soft, soft fresh, soft-ripened, processed and "ultra"-processed[3]. Rather than bore you with the definitions of each, let's just talk about ultra-processed (we've added the word ultra, because technically slicing is a process). Ultra-processed cheese, in simple terms, is a food product made from cheese, plus emulsifiers, saturated vegetable oils, extra salt, food colourings, whey or sugar.

This rather frightening definition is the reason why the stuff gets such stick, but we are open-minded people and we are going to look beyond that, aren't we?

Ultra-processed cheese tends to be cheaper, making it more accessible for the poor. Many food shamers out there are very ready to wag their freshly manicured fingers at ultra-processed cheese, all the while ignoring the fact that this is fuel for many on a tight budget, not to mention those who simply just prefer the taste of it. There is no shame in eating within your budget, even if that means eating ultra-processed cheese. What else are you meant to do, starve? These "plastic" cheeses have been necessary to sustain the poor since World War II, and in schools as early as the 1960s. In fact, there was even such a thing as "government cheese" in the US, which was provided to welfare beneficiaries, Food Stamp recipients and the elderly receiving social security[4]. To this day it is still provided to food charities. At a time when millions of Americans felt food insecurity, this famous orange cheese containing a mixture of Colby and Cheddar with curds and emulsifiers became essential; it was cheap, shipped easily and had a ridiculously long shelf life. This ultra-processed cheese eventually came to be called, simply, "American" cheese, which many of us have grown to love on our Aldi own-brand beef burgers. You know the stuff! We can't ignore the class issue behind shaming people for eating ultra-processed food, as the explanations for why they need to in order to survive are rich and complex. So the next time that Waitrose shopper wags her finger at you and gives you grief about your latest purchase of cheese strings, just tell her where she can shove it.

Although cheese is often omitted from most healthy eating guides, there is one very prominent woman in the food industry who believes, like us, that cheese is integral to living well. One of my favourite food writers, and the current restaurant critic for the

Sunday Times, Marina O'Loughlin walks me through some of her favourite cheese-related memories, so that I may imagine myself with the elegance and authority of a well-travelled critic.

"It's impossible to forget the first time I ate the pungent, raw ewes' milk cheese Torta del Casar in beautiful Trujillo, Extremadura. It's so insanely whiffy it comes triple-packaged in secure boxes. You cut the cheese's lid off and spoon it out – but there's little needed as the violent brute basically jumps out to meet you. Or the times I've watched cheese being made in Italy: burrata in Puglia, marvelling at the curds turning into skeins of snowy elastic to be stuffed with cream; this is what the angels are clearly fed on. And fresh ricotta in a tiny hut on a Sicilian farm, handed out to us still warm from its simmering. I'm afraid this made me feel mildly vomitous."

Mmm, vomitous! I breathe further into my daydream...

Talking to Marina makes me realize what a sheltered cheese-filled life I've lived in terms of quality not quantity, as her favourites extend across the world's most pungent nooks. "I adore Alpine cheese," she explains, adding that she "can't get past the great French cheese boards – the one at Bocuse in Lyon should be canonized: a myriad of perfectly kept, oozing beauties. But the UK's cheese offering is hot on its heels, the likes of Baron Bigod and Tunworth more than holding their own against their cousins across the water. I also think the incredible, unsung mountain cheeses of Portugal, created with rennet made from thistles or cardoons, which gives them an oozing, mushroomy, faint bitterness – they certainly deserve a mention."

Although mine and Marina's knowledge and standards of cheese differ greatly, we can agree on one thing. When I ask if she'd be able to cope in a cheeseless world, she replies: "No, never. I'd give up anything – booze, meat, even my beloved bread – before I'd give up the joy of cheese."

While we all know that we should be trying to eat less processed food, sometimes our cheese indulgences come at a price, and if you can't afford the more expensive ones, that's okay.

OWNING YOUR FOOD CHOICES: TIPS FROM GRACE VICTORY

Eve asks The Internet's Big Sister how she deals with food trolls and how we can eat our cheese, cake and cookies with pride.

Thank goodness there is now a stellar collection of faces, bodies and voices online, sassing about and spreading their truths in a brave, unapologetic and utterly fabulous fashion. They don't make excuses or apologies for their meals, how they look or what they feel, paving the way for you to follow suit and finally be free from judgement, restriction and misery. One such woman is Grace Francesca Victory. Otherwise known as The Internet's Big Sister, Grace is a BBC3 presenter, body positive campaigner, fashion blogger and she also just so happens to be an excellent friend of mine. Grace was one of the first social media "influencers" of her kind; honest, open and raw, and showing her 145,000 followers that it's okay not to be okay. And not in an italic-quote-about-living-for-the-moment kinda way.

I met Grace back in 2016 when I took part in a documentary she was presenting (the very same which led Laura to find me via the Twittersphere). Grace interviewed me about the contribution of clean eating and wellness blogs to my anorexia development. Over coffees with cow's milk, we simultaneously slagged off every untrained wellness guru going and have remained firm friends ever since. Here, I ask her how she deals with the inevitable Instagram comments offering unhelpful opinions on her poached eggs on toast, and how she won back ownership of both her body and her dinner plate.

EVE: *How do you eat without fear of judgement? Is it ever possible?*

GRACE: Eat what you want and what your body is asking for. Listen to hunger cues and stop eating when you are full. Your body knows what it's doing, so trust it. I'm not here to tell people what to eat as I'm not trained, but my only bit of advice is variety and colour. For me, food that looks good and is full of vibrancy means I'm more likely to enjoy it and digest all the nutrients. Eat your cookies and eat your broccoli. Life is too short not to have both.

EVE: *How have you got to a place of shunning body and food fascism?*

GRACE: Education. I read a lot and that means I am well-informed in a non-biased way. I also take everything with a pinch of salt and every morning I remind myself, "You have the permission to eat what your body wants today." Challenge people if you have the energy and surround yourself with people who get it. You deserve a life that is free.

EVE: *What are the most common tales you hear from young people about their struggles with body image and/or food?*

GRACE: Where do I begin? From disordered eating, to suicidal thoughts, to daily questions asking me how to heal, the overall theme is "How do I feel happy? How do I stop worrying, stop running from life and stop being so full of fear." People don't feel good enough and I can relate to that. It's hard to be who you are when the world tells you that it is unacceptable. Women (speaking inclusively) have lost their power and it's time we claimed it back. Our validation needs to come from within ourselves and nobody else.

EVE: *What is your response to the whole "body positivity / food freedom is glorifying obesity" assertion?*

GRACE: My response is "Go and f*ck yourself" but I guess I can't always say that. I usually reply that body positivity is about acceptance, love, compassion and non-judgement; that's the only thing we glorify. Nobody is saying, "Hello, look like me." It's more about saying you are worthy regardless of what you look like. I think it's also important to point out that there is no point wasting time trying to justify your body or size to people who don't want to understand. I lead by example and show my followers and friends that you can live the most fulfilled life – and you don't need to be thin to be happy. I also tell people to read *Health at Every Size* and do their research because many studies actually tell us overweight people live longer than very thin people. But I guess people aren't ready to hear that truth.

EVE: *What is it like to be a bigger body in this diet-obsessed culture?*
GRACE: It's a tricky one because even when I had a conforming body, I was still perceived as big. I lost 5 stone and didn't eat but the world still saw me as "other". It was hard. The opinions and voices of other people have been at the forefront of my worth for as long as I can remember. From being called fat at 12, to being called fat at 20. But none of that would matter if we didn't all believe that being fat is bad and means you're lazy, ugly and have a lack of self-control. But it did matter. I developed a full-blown eating disorder and self-harmed as a teenager, which shows just how much it affected me. It's the norm to be on a diet, and when you're free from it, people think you're the odd one. That's what I'm going through now.

EVE: *Will we EVER get to a stage where bigger bodies are seen as the ideal? Or where we don't focus on the way that women look?*
GRACE: We will...it'll just take time. Personally, I'd like us to get to a place where nobody is seen as "other".

10 REASONS YOU SHOULD BE PROUD TO BE A COW'S MILK DRINKER

1. Human beings have evolved to be able to drink cow's milk; without being able to do so we would probably still be hunchbacked, illiterate and die before the age of five.

2. Cow's milk is recommended by practically every dietary expert in the world as the most reliable, nutritious and easily available source of calcium for human bodies. The National Osteoporosis Society has expressed great concern at the increased risk of bone diseases such as osteoporosis and osteopenia due to cutting it out of our diets.

3. Without meat eaters and dairy farmers, most animals wouldn't have a life worth living. Modern standards in livestock rearing mean that farm animals' life expectancy is vastly increased, and quality of life drastically improved.

4. There is some evidence that a diet high in dairy products can protect against bowel cancer[5].

5. Dairy makes you clever! No, seriously. Milk and other dairy products are the main source of iodine in most people's diets. Studies have shown that iodine can positively impact the IQ of infants when given to pregnant women; if, on the other hand, pregnant women are significantly deficient in iodine, brain impairments and developmental foetal conditions can occur. Cow's milk is definitely best; dairy alternatives provide just 2 micrograms of iodine per glass, whereas cow's milk supplies 70 micrograms (the recommended daily amount is 150). Yes, you can get it from fruits and vegetables but you have to eat a lot and who wants to have to take up valuable brain space stressing about whether or not they've had enough iodine today?

6. If we didn't rear animals for food and milk, WHERE WOULD THEY LIVE? They'd give birth to unkempt, diseased children

who would then give birth to more children, before eventually outpopulating humans and probably popping up at your bedroom window at night to scare the absolute bejesus out of you.

7. According to government figures, it's estimated that the dairy industry contributes more than £5 billion to the UK economy every year. That's enough to clear the NHS deficit five times.

8. Two words: ICE CREAM. You're automatically winning at life if you can eat all of it (and you damn well should).

9. Eating animal produce is pretty much the best way of helping the environment and reducing global malnutrition. In his book *Meat: A Benign Extravagance*, agricultural expert Simon Fairlie explains that when animals are fed on food/waste that humans can't eat (i.e. grass), it frees up excess meat *and* grain to feed more than 1.3 billion people. The problem, he argues, is that animals are not fed effectively in terms of reducing global food waste, but if we adapted the farming system (especially in the US), they could play a fundamental role in feeding the needy. Fairlie also argues that the age-old UN calculation that 18 per cent of global carbon emissions come from livestock is highly inaccurate. He says it attributes all deforestation to cattle, rather than logging or development. It also muddles up one-off emissions from deforestation with ongoing pollution. The real figure is more like 10 per cent, and transport-generated emissions are far higher.

10. By drinking cow's milk and eating dairy products, you are actively supporting 346,000 hard-working farmers, suppliers, drivers, machinists, vets, herders, milkers, cattle hoof trimmers (and many more professions) who dedicate their lives to the splash of milk that soaks your morning cornflakes. So slurp with pride.

"11 ways gluten can damage your health"

– paleoleap.com

GLUTEN

GLUTEN MYTHS DEBUNKED

Eve wades through the nutri-nonsense that surrounds the ever-controversial – and delicious – protein and asks what all the darn fuss is about.

The fear of carbs is very much a real one. I feel as though my seemingly innate aversion to spongy, beige – and brown, white and orange, for that matter – carbohydrates somehow seeped through the womb alongside the patriarchal pressure to remove my pubic hair. Even post eating disorder, and years of therapy/ dietitian appointments/health journalism later, I'm still quietly nervous around a bread basket. Not that anyone would notice, as the chances are my friends will order a chef's salad, spouting "bread bloats me" as a totally unnecessary justification for their order. The bread and bloating thing is annoying (it's called being full) and particularly stings given that when I was forced into a state of overfullness as part of "refeeding", I rarely felt as uncomfortable after a plate of creamy pasta as I did after a protein-heavy dinner including far too many vegetables (they were "safe", so I ate a lot).

I now understand that the vilification of grains is steeped in the diet culture paradigm, and my conscious avoidance of them is a result of 25 years of messages informing me to avoid being fat at all costs. In a land of plenty, in which overconsumption is the ultimate fear, it was only a matter of time before the scaremongering rhetoric landed on carbs – just as it has done with meat, sugar and dairy.

It's therefore frustrating that the majority of the population is seemingly blind to this connection, and instead of joining feminist marches or writing letters to various newspapers every time a "FIVE REASONS YOU SHOULD NEVER EAT BREAD" article is published, they rush out and stock up on gluten-free pitta breads.

Since 2010, sales of gluten-free alternatives have doubled to more than £324 million a year[1], with 54 per cent[2] of younger consumers opting for at least one gluten-free product in the first three months of 2017. Despite this sudden hunger for gluten-free products, it is estimated that just 1 per cent of the entire UK population have coeliac disease, an autoimmune condition caused by a bodily reaction to gluten.

So what is gluten and how did it become the bad guy? A composite of proteins found in wheat, spelt, barley and rye, gluten is – as it sounds – the "glue" that holds food together, delivering that satisfyingly light chewiness you get when you bite into a sandwich, or rip apart a slice of crusty sourdough. Breads that don't contain gluten are typically flat or "unleavened". Humans have been harvesting grains (and with that, gluten) for millennia – specifically since the discovery of wild grasses in the Egyptian Fertile Crescent

– in around 8800 BC. They quickly became a staple of the human diet, and still now dietitians would recommend a healthy, balanced diet with whole grains (containing gluten) as the base for most meals. They are low in fat and sugar; high in bowel-friendly fibre, protein and a host of vitamins and minerals; and they are delicious when dressed with lashings of peanut butter, too.

According to Dr Nick Trott, a dietitian and gastroenterologist who specializes in coeliac disease, a life without gluten can be a significant health hazard. "There is absolutely no evidence that non-coeliacs need to follow a gluten-free diet. If you haven't got CD or any other gluten-related disorder, it is not harmful. In fact, [wheat is] a great prebiotic as it contains fructans and galectins. It is an important, cheap source of protein and carbohydrates.

"Most of the main sources of iron, thiamine and calcium in the human diet come from bread. Going 'gluten-free' means cutting down on whole grains, which are protective against a whole host of chronic diseases – thus increasing the risk of diabetes and coronary heart disease."

For the small percentage of poor souls who are genetically programmed to reject gluten, the gluten withdrawal process is certainly not taken lightly. Neither, I might add, is the often-debilitating nature of the autoimmune condition that causes some to end up with literal, gaping holes in the bowel.

People with CD need regular bone scans and perhaps medical treatment for their bone health. There's an effect on fertility and vitamin D levels, and risks of other autoimmune diseases is significantly increased. Unlike an allergy, which is instantaneous, there is long-term gut damage in coeliac disease. And before you all trudge down to the gluten-free aisle, note the *cause* of coeliac disease isn't down to some mystically wicked compound in gluten itself, but is down to the immune system of the person who develops the condition.

Then there's non-specific, non-coeliac gluten sensitivity. Sounds absurd, but according to the medical community, a small percentage of the non-CD population (about 5 per cent) do experience significant gut symptoms after ingesting gluten.

It's an annoying problem for both the bright sparks of the gastroenterology world and for me; mostly because it kind of shits on my whole parade. Evidence as to what causes this reaction in a small percentage of people isn't quite there yet so it remains unknown. It has been suggested that fructans (also in beans, pulses and some vegetables) are to blame, as many foods containing gluten are also high in fructans – known for causing IBS symptoms. Although no hard and fast conclusions have been drawn.

As for all those who self-diagnose as gluten-intolerant and spend the rest of their miserable lives pretending to enjoy beautifully styled bowls of pesto courgetti, Dr Trott makes to you a sobering plea: "If you are having gut symptoms, please go and get it checked out by a gastroenterologist before cutting anything out of your diet. The most worrying thing for us is that these people might have coeliac disease but remain undiagnosed. Misdiagnosis increases the risk of other autoimmune diseases and potentially replacing gluten with other, less healthy foods."

BUT...WHY GLUTEN?

If there is only a small handful of people for whom gluten is problematic, why the hell is everyone else so scared of it? Why does carotene get off scot-free? Sodium bicarbonate? Egg whites?

Some argue that the way in which wheat is now processed, and thus the effect on the gluten, is the problem. Our bodies simply aren't built to tolerate it, they say.

Well, according to research conducted by Donald Kasarda PhD[3], the king of agriculture research in the US, the method of wheat milling and breeding hasn't changed much over the past 100 years.

The president of the North American Society for the Study of Celiac Disease told *The New Yorker* that the rise in coeliac disease and gluten sensitivity cannot be linked to the genetics of wheat.

So, what then? There is a suggestion that the increase in additives put into wheat products (such as stabilizers and preservatives) may be to blame, while others cite evidence for changes in gut bacteria, which has been linked to the development of autoimmune diseases. We also know that the balance of gut bacteria can be manipulated with diet and one high in sugary, fatty foods and low in vitamins and minerals can disrupt this gut bug community[4].

Scientific evidence to explain the big gluten phobia remains thin on the ground. As for my opinion? At the risk of sounding flippant... I smell nutribollocks. Few non-coeliacs so much as looked up from their carbonara at the word gluten until about a decade ago when an American cardiologist brought out a book sensitively titled *Wheat Belly*. Advocating a ten-day detox from wheat and all its "poisonous" properties, the book posed the protein as the enemy, linking it to conditions such as eczema, multiple sclerosis and schizophrenia. None of which is accepted as fact by the scientific community, by the way. The book was so successful that other doctors followed suit. One of whom was a neurologist / celebrity doctor who wrote a popular diet book titled *Grain Brain: The Surprising Truth About Wheat, Carbs, and Sugar – Your Brain's Silent Killers*.

Rather depressingly, such scaremongering babble flew off the shelves, with the anti-gluten message spreading quickly across the seas, and several (already rich) men got even richer. All we got was an unsolvable hunger and irritating lunch dates.

It was the perfect set-up; people read the book, cut a load of food out of their diet, lost weight and discovered a simple, quick-fire way to remain thin while still eating ice cream. Coz, that's the ultimate goal, right? As far as I am concerned, the demonization of gluten is, generally speaking, not much more complicated than a rebranding of the Atkins diet. Strip back the tabloid-style headlines, the doctors in white coats and the shiny book covers, and the message is simple: carbs make you fat, so stop eating them.

My approach is a little simplistic, I admit. But one key thinker in the field is with me on at least some of my theory. Alan Levinovitz is a religion professor and author of the critically acclaimed 2015 book *The Gluten Lie: And Other Myths About What You Eat*. He takes a special interest in parallels between societal food fads and ancient religious folklore. After studying ancient medicinal practices he soon realized that promises made about restrictive diets have been circulating since day dot. Time and time again – and across many cultures throughout the world – rationale behind what we eat is related to identity, morality and superstitions rather than science. "Take sugar for instance," he poses, "when sugar first came into Britain in the 1600s and 1700s, it came from overseas with coffee and people were terrified because it wasn't British. Honey was fine, but sugar was dangerous because it was foreign. People then began to blame these foods for illnesses that they couldn't explain at the time, like scurvy."

Similarly, a bogus fear of salt arose from the 1940s study by one man, Dr Walter Kempner, and his (scientifically discredited) Rice Diet. People with hypertension ate nothing but rice and fruit for several months and lo and behold, their hypertension reduced and their weight loss was dramatic. Despite 25 people dying in Kempner's original cohort, he was somehow considered a hero and, although there were many other food groups expelled from his imposed diet, salt emerged the enemy. To this day, most US and UK salt regulations can be traced back to this one scientifically questionable study.

Which brings us back to gluten.

The undiagnosed coeliac's adoption of a gluten-free diet, with life-changing consequences, is arguably what sparked the mystical furore around gluten. Those who were plagued by an unexplained agony after eating gluten-laden foods genuinely experienced miracles from going gluten-free when nothing else seemed to work. Then they would tell a friend. Who tells another friend...and before we know it everyone is substituting pizza dough for mashed-up cauliflower. And so a dietary villain is created.

Reinforcing this vilification is the sense of dietary alarmism – a super-powerful fear that can elicit actual, physical responses in some. Known to researchers as the nocebo effect, eaters have been proven to experience negative physical symptoms after eating foods that they genuinely believe are bad for them.

An army of studies show that people who identify as gluten sensitive and *think* they are eating gluten (when in fact they are given a well-disguised, gluten-free alternative) will experience more gut symptoms than those eating actual gluten.

So it's not unreasonable to assume that the increase in gluten-related gut symptoms is largely severe anxiety that has resulted from a Western fixation on the ingredient. If anything is going to get your bloat on it's probably the 20 minutes of agonizing about whether pasta is "good" for you. If you think you might be coeliac, or are suffering with real, life-altering gut problems, go to your GP and ask for a referral to a gastroenterologist. If not, shut up and eat your pasta.

GLUTEN FACE

In an effort not to take up precious space with the completely unfounded theory that gluten could produce a reaction of the skin (it's beyond the realm of nutrition nonsense), we called on consultant dermatologist Dr Anjali Mahto to explain the deal in one short, fact-filled punch.

She says: "Facial mapping originates from ancient Chinese practice. Despite its popular use, Western science and medicine has yet to prove it works. The idea behind it is that the face is linked to other organs in the body and potentially even their ailments. Some newer variations on this theme suggest that facial skin is linked specifically to digestive health – 'wine face', 'gluten face', 'sugar face' and 'dairy face' have all been described by naturopaths. There is no rigorous, quality scientific evidence to back this up and one must be cautious about making significant dietary changes or excluding whole food groups as a single treatment for skin disease in this manner."

PLENTY OF CARBS BEFORE MARBS

Laura recounts her own holiday crash-dieting stories and explains why they just aren't worth it.

I've never been to Marbella, but I envisage it to be a destination for pasty, thirsty Brits, similar to the Greek island of Kos, where I once went with a large group of young girls, a suitcase full of naivety and an undiagnosed eating disorder. I must admit that on this holiday it was pretty easy for me to conceal my own uncomfortable relationship with food, as it would come to light that most of the girls I was spending a week in the sun with were also battling their own demons. I shared a room with one girl who wasn't embarrassed to make herself sick in the bathroom we all shared, with the door open next to where we slept. Another considered two stuffed vine leaves to be a large lunch and an excuse for her to skip dinner later that evening.

Holidays, for me, used to begin about three months before we'd even take off. The usual lonely task of developing a diet plan in order to achieve a summer body became almost joyous when shared with a group of girls who all wanted to be skinnier than the other. We were each other's competition for punishing ourselves in the lead-up to our holiday, yet we'd never admit that thanks to pride. We'd delight in sharing the different things we were going to cut out of our diets as our holiday approached in order to lose X pounds, and would collectively wallow in the trauma of realistically not sticking to such unachievable regimes, instead starving ourselves with quick-fix crash diets a couple of weeks or days before. What should have been a time spent getting excited about partying and planning boat trips was overshadowed by an overwhelming need to look our best when compared with eight other young, attractive girls.

The trouble with No Carbs Before Marbs, or any other crash diet before a holiday, is that when the holiday comes, so does your opportunity to relax, meaning you could be prone to bingeing to excess and spend the week bloated, especially if you have an eating disorder. Yearly holidays are often spoiled because of this uncomfortable bloat and the worry about how far your food baby is protruding between your two-piece.

However, it isn't only for this reason that crash diets are a load of nonsense. Performance and eating disorder dietitian and author Renee McGregor explains that everyone is looking for a quick fix when it comes to weight loss, which is why the popularity of fad approaches continues to grow. It has been documented time and time again that creating a calorie deficit is one of the most successful ways of reducing weight. So the bigger the calorie deficit, the more weight you will lose – right?

Wrong. It is important to understand that the body is a finely tuned and controlled machine; if you tip it to any extreme, it will bite back...by wanting to overeat on holiday when given the opportunity to feed itself, for example.

Renee says: "The biggest problem with crash diets in particular is that they are not sustainable; while they may seem to cause quick weight loss, in reality all that is happening is a reduction of fluid associated with glycogen stores – for every gram of glycogen you hold in your muscles, you also hold 1–4g fluid. So while this initial loss may seem like a positive outcome, the reality is that it is not 'real' weight loss, aka loss of body fat; it is a reduction in glycogen stores due to being on such a low-calorie intake. Once glycogen stores have been depleted, weight loss will plateau and this is when individuals become frustrated. This will end in one of two ways – further calorie restrictions or reverting to previous dietary intakes." This explains why the weight of crash dieters tends to yo-yo, and as a result why they spend their lives looking out for the next trendy diet that claims to be able to "cure" them of their fatness. Sigh...

If you restrict what you eat further and your body cannot cope with this, different hormonal signals will be switched on, causing the body to believe it is starving. This actually results in the body preserving energy, meaning your metabolic rate will drop and weight loss will become harder. So if you're crash-dieting in order to lose weight, you could actually be making things harder for yourself. In extreme cases, it is common for people to eat to excess when food becomes available again, as a way to overcompensate for the crash-dieting. While this is just a transitional phase, for some it can lead to a binge–restrict cycle and an unhappy relationship with food and body image.

The final issue with crash diets is that they deplete the body of essential vitamins and minerals, which are crucial for many of the biochemical and hormonal pathways that occur within the body. For example, experts say that if iron levels drop too low this can cause an iron deficiency called anaemia, which leaves you feeling exhausted, short of breath and at an increased risk of poor bone health. A lack of dietary fibre and sufficient volume of food in general can lead to constipation and other digestive complications, which doesn't seem worth it for the sake of wanting to fit into a size 8 bikini. Successful weight loss takes time, and if you're interested in achieving it, you'll just have to be patient in order to do it healthily.

Although we'd never admit it, a large part of the reason why us girls wanted to look what we considered our "best" was the prospect of having a whirlwind holiday romance – nothing wrong with that. It's just unfortunate that we all believed no one would find us attractive unless Greek sunlight could be seen between our spindly legs.

My first girls' holiday to Kos sure was a blooming period for my romantic life – the word romantic being used in the most ironic of ways. Stepping off the plane, we were mortified to learn that the bus to our hotel was being shared with 30+ rugby lads, all of whom would be staying at the hotel too. We were outnumbered, and thoroughly regretting eating those sausage sandwiches at the airport. Our first night out to a foam party resulted in me breaking my camera as it soaked up the poisonous suds, as did my throat too. I ended up getting laryngitis, meaning I couldn't speak to, let alone get to snog, any boy who seemed remotely interested in me. With my chastity belt firmly tightened and my vocal chords singed, I instead focused on the amount of food I could horrendously binge on over the week, making sure I would eat at least two sharing bags' worth of ridged, salted crisps each day, because if I couldn't talk to them none of these guys would be interested in me anyway. I committed myself to silent, hungry isolation. Thinking back to the promiscuous stories of my friends on this holiday, and the lack of STDs I brought home with me, I was better off.

If I could go back and talk to the dieting teen me, before I embarked on a savage ostracization of carbs before this Kos holiday, I'd give her a hug and tell her that crash diets are not worth it for all the reasons listed above. I'd tell her to wear sun cream, drink those sugary cocktails and zip that camera into a waterproof sandwich bag before the foam party.

AN ODE TO CARBOHYDRATES...BY THE ANGRY CHEF

Someone who is particularly annoyed by our societal shunning of carbohydrates – and gluten in particular – is writer and chef Anthony Warner, who runs the blog The Angry Chef. We thought he'd portray this rage far better than we could; so we asked him to offer his two cents so you too can revel in the unrelenting frustration both we and Anthony share every time a gym employee is chuffed to tell you their green juice is gluten-free.

Anyone can cook a fillet steak and make it taste good. Turbot, scallops, John Dory and lobster are all fine things, but if you mess them up you are just not paying attention. The basic principle is that less is more. Cook them simply and let them speak for themselves.

That is why I love carbs. They are simple pleasures that require love, skill and attention to detail. When done properly, they can achieve heights that no overpriced prime cut can ever dream of.

I have worked in professional kitchens for over twenty years, and I can tell a talented chef the moment I set eyes on them. You can see it in the way they stand, the sound their knife makes against the chopping board, or the way they take a tray out of an oven. Anyone half decent will be able to cook a piece of meat or fish and produce a delicious plate of food when presented with expensive ingredients. But it is only when you see someone produce something sublime from a few potatoes or a bag of flour that you know they can really cook. To do that, you need to understand each ingredient, and have the ability and confidence to make them sing.

It is in the alchemy of elevating something humble into something extraordinary that we find cookery's richest rewards. The crust of freshly baked bread, the silken luxury of handmade pasta, the golden top of a tray of dauphinoise, potatoes roasted in dripping, creamy risottos, crispy fried rice, freshly cooked chips, poached suet dumplings and flaking pastry crusts.

Carbs offer us comfort, happiness and memories of home. They nourish us and protect us from the cold. They cross class divides, form the centre of our finest meals and provide the canvas on which great cuisines paint their pictures. In my lifelong love affair with food, carbs are the beating heart. So if anyone wants to be my friend, it would pay not to mess with them. And if you really love food, why the hell would you?

But over the last ten years or so, something very strange has occurred. The once-obscure Atkins diet, a disordered eating pattern famous for bad breath and high cholesterol, has grown to conquer the world. As society has taught us to fear and despise our bodies, cutting carbs has become the blunt weapon of choice, a simple life hack to help us contort ourselves into a more social acceptable form. So we now have a selection of spiralized and ground-up vegetables to replace noodles, rice and pizza crusts, creating piss-poor facsimiles of our favourite foods.

Weight loss can occur when someone cuts out carbs, but only because of the inevitable restriction that results. Unsurprisingly, when we condemn many of our most delicious treats as evil, we temporarily end up eating fewer calories. Instead of fish and chips, we have fish and misery. When we have a burger, we throw away the bun and the fries. We reject a sandwich, opting for a plate of ham. And every time we do, we are sucked further into a whirlpool of joyless denial, our lives becoming a little poorer as a result.

In order to motivate disorder, those that push low-carb dieting adopt a veritable smorgasbord of pseudoscience. They tell us that carbs are uniquely harmful or fattening, and sure to make us sick. They are wrong, of course. Carbs form the basis of all great cuisines for a reason, and are at the heart of all balanced meals. There is quite simply no good evidence that they cause us harm, and plenty that they are a force for good. But those that push diet and disorder claim otherwise, often because their lives and careers depend upon it. They argue they have discovered a secret locked within our DNA, or a mysterious metabolic advantage that has eluded everyone else.

In truth, in a couple of hundred years of nutrition science, no manipulation of the carbohydrate or fat levels in our diet has been shown to be superior in terms of health, or better for people who want to lose weight. And contrary to what we are forever being told, carbs are not linked to the development of type 2 diabetes. In fact, the opposite seems to be true, as consumption of fibre (a type of carbohydrate) is known to reduce our risk.

So it seems beyond foolish to exclude our most joyous and delicious foods, the ones that bring us together and deliver us so much happiness. Because although we cannot live off bread alone, to try and exist forever without it is perhaps not a life at all.

The Truth About Fat by Anthony Warner is published by Oneworld.

BAKING WISDOM FROM RUBY TANDOH

The *Great British Bake Off* hero and long-time "eat what you want" advocate imparts her baking wisdom with this gold standard recipe for light, nutty soda bread. We've been an admirer of Ruby since the very first day she popped up on our television screens, young, sprightly and goddam beautiful. When you've finished this book, we'd recommend you buy a copy of her food bible, *Eat Up* – a necessary step in reaching the ultimate goal: eating what you want and not giving a shit.

RUBY TANDOH'S PERFECT SODA BREAD

This easy bread takes things that are abysmally dull (especially compared to the technicolour palettes of Mediterranean kitchens) and gives you a chance to magic up something magnificent from them.

Makes 1 loaf

200g wholemeal flour
50g rolled oats, plus extra for sprinkling
1 tablespoon dark brown sugar
¾ teaspoon bicarbonate of soda
¼ teaspoon salt
60g full-fat Greek yogurt
100–125ml water

Preheat the oven on to 180°C (fan 160°C), Gas Mark 4, and lightly grease a baking tray.

Combine the wholemeal flour, oats, brown sugar, bicarbonate of soda and salt in a large bowl – the brown sugar and oats add a really nice nutty sweetness.

Stir in the yogurt and just enough of the water to bring the dough together to a soft, slightly sticky mass (it's important it's not too dry and rubbery, or it won't rise). Form into a rough cob shape on the greased baking tray, sprinkle with some more oats and score a cross in the top with a sharp knife.

Bake for 50 minutes, then leave to cool slightly before serving with salted butter and jam – blackcurrant jam on this bread is the stuff dreams are made of.

Eat Up by Ruby Tandoh is published by Serpent's Tail.

"The four detox ingredients you SHOULD be adding to your water"

– popsugar.co.uk

DRINKS

WATERING DOWN THE MYTHS

Since the act of writing about water is about as thrilling as drinking the stuff we'll try to get a move on with this chapter, so that everyone can get on with their day.

Water is important, we know that already. Bear Grylls told us that we'd die within around three days of not drinking water in the Aussie outback (not sure how we ended up there), and that if push comes to shove we should squeeze the nearest hot, fresh elephant dung over our mouths and slurp up the fluid that drips down...if we want to survive. Great, what's next?

Well, even with such simple survival tips from Bear, people are still struggling to get their heads around the stuff. Even something as boring as a plain glass of water can't escape the clutches of unethical marketing techniques, telling us that the clear stuff alone isn't good enough unless it comes in a glass VOSS bottle or is mixed with a variety of organic sliced fruit. Oh, and Fit Water is a thing now? So what's the truth? What's the deal with water? Are we all going to turn to dust if we don't swap our regular tap water with purified electrolyte water? Or branded water with supposed miracle additives in it and therefore an outrageous price tag?

Not exactly, according to registered dietitian Ellen Mansfield. "The main differences between branded waters are: where they come from, how many times they are filtered and what minerals they contain. Trace minerals in water are not proven to positively affect your health." Just because water is branded or more expensive, it doesn't necessarily mean it is any better for you than regular tap water. The real differences are the appearance of the bottles and the taste, but most of us don't even notice the latter anyway.

Other trendy waters include "fibre water" and "alkaline water". Fibre water is water with soluble fibre in it, and we all know that fibre is an essential nutrient for bowel health. There are two types of fibre: soluble, which can be found in oatmeal, root vegetables, berries and legumes; and insoluble fibre, which can be found in green vegetables, seeds, nuts and wheat bran. There are many benefits of having enough fibre in our diets, but you do not need to drink fibre water to get it. Alkaline water is water with a pH of 8 or above and is generally achieved by a company or individual adding dissolvable alkaline minerals, such as calcium carbonate, to achieve a higher pH level. However, it's worth noting that there is no solid scientific evidence to prove that there are any benefits from drinking alkaline water, and it is significantly more expensive. So please, put your purse away.

Now that we know that branded water isn't necessarily any better for us than tap water…let's explore how to drink it (patronizing, I know, but bear with us). Firstly, how much of it should we be drinking a day? NHS guidelines advise us that eight glasses of water a day is generally good to aim for, although everyone has slightly different fluid needs at different times of the day. Are you exercising or particularly hot? If so, drink a bit more to balance what has been lost through sweat. If you need a little help, you can tell how hydrated you are by the colour of your urine. Generally what you are looking for is a light straw yellow colour or lighter. Be aware that some foods, supplements and medications can change the colour of your urine slightly. If your urine is very dark despite regular water intake or is not a colour on the scale (for example, pink), consider seeing a doctor. You may have just eaten a shade too much beetroot...but it's best to check.

How about water fasting – meaning that you consume nothing but water for a specific period of time. Should we be trying this at any point in our lives?

Ellen thinks not. "People claim it helps the body 'reset' and 'remove toxins' and it leads to weight loss. Human bodies do not need to reset, and most do not need help removing toxins – your kidneys and liver do this. If you do require help to remove toxins, you need a hospital, not a water fast. Water fasting not only has no proven health benefits, but is extremely risky. Possible side effects include hypoglycaemia, low blood pressure, headaches and fainting." A water fast might seem appealing if you are desperate to lose weight quickly, such as in time for a wedding or party, but as well as being bad for your health, it will not be sustainable. Any weight loss will only be due to your glycogen stores in your liver breaking down, so that your body has glucose to use when you are not eating anything. The reality is that if you fast in order to lose weight, you will likely end up bingeing – because you will be so hungry – and you will end up piling back on all the "weight" you thought you'd lost – plus more.

Great, now we've established that man (or woman) cannot live on water alone, let's get back to HOW to drink water, as if it needed an explanation...

Should we drink water before eating? Well, yes and no. This is often a dieting tip to try and stop us overeating and therefore gaining weight. If you've eaten food in the last few hours, you might need to think about whether you are hungry or thirsty. Ask yourself, how much have you drunk so far today? Does that seem like enough? Is it particularly hot and therefore are you more likely to need more water? It's about knowing your body. There is a danger that disordered eaters will try to replace their food hunger by temporarily filling their stomachs with water. As we said above, you cannot live on water alone. If you could we wouldn't be writing this book.

Another water-related dieting tip we often hear is that you should drink your water with a slice of lemon in it, as it helps to "cleanse" the body. There is vitamin C and other nutrients in lemon juice, however, you can also get these from eating fruit and vegetables. If flavouring your water with lemon makes it more palatable for you so that you drink more, that's all good, but beyond this there is no other proven benefit. And it's worth considering the impact on your teeth as lemon is acidic and could lead to erosion of enamel on your teeth – enamel being something that may already be vulnerable if you have had or currently have an eating disorder.

Another reason why you might have considered drinking more water – or even that you got this far into this chapter without falling asleep, well done – is for its supposed ability to clear up any "problem" skin. Although adequate hydration has lots of benefits, including nourishing your skin, making you appear more awake and glowy, there is no linear drink-more-water-get-clearer-skin solution, as Laura knows all too well. You can drink all the water in the world (don't do that, though) and you might still be stuck with painful, soul-destroying acne. The only thing that cured Laura's acne (twice) was a rather powerful drug called Roaccutane. This can only be prescribed by a certified dermatologist and can cause side effects such as dry skin, itching, rashes, nosebleeds, cracks in the corners of the mouth and harm to developing foetuses. If it was as simple as "just drink water", we'd all be able to live happily ever after, but although the stuff is vital for our survival, it isn't so good at curing skin conditions.

Do not trust those beauty bloggers on Instagram who profess that a miracle product or just drinking more water cured their skin. We're betting they aren't dermatologists, and that they probably have a monetary incentive for saying so. If your skin is really making you feel low, please go and see a specialist. This might be more expensive, but if your skin is making you feel that down and it's negatively affecting your mental health, it would be a worthwhile investment.

CAFFEINE MYTHS DEBUNKED

Eve asks how much coffee is too much, so that you can enjoy your venti, full-fat, caramel macchiato in peace.

My best friend Ana (with whom I spent many a night in McDonald's car park, NOT hotboxing, but destroying McFlurries and apple pies...cool) once told me that she knew I'd stopped eating when I started drinking coffee. It was an odd marrying of two events, which I'd assumed were totally unrelated. However, I was also "enjoying" those weird raw chewed-up dog food balls at the time so my judgement wasn't exactly reliable. Turns out she was right. My foray into the fashion world meant following every one of Anna Wintour's movements and never stepping foot in Primark ever again. The Primark thing I can live with, but clearly Anna Wintour's lifestyle routine didn't work out too well for me.

Anyway, Ana wasn't totally on the money. I'd actually begun drinking coffee a year or so before I became ill. I'd met a new, sophisticated man who introduced me to metropolitan ways such as sourcing Colombian bean drip-filter coffee and listening to BBC Radio 6 (as opposed to Choice FM). But regrettably, I was not yet similarly refined, and while Will sipped his rarefied filtered baby cup, I'd be banging on the end of the cinnamon shaker to add more sweet powder to the (already chocolate-covered) top of my milky caramel latte. Those were good times. Alas, then I got unwell and – as Ana quite rightly noticed – my coffee intake soared, but my milky, chocolatey goodness intake decreased. Somehow, my eating disorder had trained my brain to enjoy the oaky bitterness of a black Americano, even though it tasted, to me, like tree bark when not coupled with a pouring of Sweet'N Low.

These days, my coffee drinking remains in the marginally milky camp, but this is mainly because I am often in need of as much caffeine as my body can physically handle (turns out you have to wake up stupidly early to both write a book and hold down a full-time job). Word on the internet is that high amounts of the substance can increase the incidence of bone fractures, insomnia and heart problems. As someone who's spent the majority of her life with a permanent thunderbolt of a heartbeat pounding through her chest, the last thing I need is an anxiety starter pack in liquid form. To further confuse me, some studies now suggest that regular coffee drinkers have a reduced risk of dying. According to the American Cancer Society, coffee may lower the risk of several types of cancer, although these potential beneficial effects of coffee are not fully understood.

It's thought that the good stuff in coffee, including flavonoids, lignans and other polyphenols, are also beneficial for health. On the flip side, recent articles highlighting the "risks" caused by the inclusion of acrylamide in coffee – deemed a "probable carcinogen" by experts – have caused minor panic in the hipster coffee shop community. But don't ditch that overpriced drip-filter just yet; these articles are, of course, a safe distance from the truth. Although it is true that acrylamide is found in coffee, and there is sufficient evidence to class the chemical as a cancer-causing substance, the link between dietary acrylamide intake and the development of cancer isn't proven. Also the amount of acrylamide in coffee and other dietary sources is miniscule. The estimation is that, on average, as long as we stick to a limit of 208 micrograms of acrylamide per day, we're golden. One cup of coffee contains roughly 2 micrograms of acrylamide. So, unless you're drinking 70 cups of coffee, every day, you'll probably be all right. Two large, comprehensive studies into dietary acrylamide and cancer in 2011 and more recently in 2014 found no association between dietary acrylamide and cancer[1].

But the coffee questions don't stop there, right? How many cups *are* we supposed to drink? Will a 5pm latte keep me up all night? And do I have to drink litres of water to "rehydrate" me?

Further investigation would appear to show that, as always, recommended caffeine intake differs from individual to individual. Invariably, some will feel their heart pumping uncomfortably after one espresso, while others need four Americanos just to see them through till lunch. Generally speaking, the recommended daily limit is 400mg per day (four Americanos), according to the European Food Safety Authority. Pregnant women are advised to stick to just 200mg per day and anyone under the age of 16, 150mg. To give you an idea: there's about 120mg in an espresso; 40–50mg in the average cup of tea, 35mg in a cup of green tea, and 80mg in a can of Red Bull. "If you stay below the 400mg limit," says dietitian Carrie Ruxton, "you'll be unlikely to have any increased anxiety or heart palpitations." Hear that? Four whole cups a day, folks. Another revelation is even if you slurp down a 6pm espresso before leaving the office, it probably won't keep you awake at night. "Caffeine is out of our system within about five hours," explains Carrie. "Some people can even drink coffee right before bedtime and it has no effects on their sleep." Affogatos all round! As for that annoying girl in your office who claims to be "so addicted!" to her morning Starbucks skinny-mocha-soy-with-sprinkles concoction – she's not entirely wrong. Coffee stimulates the adrenal glands, which are responsible for making us sleepy and releasing adrenaline. Consistently high levels of caffeine (more than 400mg a day) increases the number of adenosine receptors, meaning there's a period of withdrawal when you cut down – symptoms of which include anxiety, headaches and feeling irritable. However these symptoms typically only last for about two days – hardly comparable to the fallout from a heroin habit.

Those who do need to watch their caffeine intake are people with existing heart problems such as heart arrhythmia. For everyone else, coffee boasts a range of health benefits, including elasticity of blood vessels to help with fluctuations in blood pressure; improvements in cognitive ability; better heart health and a lower risk of cancer. Taking a couple of 50mg caffeine pills before a race can increase the endurance of highly trained athletes and decrease their sensitivity to pain. What's more, coffee – when combined with water and/or milk – is positively hydrating, meaning that it counts as a source of hydration for the body (although drinking cup after cup may make you frequently pass urine, which can be dehydrating). In essence the message is this: drink coffee if you like coffee. If you start to feel abnormal after drinking coffee, stop drinking so much of it. And always top cappuccinos with chocolate powder and consume with supplementary biscuit.

LAURA BUSTS BOOZY MYTHS

There's a very them-and-us mentality when it comes to incorporating alcohol into the nutritional conversation. There's always the assumption that, in order to be healthy (when health = thin in most people's minds), you shouldn't drink any alcohol at all – not even that large, silky glass of Malbec with your steak – for its supposed ability to make you gain weight just by looking at a bottle of rosé, and for all those calories you'll consume when you lose all your inhibitions and start gorging on all that salty, greasy food.

From personal experience, the latter has some truth, what with the number of times I've face-planted a large portion of cheesy chips with burger sauce after a night out. However, when it comes to alcohol making you fat, I don't think I buy it, probably for the fact that I've always woken up after a night of boozing feeling that I looked thinner. I always believed that this was because I'd become dehydrated from all the Jägerbombs coursing through my bloodstream. I watched a Twitter Q&A unfold once, where someone asked TV doctor Dr Christian Jessen what we should drink in order to stay hydrated, and he replied anything but alcohol. That has stuck with me for years since, but interestingly, dietitian Ursula says that this might not be entirely accurate. She explains that in a recent BBC *Horizon* documentary, twin doctors Chris and Xand van Tulleken collected all their urine during a night in which Xand drank 21 units of alcohol in one sitting, while his brother only had one drink. The next morning their volumes were the same. In other words, the excessive alcohol consumption had not, as is widely believed, had a significant diuretic effect. Mind blown, right?

We've all woken up after a night out, bleary-eyed and confused, convinced that water is what we need to counteract the hangover. But the truth is that we don't exactly know if it's dehydration that causes hangovers. In fact, scientists still don't seem to fully understand what exactly causes a hangover[2], much to my own disappointment, being someone who can't function like a normal human being for days after mine. One study in the *Current Drug Abuse Reviews*, examining the link between dehydration and hangovers, actually found no correlation between high levels of the hormones associated with dehydration and the severity of a hangover[3]. The research analysed the blood and urine samples of participants. "These analyses showed that concentrations of various hormones, electrolytes, free fatty acids, triglycerides, lactate, ketone bodies, cortisol, and glucose were not significantly correlated with reported alcohol hangover severity. Also, markers of dehydration were not significantly related to hangover severity. Some studies report a significant correlation between blood acetaldehyde concentration and hangover severity, but most convincing is the significant relationship between immune factors and hangover severity." They added that several factors can aggravate severity of a hangover, including sleep deprivation, smoking, certain chemical components in certain alcohols, health status, genetics and individual differences. Basically, if you're going to drink alcohol, make sure you drink water alongside; it will help to reduce the toxic and irritant effects via dilution, but unfortunately will not stop the hangover altogether.

As a former professional yo-yo dieter, I'd always been a little confused when it came to alcohol and whether I was allowed to drink it – having fun out with my friends – or whether I'd have to sacrifice my social life in order to achieve my "dream body". Unfortunately, I decided that it was better to be safe than sorry, and spent Friday, Saturday and every other night of the week at home, trying to get to sleep at 10pm on an empty stomach.

I'd read a book called *The French Don't Diet Plan*, in which author and neuroscientist Will Clower states that small amounts of wine can be consumed as part of a healthy diet – or rather, it won't make you fat. It's a common cliché that the French like to enjoy wine as part of most evening meals, but is this the "healthiest" way to live? Does science say that alcohol can be a part of our everyday lives and won't result in an excruciating untimely death? Or should alcohol be avoided like the plague? Is it making us all fat and miserable?

As the premise of this book is to promote balance, I'd be pretty bummed if I found out I had to stop drinking that bottle of Bud after work in order to be my "best self", but thankfully, Ursula doesn't believe this should be the case. "There are several possible reasons for the beneficial effects of drinking moderately. Moderate alcohol consumption may raise the 'good' cholesterol in your bloodstream, decrease blood pressure (a major risk factor for heart disease), lower the concentration of fibrinogen in the blood (a substance that contributes to blood clots), cut the risk of diabetes (another major risk factor of heart disease) and reduce stress and anxiety temporarily." The key word there is temporarily. Alcohol is a depressant, which means it can mess up your mental health if abused over time. When I drink heavily, I tend to feel quite low for a couple of days after. My mum calls these "the holy rollers".

Elaborating on the point that moderate alcohol consumption has the potential to reduce the risk of heart disease, Ursula says: "The relationship between alcohol and cardiovascular disease is complex, and seems to depend on several factors. Light to moderate drinking is linked to reduced risk of cardiovascular disease, while heavy drinking appears to increase the risk." Alcohol consumption guidelines in the UK are currently no more than 14 units a week for both men and women.

Drink Aware, a leading UK website for alcohol advice, has further information on the possible positive benefits of small amounts of alcohol, particularly for those of middle age and older, including reducing the amount of fatty deposits in our arteries and preventing the formation of blood clots[4]. But before you run away with that information and down the nearest bottle of Malbec because you think drinking will protect your heart, know that there are harmful health effects that far outweigh the positives. Alcohol consumption is a risk factor for cancers of the mouth, throat, colon, breast and liver. The cells lining the mouth and throat are especially vulnerable to the harmful effects of alcohol. Even light alcohol consumption – one drink a day – is linked to a 20 per cent increased risk of mouth and throat cancer, and this risk increases with the daily amount consumed. More than four drinks daily appears to cause a fivefold increase in the risk of mouth and throat cancer, and also increases the risk of breast, colon and liver cancer.

Red wine, in fact, had been hailed by scientists as containing the cancer-busting antioxidant resveratrol, which is a compound that attacks cancer cells and can protect the heart and brain from damage. However, the NHS responded by saying that as it appears that red wine is almost the only source of resveratrol in the human diet, to see any benefits, a person would need to consume around 60 litres of red wine a day, which is certainly not feasible (or recommended!)[5]. Alcohol can also irritate your digestive system. Drinking even a little makes your stomach produce more acid than usual, which can in turn cause gastritis – the inflammation of the stomach lining which triggers stomach pain, vomiting and diarrhoea. The digestive system works extra hard to eliminate alcohol from the body, prioritizing its elimination ahead of other nutrients, including lipids (fats), carbohydrates and proteins.

It's useful to take all these terrifying bits of information with a pinch of salt. These are all important things to be aware of, but if cutting out the occasional drink leaves you miserable, have that occasional drink and enjoy it, remembering that if ifs and buts were sherry and nuts we'd all have a Merry Christmas.

You might be reading this as a "drunkorexic" – an individual who is a binge drinker, starving all day in order to get drunk at night. The term has appeared in media reports but is not an officially recognized diagnostic term. It's a dangerous practice, as it leaves people more exposed to the toxic effects of alcohol, which affects mood and decision-making. This often leads to a food binge following the drinking and subsequent vomiting, with low mood and anxiety the following day. If this sounds like you, drinking could be very triggering for you, and cause your mental health to spiral. You may need to seek some professional help.

Us disordered eaters have an increased risk of becoming disordered drinkers too, and so it's important to be aware when this may be affecting you and to deal with it (by seeing your GP) accordingly. Many of us feel that if we are to enjoy ourselves – to out to the cluuuurb and drink our weight in rum and Coke – we have to compensate for these calories by restricting our diets for days to follow. In terms of the myths surrounding alcohol and weight gain, "empty calories" is a term often thrown around. But what are they?

"This simply means that there is virtually no other nutritional value from alcoholic drinks, other than energy," Ursula explains. "Beer contains a similar number of calories as sugary soft drinks, ounce for ounce, whereas red wine contains twice as many. However, studies investigating the link between alcohol and weight have provided inconsistent results. It seems that drinking habits and preferences may play a role. For example, moderate drinking is linked to reduced weight gain, whereas heavy drinking is linked to increased weight gain. Drinking beer regularly may cause weight gain, whereas wine consumption may reduce it."

In the age of the Kardashians and the impossibly tiny waist, beer bellies can be one of the most cripplingly terrible threats. But it isn't a case of "if I drink beer I'll develop a gut". If you think about the lifestyle of people with beer bellies, they are people who go to the pub most nights, or they sit at home drinking – they're also likely to be snacking. Weight gain and beer bellies aren't typically caused by one factor alone – such as beer. Smoking, little exercise, genetics and overeating all contribute. When you drink beer, your liver has to work hard to detoxify the alcohol, and even harder when packets of crisps and peanuts are added. Over time, all these calories will add up and contribute to a beer gut[6].

Age and gender both play roles in determining whether you will get a beer gut or not. After the age of 35 most men's metabolisms start to slow down, and while men tend to put weight on their bellies, women's fat stores commonly go on their backside and hips.

So, what's the problem with the beer belly? Aside from it not being today's beauty ideal...

Well, research suggests that carrying extra weight around your middle presents a greater health risk than just being obese. Private healthcare provider BMI Healthcare explains that if you carry fat around your waist – known as central obesity – you have a greater chance of cardiovascular issues than if you are overweight or obese but have a normal fat distribution. "Central obesity is also linked to an overall higher mortality risk. In fact, adults of a healthy weight who carry weight on their stomach have double the mortality risk compared to overweight or obese people with normal fat distribution. The fat around your waist is more dangerous than fat deposited in the legs or buttocks because it is an indicator of having too much fat inside the abdomen, or visceral fat. This can cause inflammation to the internal organs which would put you at a higher risk of developing a chronic condition."[7] The whole "should we drink alcohol" debate rumbles on. It's fair to say that if the harmful effects of alcohol had been known when it was introduced, it probably wouldn't be legalized today. Alcohol is, in fact, a drug, and can cause irreparable harm to some people and those who love them. Some of my favourite memories have been under the influence of alcohol – storytelling with my friends in fields, travelling around Prague on a bar crawl for my 20th birthday and drinking lager every day as I interrailed across Europe – but equally, so have some of my worst. I recognize that the best thing to do is to keep my alcohol consumption low in order to preserve the state of my mental health, but I am certainly not going to deprive myself entirely, especially not for fear of it causing me to gain weight. If you're going to drink, try to have at least two consecutive days off after.

WHY YOU SHOULD ALWAYS EAT BEFORE GETTING DRUNK

Laura looks back at her own episodes of drinking on an empty stomach and explains why this isn't such a good idea.

When I look back at the years when I first dabbled with rebellion and drinking alcohol, I find it difficult to determine whether the nights that I spent vomiting into my lap were due to the fact I had been starving myself all day (or days) leading up to this, and therefore couldn't "handle" a normal amount of alcohol, or whether it was because I'd drunk 15,683 double vodka lemonades...although these memories are hazy, I have a strong suspicion that – for the majority of the time – it was the latter.

Don't be fooled by the opening to this section: I'm no partier. No, no, I'm thoroughly boring, as you suspected. However, there was a short time during the couple of years before I was legal to drink where I was a precocious and lying extrovert, going out every Friday and Saturday night with a shoddy fake ID and the sole purpose of getting "off my trolley" and attracting an equally trollied member of the opposite sex for a quick snog to Flo Rida's "Low". Romance, eh? Nowadays, life-threatening hangovers and a preference for going to bed before midnight cancel out my yearning to go to a nightclub and dance terribly...but I do sometimes enjoy looking back fondly at a time when it wasn't a "good night" unless I'd made a total arse out of myself. Instead of losing sleep to anxiety, I was losing sleep laughing with friends until the early hours and tipping the contents of my bag on to the floor of my taxi home. These friends and I would later grow apart, as my deteriorating mental health made me joyless and too much like hard work for them, but it's still nice to reminisce about a time when I was considered the life of some sort of party.

A nightclub called Snobs is a place where I keep some of the most treasured memories from my teens. Covered in scaffolding and sticky flooring, I'd waddle from room to room sharing sweaty hugs with people I half-knew and enjoying the drama of courting in the smoking area. But my favourite part of a night out was always the food run on the journey home. Nothing extinguishes a churning stomach full of alcohol like a Styrofoam bucket full of cheesy chips and a spongy chicken mayo burger. This meal was sacred, and prevented me having to pay an extra £30 to apologize for vomiting in the taxi on the way home. It felt as though this greasy meal was a magical eraser of all bad decisions.

Just as I knew of the importance of the post-night-out meal, I also knew that I shouldn't drink on an empty stomach, which is a nightmare when you're trying to quit eating in order to be skinny. The words "you need to line your stomach!" rang in my head from my inner voice of reason before every first sip of rosé watered down with diet lemonade. Sometimes I'd listen, sometimes not. As you can imagine, this threat of extra calories caused a great dilemma for someone with an eating disorder, and I believe that a strong reason why I stopped going out as much – aside from the hangovers – is because I couldn't justify the calories from eating before going out, from the alcohol I'd drunk until 4am, and then from the greasy burger after. Having an eating disorder can stop you from socializing for fear of a lack of control when you are presented with food in the outside world. This was definitely true for the young me.

I recall one particular humiliating experience of mine, where I was invited to pre-drink with a small group of girls I'd become friends with through college. We'd meet at one of the girl's parents' house, as would be routine for most of our nights out. But this time was different. Two boys were on their way too – one of them being my future boyfriend. I'd heard a rumour that he fancied me, so there was a fluttery tension between the girls, as they predicted a romance blossoming. I was unsure, but willing to comply in order to remain somewhat popular.

To the silent horror of all my friends (bar one), I arrived skinnier than ever, having starved myself for the week or two prior in preparation for this night out. Although I didn't fancy this guy at this time, I sure as hell couldn't look fat in front of him. My one not-so-silent friend exploded at me with concern, prodding me for info on how I'd managed to lose all this weight, telling me I looked "ill", and that I needed to eat right at that very second. "Make her some toast!" she bellowed, and another girl went to obey her orders. I struggled through every bite, embarrassed, before I felt I was allowed alcohol.

This memory has sat with me uncomfortably for many years since. At the time I believed "the toast incident" had happened because this friend cared about me but I now suspect that her intervention had less to do with concern for my health than I thought and more to do with the competitive nature of weight loss within a group of young girls. I think this because when I was at my worst – when I had put on weight and was struggling with a binge eating disorder – she, and many others, were nowhere to be seen.

Within that story, there are a lot of psychological layers to unpick, but without deviating from the topic at hand too much, this girl's reasoning was that I'd be sick from the drinking that was to come if I didn't eat. And, whatever her motives, she was, in fact, right. Having grown up a little since, I know now to turn to experts for advice, which is why I asked dietitian Ursula if she believes we should eat before drinking. Yes, she agrees, adamantly. A good meal that includes carbohydrates and fats will not stop alcohol getting into your system, but it will delay the rate of alcohol absorption. But don't be misled – carry on drinking heavily and you will get drunk. The Harm Reduction for Alcohol website, or HAMS, explains in more science-y terms why our bodies absorb alcohol more slowly when we eat beforehand: "The surface area of the stomach is only a couple of square feet, but because of the presence of villi [finger-like projections of tissue] the surface area of the small intestine is roughly 2,600 square feet. What this means in practical terms is that the small intestine is very efficient at absorbing alcohol whereas the stomach is very inefficient. Between the stomach and the small intestine there is a valve called the pyloric valve. When you eat a good-sized meal this valve closes to keep the food in the stomach for digestion. If the meal has a high fat content the valve can remain closed for up to six hours. Proteins pass through more quickly and carbohydrates pass through the quickest of all. So if you eat a big meal of fried chicken or pizza before you drink, the alcohol will be absorbed slowly, your blood alcohol content will remain low, and you will not become intoxicated quickly. Drinking on an empty stomach will make blood alcohol levels rise very quickly and you may well pass out or suffer a blackout."[8] So yes, please do eat before you get drunk. Not only because you don't want to get drunk too quick, but because drinking and having a good time when you're out can mean you might skip dinner, or getting in a decent evening meal, whether deliberately or through "just forgetting". We here are reasonable people. This far into this book, you should know by now that you need to regularly feed yourself and feed yourself well, and this means even when you're pissed as a fart...or about to be.

A little additional advice? If you notice that your friend hasn't eaten before you're about to go out on a sesh, please don't force-feed them. Politely nudge them, reminding them that they should eat. Offer to make them something nice, but don't be a dick.

IT COULD HAVE BEEN ALCOHOL!

Eve asks if eating disorders are an addiction.

Several gems of stupidity have been flung at me since the onset of my eating disorder. From the "OMFG BUT HOW CAN YOU THINK YOU'RE FAT YOU'RE SOOOOOO SKINNY!" to the predictable "How can you resist chocolate?", I've batted away some real stinkers. But by far, the most insulting wasn't tinged with judgement or nastiness, but with ignorance.

"Man, that shit is an addiction, isn't it?" Well, no idiot, it's not, was my immediate reaction. But when the sting subsided I got to thinking. Just as in substance, gambling, shopping – even social media – addiction, the problem wasn't that I didn't *want* to stop, but that I couldn't. Was I addicted to starving myself?

Professor Janet Treasure, head of eating disorder research at King's College London, is open to the idea when it comes to bulimia and binge eating disorder, but not for anorexia. "There is some evidence that certain foods can elicit the release of dopamine in the brain, which is similar to what we see in substance addictions. But obviously it's much more complicated than a simply physiological addiction because of the thought processes that exist within it." There are eating disorder treatment centres up and down the country that view and treat the condition in exactly the same way they would an alcoholic. None of these are NHS clinics, but some are successful in treating patients using a modified version of the famous Alcoholics Anonymous 12-Step programme.

Recently, some evidence has emerged suggesting that giving a drug called naltrexone to bulimia and binge eating disorder patients shortly after they experience the urge to purge (just call me the rhyming queen) can significantly reduce both binge and purge behaviours. The drug – currently not available in the UK – is commonly given to people in the US who have suffered a heroin overdose. Known as an anti-addiction medicine, naltrexone is an opiate antagonist, meaning that it works on opiate receptors in the brain to block the effect of the drugs and reduce the desire to keep using it. Researchers argue that the substance has a similar effect in those with eating disorders – but instead of blocking the effect of heroin, they block the brain's reward response that results from the binge–purge cycle. It's a controversial standpoint, and one that I struggle with. Yet the research is supported by Professor Treasure and appears to be showing some promising results at a time when both the breadth of medication and psychological treatment for people with eating disorders is (let's be honest) pretty pathetic.

There is some scientific evidence to show that reward pathways in the brain – including the release of neurotransmitters dopamine and serotonin – are unusually active when people with eating disorders eat food[9]. A review by researchers at the University of Colorado explains that the reward circuit is hyper-sensitive in anorexia, and hypo-responsive in bulimia. We see a similar pattern in people who suffer from addictions. However – and it's a big however – most studies show that this sensitivity diminishes with recovery, indicating that such brain changes result from the "extremes of food intake"[10]. A critical analysis of the eating-disorders-as-addiction model noted that not only is the co-morbidity of eating disorders and other psychiatric illnesses higher than addictions, but community studies – in which researchers follow an entire group over a number of years – have found very few similarities between the illnesses, or concurrence between the two.

If we're addicts, does this mean that if it wasn't food, it would have been something else? Do our rampant, vulnerable brains make us destined for a life of chasing our own individual dragons?

According to eating disorders specialist Ursula – who is less than sympathetic to the ED addiction theory – brain patterns within eating disorders are a whole lot more complicated than some therapists who advocate an addiction model of eating disorders would have you believe. "It's not as simple to say one thing leads to another," she says. "There's some evidence that bulimia and binge eating are perhaps related to addictive elements of self-soothing but the food itself is not an addiction. When you look at MRI scans and neuroimaging you see similar patterns to phobias and obsessions, but not addictions. With people with anorexia, their reward systems won't light up when they're given food. It's more of a conditioned reward response that comes from starvation."

And science agrees. A 2007 review published by the American Psychological Association stated: "The validity of the addiction model of EDs has received little empirical study and the efficacy of addictions-based psychotherapies for eating disorders remains untested"[11]. Worryingly, the paper also highlights that despite the clear lack of evidence, approximately a third of clinicians and treatment providers are still tackling eating disorders according to the addiction model. While this is based on US data, it wouldn't surprise me if the number is similar for private clinics in the UK. Countless friends – in clinics up and down the country – have told of the (expensive) addiction-based, 12-Step approach thrust at their eating disorder in the hope something would stick.

A significant problem within the treatment of eating disorders – anorexia in particular – is that we still know very little about *what works*. There's a clear, evidence-based treatment plan[12] that is 60 per cent (but not 100 per cent...) effective for children and adolescents who have had an eating disorder for less than three years. But when it comes to long-standing illness in us adults we're on pretty dry land, guys. Perhaps, through a fear of not having the answer, clinicians have spun the magic wheel and landed on addiction. Or (and just speculating here), more likely, have been able to get 12-Step programmes approved because the measurable, quantitative outcomes are convenient, readable and easy.

If there's anything we know about the treatment of eating disorders it's that it certainly ain't easy. Most recent evidence shows that the steadfast nature of the condition is not the result of a neurological addiction, but rather a malfunctioning habit.

Dr Joanna Steinglass, a professor of psychiatry at New York State Psychiatric Institute, has conducted some interesting brain imaging studies that clearly demonstrate the difference between those with and without anorexia when they make food choices[13].

Whereas "healthy" controls call on the areas of the "survival" brain, typically involved with hunger and eating, anorexia patients use the dorsal striatum, which is indicated in decision-making, reward and habitual behaviours. Hence, we're no longer eating with our innate, biological senses, but with our cognitive skills. Once this pattern of thinking is practised, it becomes a force of habit or – even worse – a *routine*. It's a well-known fact within the psychological literature that once a habit is formed in the brain, it's astronomically difficult to shift. But not impossible.

Having been forced to reprogramme my inner autopilot, it's only this theory of eating disorder maintenance that has ever rung true. I'd spent two years ruminating over every edible action – and constantly drawing on a life's worth of snippets of "information" that had been bestowed upon me at one time or another. This was now inherent to my everyday functioning, so much so that I can't even provide memorable examples. It's what makes recovery so easily marred with self-loathing and guilt – I was 100 per cent committed to getting better and endeavoured to do all I could to ease the tortured, helpless pain on my mum's face when she looked at my sinewy forearms. But, for some unknown reason, I just couldn't. Until, that is, it was done for me. You can have the most controlling, meticulous parental team in the world, but trust me, if a person has an eating disorder, there's little chance that they won't be in control of what they eat. As much as my powerhouse mother prepared perfectly basted roast chicken with dietitian-instructed portions of potatoes, she couldn't stop me skipping lunch at work, or walking the long way back from the tube station. She could help, but she couldn't do it for me.

It took the mutation of my whole world and comfortable existence to squeeze my anorexia out through my ears, replacing it with anxiety and terror – at first – and then later, courage. That first bowl of orange sweet-and-sour chicken on a bed of bright white rice (neither of which I would have touched willingly) brought about an immediate freedom. I was too overwhelmed by the sudden overhaul of my environment to kick back, and within two mouthfuls – as if by magic – a plateful felt doable. If I could eat an entire plate of white (the worst) rice and sugary, battered chicken and not gain 10 stone overnight or die of a heart attack, then perhaps I'd rather enjoy a peanut butter sandwich too. And I did...a fair few, in fact. Gymming off the expected calories wasn't an option either; I wasn't allowed to move from the four walls of my room for at least five days on admission to hospital. And if my anxiety peaked to such a point that I felt the unfamiliar urge to purge, five sturdy nurses would accompany me for every trip to the toilet from there on out. The one thing that scared me more than macaroni cheese was taking a shit in front of someone.

While the way in which the nurses went about this left a lot to be desired, I understand that by forcing me to shun my habits, they quite possibly saved my life. But it takes practice to instill new behaviours as your go-to, and the help of supportive carers is absolutely key to success.

I fear that if my eating disorder was treated like an addiction – which presumably elicits a more punitive, simplistic style of "withdrawal" – the opportunity for habitual change may have been sacrificed for emphasis on the food itself. Affiliating addiction with food ultimately brings you to a dead end, both in terms of treating

eating disorders and for preventing them. One cannot abstain from food. Nor should anyone be encouraged to. As psychologist Kimberley Wilson says: "To call eating disorders an addiction is to reduce it down to something much smaller than it is."

HOW TO KNOW WHEN YOU'VE HAD TOO MUCH AND WHAT TO DO ABOUT IT

According to the charity Action on Addiction, one in three people is addicted to something. The NHS defines an addiction to alcohol as not having control over your drinking to the point where it could be harmful to you. Being addicted to something means that not having that thing causes withdrawal symptoms (or a comedown) and, because this can be unpleasant, addicts find it easier to carry on indulging than to stop, and so the cycle continues. But perhaps a more practical definition comes from an anonymous addict who said that he knew he had a problem with alcohol when he realized he needed to drink as soon as he woke up. His life had fallen apart around him without him even noticing, as alcohol had become his shield from reality.

Talk to Frank[14], a confidential drugs advice service, says that psychological and physical dependence on alcohol can creep up on you. "Your tolerance to alcohol gradually increases the more you drink, so you may find that over time you need more alcohol to get the same effect, you may seem to be getting better at holding your drink when that's really a sign of a developing problem."

As Eve explained above, addictions to food are complex and uncertain when discussing eating disorders, but alcohol addiction is clearer cut. It is a legal drug but is not something you need to consume in order to survive, unlike food. With eating disorders, alcohol is often used as a meal replacement, and may be an unhealthy tool for suppressing weight gain. It therefore makes sense that in a book focused on healing our disordered relationships with food, we discuss alcohol addiction, when to recognize when you have a problem and how to get help.

Alcohol addiction can be dangerous for many reasons, and at its worst can be fatal. It tends to exaggerate whatever mood you're in when you start drinking, and so if you drink angrily, you might end up doing something you regret. Talk to Frank explains that alcohol contributes to all kinds of problems in Britain, from violent crime to domestic violence to car-related deaths to missing work and unemployment. In terms of the harm alcohol addiction can do to your body, it is a depressant and generally slows down brain activity. The short-term risks associated with heavy drinking might include injuries and accidents such as head injuries, fractures and scars. There is also the risk of alcohol poisoning – when you consume far too much alcohol on a single occasion – which could put you in a coma or even kill you. On the other end of the spectrum, long-term risks come from regularly drinking alcohol over a long time (over 10 to 20 years or more). Then the risks of cancer, stroke, heart disease, liver disease and damage to your brain and nervous system increase.

Sarah Herbert, a mental health dietitian who specializes in eating disorders and substance misuse, explains that alcohol can become a coping strategy for many areas of life, including emotional issues, sleeping habits, socializing and other stress at work. If and when those issues and stresses increase, so does alcohol intake; the ability to cope with progressively more alcohol is due to adaptive tolerance. As with those who have an eating disorder, someone with a problem with alcohol can neglect self-care, especially when it comes to diet. Food becomes less of a priority when your day is planned around alcohol. Many people will often start to drink alcohol when they wake up in order to cope with withdrawal symptoms. This displacement of food can therefore create a progressive issue.

Having an eating disorder as well as a dependency on alcohol – the two are often related as the stress of having a mental health problem can sometimes lead to the sufferer seeking solace in other destructive methods – can be a slippery slope. Alcohol can, like food, be filling and confuse appetite signals, telling the brain that you are full. It also contains lots of calories – more than any other food except for fat. Abusing alcohol when you have an eating disorder can put you at higher risk of poor nutritional and physical status, because you are not eating what your body needs to function properly. Alcohol does not have any nutritional value, so it will provide the energy for you to function but nothing else – and that's scary.

Like with any addiction, it could take a long time before you are ready to admit that you have a problem. So when you do, you may feel like you have "missed the boat" with regard to seeking treatment. Sarah doesn't believe this to be true. "The first step is to admit there is a problem you need support with," she says. "Whether you attend a mental health detox withdrawal unit or become admitted for physical health problems as a result of alcohol intake, aim to be open and honest about the situation and know that there is always help and support."

If you feel you need help with alcohol dependence[15,16], the first thing you should do is talk to your GP. If they think you are regularly drinking more than the current UK guidelines, then they can help to figure out why that may be. If there is evidence of mental health problems, your GP can refer you to counselling, cognitive behavioural therapy (CBT) services or community mental health teams for different types of therapy and support. These teams can facilitate recovery, and if they feel you may need more specialist support, they can refer you to (or you can self-refer to) a community drug and alcohol team (CDAT), who can support and help with substance misuse.

If using alcohol has become an even bigger issue that is significantly affecting your or someone else's life, and you are therefore becoming at risk of being mentally and physically unwell, CDAT teams can refer you for an alcohol detox withdrawal. This usually means a stay within an NHS hospital on a specialist ward that will support you through medically managed alcohol withdrawal. During this time, you're likely to receive support involving psychological factors, such as relapse prevention. You may also, if you're lucky, have access to a specialist dietitian who will assess your nutritional and physical status, since alcohol can obviously have very damaging effects on the body. The idea is that they will support you with your diet on the ward and prepare you with practical ideas around eating when you are discharged.

You might have heard rosy stories about the possibility of recovery without medical intervention, but the evidence to support this is slim. In the case of alcoholism, it is best to trust the experts and seek help when you need it. There is no shame in admitting when you are struggling – it could save your life.

*"Exercise for 55 minutes,
five times a week to lose weight."*
– Telegraph

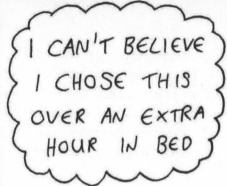

I CAN'T BELIEVE I CHOSE THIS OVER AN EXTRA HOUR IN BED

EXERCISE

HOW MUCH EXERCISE IS ENOUGH?

As a lifetime physical activity dodger, Eve wonders how much exercise is really necessary to keep her healthy and if daily gym trips are actually just a big, sweaty waste of time.

If I see one more sign on public transport informing me of my "unlocked physical potential", I think I'll have an aneurism. Thanks for your blind faith, instructor Carl (your guns say "personal trainer" but your terrible shell suit says "mechanic"), but I've met me and am therefore well aware that this feeble, Jewish body will never ever be "good" at exercise. I'm the kid who shields her head with her hands when walking within a mile of a friendly football game. I get stitches just from clenching my bum cheeks too hard, and I will do anything within my power to avoid taking the rubbish out (it involves a 30-second walk). I literally once cried because it was cold. Fitness is not my thing. I'm not sure if the gene for muscle movement was left out from my DNA, or if it was being raised by parents who never owned a pair of tracksuit bottoms; whatever the reason, physical activity will never be one of my strong points. And I'm okay with that.

When I became ill, exercise "purging" wasn't a huge concern for those who know me well; even at my most sick I'd struggle to spend more than 40 minutes at the gym. When my weight became a little more stable, I began dipping my toes into gentle exercise via the rather decadent rooftop pool at a local member's club. It was partly because I was curious as to what my now healthy-ish body could achieve, and partly because said member's club gave out free sweets.

Three weeks into my twice-weekly swimming routine – and I'm talking scared-to-put-my-head-under-the-water swimming – I'd lost almost a kilo. "But I can't even do front crawl!" I'd protest to my consultant. It would seem that only an hour of leisurely swimming combined with power walking to and from tube stations, marching up and down stairs and dancing until the wee hours in seedy nightclubs was more than enough exercise to keep my body burning up my daily calories...and then some.

Granted, it is true that those who are underweight or are in recovery from a restrictive eating disorder may lose weight faster than others. However, the information collected by my phone's "health" app enlightened me as to the exercise we do when we're not even aware of it, probably because we're not dressed in activewear and surrounded by gurning idiots. The constant rhetoric of "not doing enough" that we're lambasted with by news articles, government schemes and social media may apply to some, but not everyone. And even for those who are permanently parked on their leather recliner (the dream) – is constantly shaming them and ordering them to adopt a habit they clearly don't enjoy even helpful? Too many of my slender friends begrudgingly ferry themselves to the gym before sunrise every morning to prevent the dreaded extra inch of tummy fat, but is there even any point? Or, more importantly, could my fitspo-focused pals be causing themselves harm?

One thing's for sure: spending the best part of your Sunday afternoon cooped up in a clammy gym is definitely a waste of your valuable roast-eating time. According to a new study by McMaster University in Ontario, Canada, in which a group of "out-of-shape" men tried different exercise regimes, just 1 minute of intensive exercise has the same physiological effects as 45 minutes of mid-level sweating.

According to the authors of the study, 3 minutes of intense intermittent exercise, within a total time commitment of 30 minutes per week, is as effective as 150 minutes per week of moderate-intensity continuous training. The study only included results based on 25 men but, nevertheless, it provides pretty substantial support for the benefits of short bursts of exercise. So can the same be said for all of us?

I sought the advice of seasoned fitness professionals (neither of whom have a fitspo Instagram account to plug) for the answers. Susan Hunter, clinical dietitian and nutritional consultant to the Scottish women's rugby team says that 40 minutes each day is usually enough – and that can be a brisk walk. She also adds that the proposed guidelines – as suggested by the government and NHS England – may vary depending on the individual.

"Everyone is fixated on numbers," she says, "the 30-day squat challenge is an example. That's not promoting a healthy relationship with exercise. Sometimes, for whatever reason, you can't exercise. It's about what is right for you and what you want to achieve." Susan's comments reiterate what I already know about all the scaremongering messages that bombard us, warning of chronic disease should we enjoy a hungover duvet day. Although the messages are everywhere they're not meant for anxious, middle-class health writers like me. The target audience most likely have much bigger, more pressing priorities than calculating their macros and scheduling in a Pilates class. The reasons why their health is compromised are far more complex than mere laziness.

Regardless of who the government aims to target with these initiatives, tribes of the "worried well" soak up the memos like sponges and, despite the weekly spin/yoga/boxing classes, remain convinced that they're not doing enough. When my illness took hold, I thought I'd need to get to the gym at least three times a week just to counteract the hours I spend sitting on my arse, at a desk, eating Colin the Caterpillar cake.

While Susan says it's realistic to make it to the gym three times a week, she also points out that the frequency very much depends on a) if activity is a part of your lifestyle (walking to the tube, for example) and b) what your personal goals are. Weight loss is just one consequence of exercise and should not be the sole reason that anyone gets their body moving. "Exercise has so many positives," she says, "neurally, it promotes positive mental health and there's also a great social aspect."

Dr Stephen Mears, a sports scientist from Loughborough University, is well versed in the world of performance, Olympic-level exercise. The crème de la crème of performance level is pretty rare, according to Mears, despite what the Instagram gun show may have you believe. "Very few people get to that level of performance relationship exercise. For most people, it's about getting exercise into your routine – some is better than none. The American College of Sports Medicine recommends sticking to about 150 minutes per week of moderate exercise. This can be anything from a brisk walk to a leisurely bike ride."

That's as little as 20 minutes per day, which I've already done by the time I sit down at my desk at nine in the morning.

And if (for some weird reason) you're wedded to a weekly spinning class, that 150 minutes of moderate exercise per week can be reduced down to 90. Spinning, as well as HIIT training (eew) or long runs are all classed as vigorous exercise (vigorous is anything that raises your heart rate by around 80 or 90 per cent) and just one single session a week means you'll smash your 150-minute target in just a couple of days.

If running's your bag, and you're keen to get good at it, Dr Mears recommends downloading the hailed NHS Couch to 5K app and heading out on two to three runs per week. And yes, that *is* enough.

All that moderate exercise builds up an appetite (well, for me anyway), so what do the experts recommend that we fuel our body with pre- and post-gym session? Pints of protein shake and green smoothies, right? The substance used to refuel some of the fittest female athletes in the country may come as a surprise. Yes my friends, I'm talking about carbs.

"The night before a game, the team have plenty of carbs," Susan tells me of the diet she prescribes for the women of the Scottish rugby team. "The carbs will be low in fibre, so perhaps mashed potato with no skins. There's bread and porridge for breakfast and then about three hours before the game, the girls make their own sandwiches."As for protein shakes, both Susan and Dr Mears agree that they have their place within elite sport but only when, for whatever reason, you're unable to source protein from your lunch or dinner.

Both experts make it crystal clear that a food source is always preferable to the liquid, milkshake version. "You should be having a good source of protein with every meal and more carbohydrates if you're exercising," Dr Mears says.

The good source he's referring to? About 20–25g of protein, so about one chicken breast. You hear that, abs freaks, with your three-steak lunch on "legs day"? ONE CHICKEN BREAST WILL DO.

Any excess protein – the very same found in your overpriced tubs of protein powder – will be urinated out. The term pissing money away springs to mind.

But if you don't have an unlimited supply of cooked poultry, there's another ingredient which experts hail as useful for aiding the regeneration of cells after exercise. And it's available everywhere – milk. Susan gives milk to the girls after training as it's great for helping to generate muscle.

Supplementary energy gels are another minefield – do the drinks, powders and energy balls deliver the firecracker of speed they promise? "Most of them are essentially just sugar," Dr Mears says. "Energy gels are good in certain circumstances, if you're in the middle of a marathon or triathlon, for instance." And sugar is sugar is sugar, meaning that there are much easier (and tastier) methods of re-juicing. "Jelly Babies are a good option too," says Mears. "A lecturer here recently did a triathlon and fuelled himself only on Percy Pigs." Excellent.

The little kid inside me who had a permanently "sprained ankle" for every school PE lesson is delighted that she doesn't have to run a marathon every year in order to be healthy. Exercise doesn't have to be goal-oriented, performance-based or even remotely intensive. In fact, the healthiest form of exercise is a hell of a lot simpler, and less expensive than attempting to combat those army tank machines at the gym. If you're exhausted, in pain or losing weight unnecessarily, you're probably doing too much. If you lead a relatively active life, eat a normal balanced diet and walk a bit more on the weekends, you're probably doing enough. But if you're strongly passionate about running and genuinely enjoy spending entire weekends burning iron at the gym...well, that's up to you.

WHEN SHOULD WE EXERCISE?

For some strange reason, Laura actually enjoys the occasional run. Before she explains why, she ponders the question, when should we be exercising?

Exercise: that lovable rogue now brave enough to pound on your bedroom door – thanks to social media and a "do it all" culture – and drag you out of bed by the scruff of your neck. The inescapable popularity of fitness fills our Instagram feeds by the minute and is unwilling to let us forget our awkward PE memories from school – like Eve's imaginary sprained ankles. The very notion of participating in sports seems to fill some with delight and makes others tremble and sweat before managing even one star jump. Protein powders, #gains, Nike, gym shorts, mirror selfies and lifting heavy – these are the foundations on which successful people in a postmillennial world are built, aren't they?

The delights of "wakey wakey eggs and bacey" or enjoying your eggs with a kiss in the morning seem to have been elbowed out the way to make room for an early workout. Social media had me convinced that everybody else had already been up three hours before me to complete their hot yoga classes, leaving me paranoid that I wasn't doing enough – even though at the time of this short gym obsession I was working a full time job, walking to the tube every morning and having a social life. A chance to "tighten those abs", "work those glutes" and "banish the bingo wings", I admit, got in the way of my spontaneity and work/life balance for a while. At the time of Not Plant Based's birth into the blogging world, I had developed a slight obsession with working out, something I didn't realize my eating disorder had latched on to in order to retain some kind of control over my health. I felt bad if I didn't go to the gym at least five times a week and I'd frequently cancel plans so that I could squeeze in an outrageously long exercise workout I'd found online

– totally unsuited to my abilities, might I add. I should have known, considering the website I found it on was called bodybuilding.com. My day revolved around when I was going to work out and all my meals were planned accordingly, because I sure as hell didn't want to be that girl who splashed vomit on the treadmill because she ate a bucket of potato salad on the way over. I also will admit now that this control over when I ate around exercise allowed for more opportunities for me to "go hungry" in favourite of squatting.

Thankfully Not Plant Based helped me snap out of this way of thinking fairly sharpish, but the obsession with exercise and allowing it to control your day isn't an unfamiliar story. Many of my friends, and family members too, now plan their day around when they go to the gym and therefore their meals so that they can have the supposedly maximum amount of energy available to them squeezed from their sweet potatoes.

To me, it is a depressing thought that the need to look good (and let's face it, that is why most people go to the gym) is more important today than our desire to take our time eating well, to mull over which tomatoes to buy at the market, to cook and be kind to ourselves without the worry of wiping out the gains we earned at the gym. I'd much rather spend my time making pancakes and lying horizontally, I realise now.

Nestled in the core of a serial dieter's brain is a niggling voice chanting that if we are not exercising until we drop each day, we are not reaching our "full potential" – whatever that means. It became apparent to me that exercise had turned into a form of competition with myself, a one-upmanship game rather than a way to possibly improve and regulate my mental health. Once I realized this, I was able to nip it in the bud with an email terminating my gym membership in favour of long walks and Netflix.

During the pubescent years of my eating disorder, workout DVDs and fitness gurus would advise me to "get it out the way", to get up and moving before work so I'd be able to flourish by 10am. I remember reading that exercise was a vital component for weight loss and good health, so I binged and bought myself a pile of cheesy celebrity-endorsed fitness DVDs. As a result I was routinely reminded that to exercise at the beginning of the day was the best way to get the most out of the workout. In my head, if I hadn't exercised in the morning, I had failed.

At the age of just 17, in addition to bulimia, Davina McCall became my kryptonite, although in fairness I could have fixated on any celebrity Tom, Dick or Harry, as long as they were leading me on the path toward thinness. I would come home from college and lock myself in my parents' room, much to their annoyance (they had the DVD player), and pound away to a boxercise workout for half an hour each day. Now, that may not seem particularly excessive, and it might not have been, had I not been sustaining myself on just two bananas and two cups of white tea a day at that point. Although I very much enjoy exercise now (in moderation), back then it was a tool solely to aid rapid weight loss, rather than a way to improve my crumbling and vulnerable mental health. A few years on and I now acknowledge and attribute my disordered eating to anxieties and growing up in a society that only seemed to value girls if they were good-looking, but a few years back I could only be cruel to my body – unsympathetic to the real root of my fixations.

I had unfortunately lost a grasp on all the sporty things that made me feel good throughout my childhood, like riding ponies, running through fields for the hell of it as the long grass scratched my knees and swimming with my little brother on holiday until my hands looked like prunes. Exercising with an eating disorder only created more things to get hung up on and control, and one of those things was when exactly I should exercise during the day. I now realize that perhaps my thinking was a little clouded...but it does still raise the question of when is the best time of day to exercise?

Science suggests that there are in fact specific times during the day when we might be best able to exercise. With sleep dictated by our circadian rhythms (body clock to me and you), most of us have a cognitive peak at 9ªm, a dip at 2pm and a physical peak at 6pm – which could be why more world records are broken in the evening than daytime. As our ability to do complex cognitive skills peaks earlier in the day and our motor skills peak later in the day, ideally one would focus exercise to match those times. In other words, learning new skills or techniques in the morning and tackling endurance or fitness work in the evening could, scientifically speaking, be the answer.

However, there are studies to support the argument for exercising in the morning. One published in *Medicine & Science in Sports & Exercise* evaluated women after working out (a brisk 45-minute walk) first thing. They found that on the days that participants exercised in the morning, they also increased their physical activity throughout the day, more so than days they didn't. Additional benefits to this early-bird exercising included an increased metabolism, which is the rate at which our bodies convert the fuel in the food we eat into the energy.

A different study's findings also favoured the morning workout, as it suggested that revving up your fitness regime in the evening could compromise your sleep – something that could be an issue for you anyway. This is because exercise increases your heart rate and body temperature. There is evidence to show that working out at 7am, compared to later in the afternoon or evening, could help us get a better quality sleep at night[1].

As with most things concerning our health, diet and bodies, when to exercise is as much down to individual preference than any other factor. Some people are night owls and feel much more awake in the evening, others are larks and feel better first thing. Oh, and some people have that minor annoyance of a full-time job that means you have to organize your workouts to fit around it – or rather, scrap them altogether.

Another area of interest – or perhaps it's a concern for the disordered eater – is when to structure meals and snacks around exercise. The truth is that there isn't a specific, set formula for when to eat, how much to eat and how long to wait after eating to exercise – no matter what the health magazines tell you. Again, it comes down to personal preference and good old-fashioned trial and error.

I've got a confession to make. When I quit my gym membership (I've now rejoined, but only go when I feel like it) and gave up the five-times-a-week workouts, I didn't feel any less healthy. I didn't struggle for energy; in fact, I felt far less tired without pounding away on a treadmill. I didn't have any anxiety about when I would be able to squeeze in a workout today, but most importantly for me, I didn't feel like my life was over now that a small cushion of fat had enveloped my abs.

If you came here with pen and paper poised, ready to list down the exact times you should be exercising and when to eat your post-workout snack, I can only apologize. It's down to you to discover how best and when best you feel you'd like to move your body. Whether that's a midnight dance-off with a stomach full of tequila or a run bright and early in the morning, as long as you feel good about doing it, that's really all that matters.

LAURA EXPLORES THE DANGERS OF INSTY #FITSPO

Can I tell you guys a secret? Without you all judging me?

(*Signals for you to come closer.*)

Before Not Plant Based launched, in the very early days (looks over shoulder in case Eve is ready to sniper me), I had visions of Not Plant Based being a "fitspo" blog. A blog where I could post about my recovery, but only in terms of my ability to "stay skinny", and the mythical formula I used to get there, without pranging out about my very current – at the time – eating disorder, and with the hope that fitness could be a way to "cure" my binge eating.

(*Ducks a bullet.*)

I know...can you imagine?

As if the world needed another one of those vapid wellness blogs riddled with photos of my abs. But hear me out! I was a mess at the time. I wasn't thinking straight. My obsession with going to the gym too many times a week had bled dry any sense from my brain, and I was left only thinking selfishly of the sort of blog that I could run where people would actually be interested in reading – or looking – at me, me, me.

Thankfully, Eve shook some sense into me, and made me realize that there is life beyond fitspo and wellness, and welcomed me with loving arms into a community of others who were sick of this Instagram culture. This meant that my eating disorder recovery – my REAL recovery – was able to begin.

I'm not the only person to have been swept up by the fitspo culture. I think everyone with an Instagram account – the millions of us – have fallen prey to Bootea-sponsored adverts and paying for gym memberships we can't afford at some point or other in order to look "healthier". Haven't we? Even some of the big influencers have admitted to buckling under the pressures of having to maintain washboard abs every single day.

Remember Essena O'Neill? In 2015, at just 18, the Aussie influencer with 574,000 Instagram followers, 250,000 YouTube subscribers and 250,000 followers on Tumblr had a digital breakdown via social media, announcing her early retirement from it in a bid to protect her mental health. Essena went through her social media feed revealing the truth behind the images of her "perfect" body and beach-blond waves, explaining how in one photo she made her sister take hundreds of photos of her, after not eating all day, so that her abs were visible.

In one of my favourite TEDx talks titled "Me, My Selfie and I", psychologist Dr Linda Papadopoulos notes that the Instagram pages, or "adverts", of young girls and boys tend to be following a pattern. The boys try to portray themselves as hyper-masculine, and the girls hyper-sexualized. These young girls and boys appear to be searching for "off-the-shelf identities" to gain approval from these enormous audiences – in mine and Essena's cases, to look "fitter".

If someone as typically gorgeous-looking as Essena can't even cope with the pressure, how is everyone else meant to?

Dr Chris Stiff, a psychology lecturer at Keele University, believes that none of us are immune from being influenced by what we see online, and that includes Essena. He says, "Research suggests that an online context can be just as persuasive as an offline context, and more so in some cases," adding, "the algorithms used by a lot of news aggregation sites lead to *confirmation bias*. For example, say I search about flat earth theories...that search is tracked, and then articles about flat earth start appearing in my browser. I will probably click on these, exacerbating the cycle. Suddenly, all the sources I come across are just confirming my ideas (as they are designed to get me to click). My ideas about a flat earth become more and more entrenched because nothing I 'find' refutes it."

With regard to why social media has the ability to make us view ourselves negatively, Chris explains: "The main issue is that we choose what we put on social media. So, your feed tends to only have the good stuff in it! People view the feed of others and think that reflects an accurate picture of their life when of course it does not. The actor–observer bias argues that we tend to attribute others' actions to their disposition, but our actions to our environment. So if we see other people having a great time on Facebook, we tend to think, 'They must be a great person, and have a great life', ignoring the role of circumstance. This leads to unfavourably social comparisons, and makes us feel bad." Ain't that the truth.

Through my own experience, I have learned to recognize Instagram as a virtual shopping place, where fitspo and wellness influencers can promote themselves as products without the obvious guise of an advert in a magazine, as they appear to just be living their "normal" lives. Women and men, often who have had surgery, are selling products and packages to vulnerable people who want to look like them. As you can imagine, this has become a dangerous method of marketing for a generation that is seeking approval online.

Samantha Smith – a woman who, funnily enough, I found on Instagram – admits that fitspo culture really messed up her mental health. "I became so consumed by the wellness and fitness industry and striving to look like the fitness models that are so dominant online now, or the personal trainers in the gym where I exercise that I ended up with pretty crippling body dysmorphic disorder (BDD). My whole life revolved around exercising, making sure I was tracking my macronutrients and eating my calorie allowance. I've missed out on numerous social events like friends' birthdays or celebrating the end of university exams because it meant losing progress and not seeing the results I was after as fast. It was my whole life for at least two years.

"As a result of this fixation, I now receive psychiatric help and participate in regular cognitive behavioural therapy sessions with my psychiatrist. I hated myself and my body so much that I was diagnosed with clinical depression and anxiety. [Fitspo] just played on this belief system that I am not and was not good enough, because I did not have a stomach as toned as some of the most popular fitspo girls."

Despite what you might think, there are actually people within the online fitness world who are dedicated to promoting safer messages about fitness and building positive body images for their followers. Two of my favourites are UK-based personal trainers Tome Levi and Hannah Lewin. We connected through the internet, ironically, but gravitated toward each other because of our shared opinion on how toxic the fitness community can be online. Tome explains that Instagram is being abused as a platform by the fitness industry and "wellness warriors" to make users believe that their bodies are unacceptable as they are, but the reality is that there is no such thing as an ideal body type. "The irony here is that an industry that should be promoting health and wellbeing is instead creating a potentially very harmful environment. The obsession with conforming to this so-called ideal body type brings with it the potential dangers of overtraining, disordered eating conditions, physical injury, exercise addiction and an overall detrimental impact on mental health."

It's rare that Instagram stars with rock-hard abs selling their "one size fits all" plans talk about the role that genetics can play in the speed at which muscle definition occurs, nor do they speak realistically about the low body fat percentage that people have to achieve in order to display clear muscle definition. Hannah explains: "This low body fat percentage is generally achieved by long periods of restriction, which obviously can be extremely triggering for many and cause damage, or further damage, to their relationship with food." Everyone's body is genetically different, and this needs much more recognition.

It's no secret that the fitness industry on Instagram is huge business. All you have to do is hit the explore button and you are confronted by countless influencers with inadequate qualifications all attributing their six-pack abs to the newest "fitness" product on the market. Although we understand that people have to make their money somehow, what grieves us is the promotion of faddy products that have no scientific basis. The problem arises when such products are sold under a series of manipulative circumstances. Customers are made to feel inadequate and unhappy with their bodies, and suddenly a product pops up on your phone that promises a solution to a problem you didn't know you had minutes before. While this marketing tactic can be deemed harmless when buying shampoo, the same cannot be said for nutritional supplements, diet pills, waist trainers and "one size fits all" fitness programmes.

The reason we feel it's important to call out such unethical marketing techniques is not out of jealousy (I'd have abs too if I exercised for three months straight, jeez!) but because I know first-hand how dangerous these ethically wobbly adverts can be for vulnerable people. I don't believe the fitness industry on Instagram caused my eating disorder, but it certainly fuelled it, as I embarked on dressed-up fad diets that I thought could cure me. Surprise, surprise it never did. Tome agrees: "Wellness and fitspo often deliver messages which can be detrimental for people who struggle with their relationships with food. Watching what-I-eat-in-a-day videos and generic bikini prep meal guides can be triggering for individuals who have a history of disordered eating."

Hannah believes that unrealistic imagery, restrictive diet plans and unqualified advice can be extremely dangerous to many people, and this is sadly reflected in the extreme rise of orthorexia (an unhealthy preoccupation with eating "correctly" or "healthily") as Instagram users have increased. "There simply isn't enough policing of these types of accounts that can cause harm, or support for more vulnerable users."

So, if we are those people easily influenced and prone to disordered eating, does that mean we should just throw our phones into the nearest bin and cry into our pillows? Not quite.

If you use Instagram, the first piece of advice I would offer is to unfollow anyone who either says or advertises anything that makes you feel less than worthy. Your feed breeds the energy you put out, so if you are searching for weight loss videos, your feed will be full of other similar video suggestions. Seek out accounts focusing on positive health and fitness that are run by professionals who care about the consumer. If you see an image that looks altered, read a caption that doesn't stack up scientifically or read advice from someone who isn't qualified to give it, recognize that it is almost certainly what you suspected: a big fat lie. The trouble with Instagram is that accounts appear to show the real lives of perfect people, unlike magazines, which present glamorous situations which have more obviously been meticulously planned. When you realize that the influencer you admire has probably had surgery or other procedures – not to to mention a healthy dose of Photoshop – to look the way they do, you'll finally be able to relax into using the platform more freely.

HOW TO EXERCISE WHEN YOU HATE EXERCISE

Eve hates exercise. But she accepts that, occasionally, she may need to peel herself away from Love Island *repeats and get active. Here, she shares her tips on how to do so without crying pathetically aboard a treadmill.*

Firstly, I'd like to start this section with a caveat: you should not, under any circumstances, feel forced or pressurized into taking part in any activity that you do not want to do. Only if you genuinely feel that your mind and/or body would benefit from injecting an amount of physical activity into your life should you follow the advice that I am about to deliver. Note that, if you are suffering from an active eating disorder, the following section is not relevant or helpful. It is crucial that those who have experienced an eating disorder check with their medical expert or GP before embarking on any exercise routine.

If you're looking for a revolutionary solution to an entrenched loathing of physical exertion you won't find it here. Nor will you get a quick-fire set of instructions that burn fat fast without you feeling so much as moist under the armpits. If you're looking for a Fit4Lyf plan, may I suggest navigating to your nearest branch of Lululemon, or indulging in a scroll session of Kayla Itsines' Instagram page. I'm joking – please, for the love of god, do not do either of those things. What this section will provide is helpful pointers on how *not* to freak out at the mention of the word "exercise", and how to boost your mental health using your body. Only if you want to, of course.

1. WALK IN PRETTY PLACES

Whether it's country walks with a cute doggo or a pilgrimage to your favourite posh charity shop, make the best of your journey from A to B. Mindful walking is an easy way to fit some mindful meditation into the daily routine without it feeling too Deepak Chopra. Concentrate on the weight of your foot on the ground, the sounds, the smells, the woman over the road who has that handbag you really want – anything outside of your head. If you want to, play around with different paces of walking depending on the song you're listening to. Go slow and steady with Sampha, and march like a rampant terrorist with Lady Gaga. Or, if you're the thinking type, download a great podcast to keep you company. My favourites are the BBC's *Woman's Hour*, *The Adam Buxton Podcast* and *The High Low*.

2. TAKE THE STAIRS

I know, I know, I sound like a government public service announcement. If (like me) you work in a busy office and would rather die than spend your lunch break at the gym, using the stairs whenever you can offer a short but meaningful challenge for your body – with minimum effort from you. I try and mix up my flight of choice; try and find all the different routes to your desk and opt for a different one each day. If you're tired, aching or you're wearing hurty shoes, don't be a fool – take the lift, for god's sake.

3. TAKE A BEYONCÉ DANCE CLASS

Yes, such a thing does exist and thank the heavens for it. Have a google to find a location for your nearest 90s/00s/pop dance class. Then bite the bullet and go and try one out. They are utterly ridiculous but are guaranteed to have you both sweating and giggling by the end. Plus you'll be so busy trying to control your flailing arms so as not to smack the yoga-bunny next to you that the brain messiness will fade into a subtle murmur – for an hour, at least.

4. HAVE A NIGHT OUT

Partying until 2am with the girls – G&T in hand – is basically one and a half gym sessions without the monotonous hum of Absolute Radio and with marginally less stinking, wife-beater-wearing men. I always find myself in wild, harmonious spirits the morning after a night out with my favourite gal pals. Make sure to pick somewhere where dancing is actually a thing – there's nothing worse than toe-tapping to Whitney Houston. Also don't wear stupid shoes that are going to hurt you all night and always come armed with a reliable blister plaster.

5. TRY OUT DIFFERENT CLASSES

At the risk of backtracking, I do actually enjoy the odd exercise class myself. You will never find me weight training or putting my poor vagina through a spin class (I need at least two bike cushions, which, frankly, isn't natural). The odd yoga, Pilates or stretching class, however, I can often get on board with, mainly because these classes involve a lovely amount of sitting down time. If you think of it as an exercise class, the chances are you're going to either avoid it like the plague or spend every minute leading up to it overcome with dread. Shift the perspective so you're looking at it as an "activity" or "afternoon out". Switch up the different classes and never be afraid to try something new.

6. SWIM! (ON HOT AND COLD DAYS)

Again, not one to necessarily categorize as "exercise". On hot days, you're sunbathing! On cold days, you're mastering the Scandinavian tradition of *sisu* – challenging yourself to try outdoor activities in a bid to boost wellbeing. Studies have shown that a dip in ice-cold waters can ease anxiety, depression and even physical inflammatory responses in the body[2]. Probably because once you've experienced your nipples crawling back inside your body, nothing else seems as scary. If anything, do it for the sauna afterwards.

"A plant-based diet is 8 times more protective against cancer."

– collective-evolution.com

FRUIT AND VEGETABLES

HOW MUCH FRUIT AND VEG SHOULD WE EAT?

We miss the simpler time when we only had to try and get our five a day and eight hours' sleep a night in order to live healthily. Now it's ten or more portions of fruit and vegetables a day, it's fruitarianism or die, and it's plant-based...unless you don't give a shit about the environment, you horrible, soulless human.

Major publications have reported findings of a 2017 study led by Imperial College London that claims that eating ten portions of fruit and veg a day instead of five could prevent up to 7.8 million premature deaths worldwide every year. It's no wonder then that people are clambering to Instagram in order to follow vegan accounts posting rainbows of vegetation in a bid for eternal life.

Life is confusing enough without being unable to eat a banana unless you eat the entire bunch…so what is the truth? How much fruit and veg should we be eating a day? And what happens when ten portions of fruit and veg a day is just too expensive? Or you just don't like oranges and avocados? Are you destined for a tortured death if you can't stomach strawberries?

It's half true that fruit and veg is life-altering, due to the amounts of fibre, vitamins, minerals and antioxidants they contain. According to the British Dietetic Association: "Studies have shown that people who eat plenty of fruit and veg have a lower risk of developing many diseases, including high blood pressure, obesity, heart disease and stroke and some cancers (including mouth, throat, stomach, bowel and lung cancers). In fact, it has been estimated that diet is likely to contribute to the development of one-third of all cancers, and that eating a healthy, balanced diet, with more fruits and vegetables, is the second most important cancer prevention strategy, after stopping smoking.

"There is evidence to show that for every portion of fruit and vegetables eaten there is greater protection against heart disease and strokes (by up to 30 per cent), and some cancers (by up to 20 per cent). Other health benefits found have included a delay in the development of cataracts and age-related macular degeneration, reducing the symptoms of asthma, improving digestive health, better management of diabetes and the potential for improved bone health."[1]

Fantastic, that explains why your parents wouldn't quit smuggling broccoli into your cheesy pasta when you were little. But do we really need to be going nuts over getting more greens and other "good" stuff into our diet?

Registered dietitian Dr Suzanne Barr thinks so. "The five-a-day message is based on World Health Organization guidelines from evidence relating to prevention of chronic disease, but also on current population intakes. Because people weren't meeting the recommended intakes, five a day was seen as a realistic goal to aim for." Since the introduction of the five-a-day campaign, intakes increased but have now plateaued. And as for ten a day? There is good evidence that going beyond five a day could have additional benefits to health[2].

It's also worth noting that there isn't necessarily a direct cause and effect in studies regarding fruit and veg and the amount we eat in order to improve our health. For example, people who eat a lot of fruit and veg probably live healthier lifestyles, and so the results of such studies are likely to show that these people are, well, healthier people.

Okay, fair enough, we should all be trying to eat more fruit and vegetables...but what happens if you're on a budget? Does it matter if the fruit and vegetables we eat are fresh, frozen or canned? Fresh is ideal, but frozen and canned are also great, particularly for those people who aren't able to chop and prepare fresh produce, for example, people with arthritis, or where they don't have easy access to fresh. Plus, these varieties of fruit and veg tend to be cheaper. However, it's worth being aware that canned fruit and veg can also contain things like added salt or sugar.

What happens if you only like one type of fruit or veg? Take strawberries, for example...can we just stick to eating those all day every day to make up our recommended daily intake? All fruit and veg are beneficial in some way, and contain different levels of nutrients and different bioactive compounds depending on the type. The main thing is to make sure that you have a variety of fruit and veg in order to eat a range of these nutrients, so in short the answer is: ideally, no.

When it comes to children – and some of my adult friends – convincing them to eat more fruit and veg can be a nightmare. One of the tricks to get those who don't like eating fruit and veg to eat more of them is to cover them with something they do like (much like hiding a dog's medicine in a clump of meat), such as sugar or chocolate. But does this cancel out the benefits of eating the fruit and veg? Well, this isn't an ideal method to eat more fruit and veg, from a sugar intake point of view...but it also isn't a completely yes or no answer. If it's dark chocolate, there may be added benefits. Having chocolate *and* fruit is better than chocolate alone and will still satisfy a craving. So if you want your fruit covered in chocolate, then have it occasionally and aim for a small amount.

If you really can't imagine ever being able to stomach five portions of fruits and vegetables a day, or more for that matter, you might have considered taking supplements instead in order to get all the nutrients you need...but this isn't advisable. Dr Barr says: "There are still many bioactive components of fruit and veg that we don't exactly know how they work, but are very likely important to health, so a supplement will never replace these. Also a supplement isn't a substitute for the fibre and the 'filling' effects of eating whole fruit and veg. However, if like above, someone is avoiding or can't eat whole fruit and veg (such as swallowing or appetite difficulties) and are at risk of malnutrition, then an altered diet or vitamin/mineral supplement may be necessary to avoid deficiencies."

Although we are not likely to turn into vegans or fruitarians any time soon, you can't argue with the science behind the importance of upping your daily intake of fruit and veg. Whether you stir some broccoli into your pasta, top your sandwich with tomato or add raspberries to your porridge – as long as you are trying to eat more colour, that's the main thing.

TO JUICE OR NOT TO JUICE?

Laura thinks back to her own dabbles with juicing, and wonders if there was any truth to the myth that it can make us godly. Spoiler alert: nope.

Ahhh juicing, my old friend. Whoever said they were happy to get out of bed half an hour earlier to chop and wash kale and blend it into their morning green juice was lying through their bleached teeth, because my experiences of juicing at home have been nothing short of a pain in my arse (and not because of the high fibre).

Juices are the backbone of the wellness community's preachings. Whether in bowls, blended and sprinkled with edible flowers – for Instagram purposes only – or neon green, fluorescent and shining in a clear plastic cup, because we can't be trusted to get our five-plus a day, along come some beautiful people to tell us that the solution is to blitz our greens instead. Given the undeniable science shouting about the health benefits...maybe they've got a point?

Firstly, let's clarify what juicing is. Juicing is extracting the juice from a fruit or vegetable; the difference between a smoothie and a juice is that smoothies are thicker, as they tend to contain more fibre. Both – for the purposes of this chapter, anyway – fall into the same category, as they are both made of blended fruits and veg.

Although juices and smoothies themselves are fairly innocent, there is undeniable pretension when we talk about them in terms of nutrition. According to the British Dietetic Association 150ml of unsweetened 100 per cent fruit or vegetable juice (or smoothie) counts as one of your recommended five a day. So can we just drink five glasses of OJ a day and be done? Unfortunately not, because the juicing process removes most of the fibre from the fruit. It's also worth noting that if you juice the fruit and veg and leave it for a while, it will begin to oxidize and eventually go off, but if you drink it straight away then the nutrients will be preserved.

Juicing has, through no fault of its own, become a food trend, popularized on social media. There is almost a hierarchy around juices, in the sense that they're only as good as the amount of superfoods in them (superfood being a made-up word in order to market certain foods as being better than others). According to the internet, you'll need nothing less than a Nutribullet, a juice is pointless without the addition of a £14.99 putrid pot of spirulina, and a juice cleanse should cost you an arm and a leg to undergo. I should know, I sold both my arms and legs during my "wellness" phase, but luckily I drank enough superfoods that they all miraculously grew back...

As you can tell, I'm not keen on this moneymaking fad, mostly because I was once a sucker for it. It's hard not to be, given that all of the women I wished I looked like seemed to drink them (on social media) for breakfast lunch and dinner. It's no wonder they all looked so slim.

I once attempted a seven-day cleanse, which was peppered with smoothies and juices, but had to give up on the second day, as I couldn't find a whole artichoke to roast for lunch. I don't think anyone in the small, working-class town where I shop even knows what an artichoke is. I remember the rage of coming home from that shopping trip empty-handed, feeling like a failure because a way of eating was inaccessible to me. (The fact is that you don't need to cleanse your body anyway, because that's what your liver and kidneys are for.)

Let's take a look at the ingredients needed to make just one typical juice:

E3live – £36
Spirulina powder – £14.99
Coconut water – £1.99
Spinach – £1.40

Papaya – £1.50
Pear – 28p
Chia seeds – £1.44
Ground flaxseeds – £3.99

Total cost: £61.59

Hahahahhahahahahahahahahahahaha!

A quick word on spirulina, the most expensive (by weight) product in the smoothie (which I bought and used once...in this smoothie): it's a microalgae that has become a popular superfood due to its high nutritional value and supposed health benefits. It contains lots of calcium, niacin, potassium, magnesium, B vitamins and iron, and also has essential amino acids (compounds that are the building blocks of proteins).

However, the National Institutes of Health in the US says there is not enough scientific evidence to determine if spirulina is effective in treating health conditions, as some claim. Heather Mangieri, a spokeswoman for the Academy of Nutrition and Dietetics in the US, said that a person would have to take spirulina supplements all day to come close to the recommended daily amounts of the nutrients it contains. "There's lots of foods that, yes, they have a lot of nutrients in them, but we don't necessarily know the bioavailability so we don't know how much of that nutrient you are actually getting."[3] Something to consider before handing over your hard-earned cash in exchange for so-called superfoods.

One of my main motivations for wanting to "cleanse" my body through juicing was the hope that it would help me lose weight. I'd watched a documentary about juice fasting where the presenter claimed to have successfully lost the weight and cured various ailments along the way. Had I already founded Not Plant Based at the time of reading this, I would've rolled my eyes and called bullshit on anyone jumping to the conclusion that they might be able to cure diseases with blended fruits and vegetables, but with an eating disorder all I was interested in was the ability to lose all that weight through juicing, and I wanted a slurp of that. I did try to swap my breakfasts and lunches for a juice, but stopped when I wanted to kill every human I came into contact with.

Thinking about it, if you only drink fruit and vegetables for a sustained period of time, of course you will lose weight, because there will be a calorie deficit. But if three glasses of juice is in addition to a normal diet, you'll put on weight. If the three glasses of juice replace something else in your diet of the same energy value, you will maintain weight.

It's worth noting that most of us won't be able to function on juicing alone, as we will be starving. Juice will be less filling than the equivalent whole fruit or veg as the fibre is removed, so it will likely lead to overeating. You could technically live off juicing alone for, say, a week...but you wouldn't want to. Your body would start using protein reserves, which would lead to unpleasant side effects, such as headaches, fatigue and weird smells. Oh, and being absolutely miserable. Your body needs things like protein and calcium, which juice cleanses neglect to provide.

There are many far-fetched health claims about juicing and one of them is that drinking juices is a faster way to absorb nutrients. Sounds fantastic, right? Well, Dr Barr says, "As the fibre is removed and the cell walls are broken, there will likely be more nutrients available for absorption and this may occur faster than eating whole fruit, but I don't know why you would need to absorb nutrients quickly?" Whether you absorb the nutrients half an hour faster than you would've done previously, it seems that a) your body doesn't give a shit, and b) as long as you're getting nutrients, that's all that matters.

I could never justify spending close to £100 for a state-of-the-art juicer, given my preference for the convenience and taste of sweet shop-bought Innocent smoothies. But if you do like juicing at home – in addition to eating real food, please – as a way to up your fruit and veg intake, you don't have to spend money you don't have on expensive juicers just because the wellness blogger you love is paid to do so. Depending on how the juicer works, some juices may have higher nutrient levels than others, but everyone digests and absorbs nutrients differently, so the actual difference in nutritional status will likely be minimal.

Juice because you like the taste, because you find chopping up bananas and strawberries soothing, because you enjoy them in the morning. But please don't juice because you think it will give you eternal life or help you lose weight fast. Juice cleanses are dressed-up crash diets, and we've already learned that they're a pile of shit. They also deny us the best thing about fruit and veg, which is their fibre and filling effects, which juices don't give you. Spend your money elsewhere, and have some toast instead.

EVE ASKS: ARE HUMANS SUPPOSED TO EAT MEAT?

I will always remember the first time I ate bacon. I was 14 and had spent the night at my best friend Kelly's house.

I woke up top-to-tail in a single bed, with the woody aroma of unfamiliar meat tickling my nostrils. Kelly's house was smaller than mine, meaning kitchen smells travelled up the stairs and through door hinges faster and stronger. I didn't know what it was – pork, I guessed – but what I hoped to god was that I would be offered the chance to eat it. And, because Kelly's family weren't sometimes Jewish like mine, I was indeed plated up a glorious breakfast of charred, fatty bacon inside a cave of ketchup-slathered, white, thick-sliced toast. As the salty, rubbery pig belly made its way past my taste buds and slid down my gullet, I remember being overwhelmed with pity for my parents. Imagine going your entire life without a single bacon sandwich?

The cured pig meat has lost its exotic appeal to me over the years, and these days is most likely replaced by sophisticated smoked salmon. However, on the odd hungover Sunday morning, when my fake eyelashes are buried inside my bra, bacon – and only bacon – is best. While it's not an essential component of my everyday menu, I'd never live entirely without it. On the infrequent occasion that I'm graced with a succulent slice of roast lamb, or melt-in-your-mouth meatballs, I'm transported right back to Kelly's kitchen table; the promise of new, heavenly flavours taking my culinary experience to Michelin-starred levels of deliciousness.

It's this that saddens me about those who make ill-informed dietary commitments for no fully formed reason beside following a superficial trend. And before the Twitter trolls come in thick and fast – I am obviously not condemning vegetarianism or veganism. The vegetarian movement has played an intrinsic role in promoting environmental issues and sustainability, and uniting communities since the 19th century. For those who passionately believe in maintaining the lives of animals and don't wish to eat them, it's as commendable a lifestyle choice as any other. Yet, all too often in this weird, narcissistic, social-media obsessed world, food choices – especially restrictive ones – are made in a bid to belong to a tribe.

According to the organization PETA (People for the Ethical Treatment of Animals), "The bloody reality of killing and eating animals is innately repulsive to us." The animal rights group – which boasts more than six million members – claims on its website that humans are revolted by the sight of blood; have non-carnivorous teeth and possess a long digestive tract which is intended to give the body more time to absorb the nutrients from plant-based foods. While I'm sure that PETA content creators have done a sterling job of gathering and reporting the evidence, I thought it best to request a second opinion...just in case.

A wealth of evidence from anthropological studies shows that human beings, in their earliest form, existed on a preagricultural diet of foraged vegetables and meat. According to Harvard anthropologist Dr Richard Wrangham, early man (and woman) survived largely on root vegetables such as yams and carrots, with their main source of calories derived from available meat, such as goat and some fish.

Well-accepted literature from researchers at Harvard University and the Complutense University of Madrid note the importance of meat and fish to the evolution of human beings, with evidence (including stone tools) dating back 2.6 million years in support of the diet staple. Dr Wrangham's influential book *Catching Fire: How Cooking Made Us Human*, published in 2009, draws on centuries of anthropological science to explore how our diet developed sufficiently enough to land us the position of all-powerful, long-lasting living creature. He explains that both the introduction of meat and the discovery of cooking it (i.e. fire) boosted early humans' caloric intake enough to assist in the development of the brain and the ability to outlive our predators.

Another report by anthropologist Clark Spencer Larsen, published in *The Journal of Nutrition*, notes that about two million years ago, humans began hunting cooperatively for larger species such as wild game. This team effort resulted in a significant increase in human height as well as an estimated 44 per cent increase in average body size. Then, about ten thousand years ago came the development of agriculture, injecting more grains, fruit and vegetables into the human diet; and a reduction in meat. Human height remained stable after this point, and archaeological evidence shows a decline in human health. Researchers explain that the increased morbidities, iron deficiencies, bone loss and infections detected from this point onward are most likely a result of an increased emphasis on foods (plants) with poor nutrient content.

Dr Carrie Ruxton, a dietitian and food advisor to the Scottish Government, says that human beings have evolved by eating meat. "Our digestive tract is much shorter than that of a herbivore such as a rabbit or cow, but longer than some other carnivores', such as gorillas'. We've developed to digest both animals and plants. We share 99 per cent of our genetic material with animals, which is why it is easy for our system to digest meat and incorporate all nutrients into our bodies. Plus we have grinding teeth at the back, and canines for biting and chewing – all of which comes from our natural ability to eat meat." Relying solely on our ancestors to inform dietary choice is pretty silly. The very reason why human beings have succeeded in conquering the world, where other species have failed, is due to our relentless ability to adapt to the changing environment. Comparing our existence in the days of hunter-gathering to our modern-day lifestyles is like taking hygiene advice from a horse. Paleos, I'm looking at you. If it was good enough for literally every generation before us, it's safe for us too.

IS MODERN-DAY MEAT SLOWLY KILLING US?

In the past few years, a collection of studies have emerged showing the potential links between diets high in processed red meat and incidences of colorectal cancer. The theory is that nitrates in these processed foods interact with the gut and can stimulate rapid cell growth, which can lead to tumours. This evidence is widely accepted by the medical community and has since resulted in both the NHS and the World Health Organization introducing recommended limits of processed red meat (70g per day) to international communities.

A World Health Organization report estimates that, for each additional 70g of processed red meat included in the daily diet, the relative risk of colorectal cancer increases by 18 per cent. Note the term "relative". The risk relates to how much a daily intake of processed red meat will exacerbate your current lifetime risk of developing colorectal cancer, which we know is also determined by several other, much more influential, factors.

To put this in perspective, here are a few (non-scary) numbers. In the UK, just six out of a hundred adults are estimated to develop colorectal cancer at some point in their lifetime – typically over the age of seventy. If all one hundred of those adults ate more than 70g of processed red meat a day (about two small slices of bacon), then one more out of those one hundred people would develop colorectal cancer – in other words seven out of a hundred. Similar figures have been acknowledged for processed meat-related bowel cancer risk. In the interest of further perspective: the risk of developing lung cancer in smokers is twenty out of a hundred.

And it gets even more complicated when you consider the nature of such studies. Most are epidemiological, meaning that conclusions are based on associations rather than a proven cause and effect. Typically, groups of people are studied for a significant period of time, and their meat consumption is measured. There are a million other factors that are known to significantly increase the risk of developing such cancers and these will alter a person's lifestyle risk, alongside the influence of meat consumption. What's more, it is often overweight, unfit, middle-aged men who tend to eat a diet high in red meat – a sample that already has a higher risk of developing cancer. Perhaps it's not the processed meat itself, but diets high in certain foods that are the problem. Burgers, steak and stews may not be the issue; but the (often shop-bought) high-calorie and high-fat pies, sandwiches and ready meals probably are.

What's more, the cancer-inducing reaction between the nitrates in cured meats and gut bacteria has also shown to be countered with adequate levels of fibre in the diet. According to Dr Ruxton, "plenty of randomized, controlled studies – which are considered the most reliable form of scientific study – have shown that people eating as much as a kilogram of red meat each week as part of a balanced diet with plenty of fibre have lower levels of cholesterol and blood pressure than non-meat eaters; especially if the meat is lean and eaten with a variety of fruits, vegetables and whole grains."

In essence, the conclusion still boils down to the same old boring message that (qualified) dietitians have been wheeling out for years: as long as you're eating a balanced diet, with plenty of variety, you will be as healthy as you can possibly be.

MEAT AND FISH: THE ORIGINAL SUPERFOODS

While there may be some early evidence that a certain type of *processed* meat may, for some people, be linked to certain diseases, the nutritional benefits of meat for the human body are proven, measurable and, in my opinion, far outweigh the ever-so-slight risk of possible danger.

Ironically, according to the statistics, your health is far more likely to suffer if you abolish meat from your diet than if you eat an extra sausage on a Saturday. Dr Ruxton states that if people were scared off animal products entirely there would be much more nutrition and vitamin deficiency. Such vitamins, minerals and nutrition being the following (*clears throat*):

Vitamin A
B vitamins, including
    vitamin B12
Folate
Vitamin D
Calcium (in fish)
Iodine (in fish and dairy)
Iron (mostly in red meat)
Protein
Chromium
Copper (in shellfish
    and offal)
Magnesium
Phosphorus
Potassium
Selenium
Zinc
Sodium chloride (salt)

All of the above are essential for the development and maintenance of just about every single cell in your body (including the brain). It is unlikely that a healthy child would grow into a healthy adult without a sufficient daily dose of every single one of these chemical compounds.

But many counter-arguments to this are not to be discounted. It is indeed possible to source most of the above nutrients from plants, apart from perhaps vitamin B12 (crucial for the production of red blood cells and for energy from food) and bone, teeth and muscle-building vitamin D. The Vegan Society advises visitors to its website to supplement their vegan diet with a vegan-friendly tablet of vitamin B12, selenium, iodine and perhaps vitamin D, should they also be lacking in exposure to sunlight.

While plants may well serve as a source of many nutrients, the problem is that you have to eat a hell of a lot of produce to match the meat equivalent. Take iron: essential for creating red blood cells and maintaining energy levels. It's estimated that two-thirds of the entire human population don't get enough iron in their diets (the recommended amount is 8.7g for men and 14.8g for women). Liver and other cuts of meat top the NHS list of sources abundant in the stuff as meat sources contain a type of iron called heam iron, which is easily absorbed by the body, opposed to non-heam iron derived from plant sources; the body finds this much harder to break down and you only absorb about 10 per cent of what is in your food. About 100g of cooked lamb's liver contains around 7.7mg of easily absorbed heam iron whereas in the same amount of cooked lentils, you'll find about half the iron content, while in 100g of cooked spring greens there's roughly a quarter.

Another example is calcium. The building blocks for bones, teeth, hair and nails, this mega-nutrient also plays a major role in muscle regulation and ensures our blood is clotting appropriately (see Dairy, pages 44–59). Deficiency can cause serious problems including brittle bone diseases such as osteoporosis and osteopenia, rickets or scurvy and, in severe cases, heart malfunction. Many argue the case for kale, spinach, okra and broccoli. They're right; all of the above do indeed contain calcium. An entire 200g bag of kale contains around 230mg of calcium. You'll pack in about 60mg from 10 ladies' fingers (okra). There is 375mg of calcium in just three sardines, and 240mg in a single glass of milk. Pretty big difference, right?

And then there's the issue of vitamin D – essential for our bones' ability to actually absorb calcium sufficiently. They're kind of like an invisible tag team. Vitamin D is also available in non-animal foods – some breakfast cereals and soya products, for example – but by far the best, most available source is animals.

The only foods (other than some supplemented malt drinks) to provide more than three micrograms of vitamin D per portion (the recommended daily dose is 10 micrograms) are sourced from animals. Weighing in at almost 20 micrograms is a scrumptious plate of...grilled herring. Okay, maybe not as delicious as it is nutritious. However it's closely followed by grilled and canned salmon (12 micrograms), smoked mackerel (also 12 micrograms) and an omelette (2 micrograms).

What about protein? Firstly, protein (crucial for cell renewal and repair, hormone function, muscle formulation and wound healing) is made up of lots of different amino acids, and in order for them to do a sterling job the body requires a varied combination. Meat protein sources combine all of these amino acids and deliver them in one hit. Vegetarian sources of protein require a mix-and-match approach to ensure you're getting a sufficient variety of amino acids. Point two, again, relates to quantities. The gold standard of protein power comes not from an industrialized tub of chalky powder, but from a single, grilled chicken breast. A grand total of 31g of protein (we need 40–50g daily) will soon be running through your veins after chowing down on just 130g of the plain, cooked bird. A bowl of chickpeas will provide just 18g.

It is possible to have a healthy, balanced diet as a vegan or vegetarian; it may just take some forward planning. I am not slandering vegetarianism here, rather celebrating – and giving thanks for – the myriad of animal produce that remains permanently at our fingertips and has the seemingly magical power to effortlessly sustain an entire human body. Plus, when it's slow-cooked with pungent spices, dry rubbed and roasted in a tandoor oven or tenderized until it melts on your tongue...it's the best thing ever.

It somewhat saddens me that the food trend *du jour* is a nationwide rejection of all things meaty. Melt-in-the-mouth, slow-cooked lamb; perfectly moist chicken breast; smoky and sweet pulled pork, CHRISTMAS TURKEY!

I know it's not particularly trendy, but I am a passionate advocate for the crucial place that animal products hold in the modern, British diet. Sure, a bowl of slow-cooked lentils lovingly stewed for hours in aromatic spices is tasty, providing you have the time or, indeed, can be arsed. A packet of lean mincemeat, on the other hand, is perfectly delicious – and nutritious – in just 15 minutes with the help of a tin of tomatoes and a sprinkling of seasoning. For those who are strapped for cash and may not be well versed in the art of whole-roasted cauliflowers or bean burgers, a single packet of meat can easily feed several hungry mouths with the nutrients they need to satisfy rumbling tummies.

MEATY GOODNESS WITH ANGELA HARTNETT

In dedication to adventurous carnivores, we enlisted Masterchef judge Angela Hartnett to gift us a recipe that showcases animal produce in all its scrumptious glory. We love you too, veggies, but what can you do? A girl's gotta have her meat.

If you don't have chorizo, sausages – cut into small discs – will do just fine.

ANGELA HARTNETT'S CHICKEN AND CHORIZO WITH PEPPER AND SAGE

Serves 4

1 large corn-fed chicken, jointed
3 tablespoons olive oil
3 red peppers
100g chorizo, skinned and sliced
2 garlic cloves, crushed
1–2 tablespoons chopped sage
2 teaspoons chopped thyme
1 lemon
sea salt and freshly ground black pepper

Preheat the oven to 180°C (fan 160°C), Gas Mark 4.

Season the chicken with salt and pepper. Heat 2 tablespoons of the olive oil in a large nonstick frying pan and brown the chicken pieces on both sides for 4–5 minutes. When all the chicken pieces are golden, remove them from the pan and set aside.

Cut each pepper into four lengthways and discard the seeds and white flesh. Roughly dice the peppers into 2.5-cm squares. Heat the remaining tablespoon of oil in a frying pan and cook the chorizo for 2–3 minutes. Add the peppers, garlic, sage and thyme to the pan and cook for another 2 minutes.

Pour the chorizo and pepper mixture into a roasting tin and place the chicken pieces on top. Zest the lemon and sprinkle over the chicken, then cut the lemon in half and squeeze over the juice of one half. Bake in the oven for 40–45 minutes, turning the chicken pieces halfway through the cooking time.

*"[Sugar] can disrupt
the bacteria in your gut,
triggering pimples."*

– elle.co.uk

SUGAR

WHY QUITTING SUGAR IS STUPID (ACCORDING TO SCIENCE)

Eve explores how sugar became the enemy and asks dietitians if the best ingredient like...ever...is even that bad after all? It's not, by the way.

Sweet treats are a hot topic of conversation in magazine offices. In the five years that I have been in my media bubble, I've lost count of the number of times I've overheard women (and men for that matter) berate themselves for daring to indulge in a couple of handfuls of dark chocolate over the weekend.

With the UK government's newly introduced sugar tax charging drink companies an extra 18p per litre if they produce beverages containing 5g of sugar or more (per 100ml), and actual books telling you to quit sugar like it's crack cocaine, it's hardly surprising that we hate to love the sweet stuff. The theory, according to the government, is that the more drinks manufacturers have to shell out, the bigger the incentive will be for them to reduce the amount of sugar in their recipes. Whether the tax will have the desired effect – reducing the nation's sugar intake – remains to be seen, but a change that's almost certainly guaranteed is our attitude to sugar. The inference of such a tax is that sugar is bad, unhealthy and a problem to be tightly controlled. Next comes the influx of celebrity chefs jumping on the bandwagon, suddenly developing a passionate interest in the nation's health (which is coincidentally aligned with the release of their latest sugar-free cookbook).

While it may be statistically true that we – as a country – are probably consuming a bit too much sugar, the current moral panic is both uncalled for and unscientific. For one, there are many complex reasons as to why the population consumes too many calories (by way of sugar and other foods), and to single out a single ingredient is both reductionist and lazy.

After witnessing one of my all-time favourite TV personalities refer to sugar as the devil on a popular Saturday morning cookery show, I decided that if she could spout "facts" about sugar, then so could I. The difference, of course, is that my take on the sugar debate would be based on the knowledge of qualified medical professionals.

For context, let's start with some history. According to religion, philosophy and science professor Dr Alan Levinovitz, an irrational fear of sugar is nothing new. When sugar first came over to Europe from the Caribbean and Brazil, people were afraid of it because it was foreign. Then in the 1600s and 1700s people would blame sugar for conditions that they didn't understand, such as scurvy. Even as recently as the 1800s, British author James Redfield blamed sugar for unwanted or uncomfortable sexual desires, and warned that children were particularly at risk of being influenced by sugar's corruption and that consumption of "processed" sugar could weaken their nerves. All pseudoscientific nonsense, obviously.

The theory of sugar as an "addiction" (it's not) is also steeped in history. Nineteenth-century evangelists argued that a taste for sugar was a prerequisite for a developing a drug habit. Traci Mann, a health psychologist, recently wrote in a *Behavioral Scientist* article about 1970s nutrition publications that claim: "The only difference between heroin addiction and sugar addiction is that sugar doesn't need injection, is readily consumable because of its availability, and isn't considered a social evil."[1]

Then there's the ADHD theorists who lambast foods high in sugar for attention deficit problems and behavioural conditions. You know the parents who refuse to give their kids blue Smarties for fear that little Jimmy will be bouncing off the walls? Those guys.

Both the addiction and the hyperactivity hypotheses are void of any scientific support. While highly sugary foods cause a spike in blood sugar and therefore may provide a sudden burst of energy, the same is true for many other foods. Studies in which two sets of children are given either sugar or a placebo ingredient and their resulting behaviour is analysed show no difference whatsoever between the two groups[2].

A 1994 study published in the *New England Journal of Medicine*, looking at the amount of sugar in overall diet and correlation with the "bad" behaviour of 40 children, found no link between a high-sugar diet and challenging behaviour or cognitive ability.

Unsurprisingly, the sugar addiction notion is pretty void of evidence too. For starters, according to the definition of addiction, withdrawal and tolerance are necessary characteristics. Neither has been proven, by studies, to exist with regards to sugar. Most of the studies showing that similar areas of the brain light up when cocaine and sugar are ingested are conducted on rats – not humans – and according to a hefty scientific review into these neuroimaging studies, when it comes to human eating behaviour, they are "inconsistent and weak"[3]. Plus, it's near impossible to ascertain if this reward/pleasure reaction in the brain is due to sugar or to food in general. Humans are designed to feel rewarded when they eat – the more energy, the bigger the reward. It just so happens that sugary foods tend to be pretty high in energy (in other words, calories) so no bloody wonder our brains are loving life when they get a hit of energy that could help us escape from a hungry lion. But does this mean we're addicted? No, for god's sake.

But what actually is sugar and how does it work in the body?

According to the World Sugar Research Organisation, all sugars are a type of carbohydrate and hence, once digested, are converted into single, molecular sugars. These are then absorbed into the intestine and used as energy for cellular functions. In other words, dietary sugar is converted to molecular sugar, whether you get it from a packet of Haribo or a tablespoon of agave nectar.

Here's another science-y bit and then I promise I'll stop with the big words. There are three different types of sugars:

MONOSACCHARIDES – blood sugar, fructose and galactose
DISACCHARIDES – sucrose (aka table sugar) and milk sugars
POLYOLS – sugar alcohols, artificial sweeteners that contain fewer calories than other sugars
Note: This is an extremely simplified definition of sugar. There are lots more intricate details and chemicals that play an important role which I do not understand and cannot pronounce.

Most of the panic-stricken discussion relates to sucrose, or refined white sugar. This essentially means that all the fibre, nutrients and other microscopic good stuff has been stripped away. Sucrose is also often referred to as "free sugar" or "added sugar". It's this stuff that health officials are constantly advising us to cut down on – specifically, to constitute just 5 per cent of our daily calorie intake.

Free sugars are added by manufacturers and used by consumers to sweeten foods – cereal for example. They are also a key ingredient for the good stuff: cakes, biscuits, sweets and so on. The UK population, on average, consumes over the recommended guidelines of 30g (about seven sugar cubes) of free sugar per day.

This free sugar rule does not apply, however, to fruit or the naturally occurring sugars found in milk. It does apply to dates, other dried fruit, honey, agave nectar and any other "natural" unrefined sugar alternatives. IT'S ALL STILL SUGAR...and your body can't tell the difference between the two.

Despite the government's action on sugar, dietetic experts still encourage including free sugar as part of a healthy, balanced diet (up to 30g a day). And remember that doesn't include whole pieces of fruit or lactose, found in milk and dairy products. So basically about six chocolate digestives.

I'm not telling you to eat six Hobnobs every day (but nor am I telling you not to), my point is that if you do happen to eat a few biscuits or a cupcake – even a chocolate bar – once in a while, it's perfectly healthy. Even the experts say so.

"Eating the odd sugary food, like cake, biscuits or sweets is not bad for your health," says Kirsten Crothers, a registered dietitian and IBS specialist from the British Dietetic Association. "For most people, following a sugar-free diet long-term is unrealistic and therefore doesn't provide any real long-term health benefits."

As for the hidden sugars supposedly sneaking into our dinners and making us all morbidly obese, the issue is far from as simple as the headlines suggest. According to BDA spokesperson and dietitian Dr Frankie Phillips, the reason sugar is portrayed as causing dietary problems isn't really a direct attack on sugar itself, but rather on the nutrient-poor foods that are high in sugar, for example sugar-loaded drinks. It's not sugar itself that puts you at risk of obesity, but what it does or doesn't do for your hunger.

Is sugar the main culprit to blame for obesity in the UK? Obesity has many factors – genetics, mental health, education, lack of exercise, income, fat, sugar, cooking skills, access to gyms and parks, environment, family life. People become obese when they continually eat more calories than they burn, regardless of where these calories come from. The experts are loath to discuss any one factor, or ingredient, in isolation.

Take the humble baked bean. You wouldn't necessarily lump a tin of sauce-covered beans into the same category as a salmon fillet or green salad but, nutritionally speaking, it's pretty much on a par. "Baked beans are a great, easy meal to make," says Dr Phillips, "with low-sugar varieties, you get all the nutritional benefits from the fibre, as well as the vegetable protein." Breakfast cereals are another example – even the ones that contain a small amount of sugar. "This is because many of them are fortified with vitamins," she says, "which means some vitamins are put into the grains. Two Weetabix contain just under 2g of sugar, yet despite the free sugars, it's a more nutritious breakfast – due to the iron and B vitamins – than your instagrammed bowl of sugar-free porridge.

"It's a case of throwing away the baby with the bathwater, you're not achieving good nutritional balance [by cutting out sugar]. You might not be getting enough iron, or zinc – you're replacing sugar with another problem."

Which leads us nicely on to the sugars in juice.

One popular health blogger loves to harp on about the benefits of low-sugar fruit and advocates substituting fruit juice for half a litre of thick, green, liquidized shrubbery. Although, according to the actual experts, fruit juice SHOULD be included as part of our healthy, balanced diets.

"As well as the free sugars in juice," says Frankie, "you get all the benefits of the antioxidants, the vitamin C and the minerals. Whereas with flavoured drinks, you don't get any of the nutrients." Basically, if you're a fan of fruit juice, drink it. Keep your portion to about 150ml daily and you'll get all the goodness without too much of the excess sugar. And while we're on the subject of fruit and juices, here's a gem of wisdom: PUTTING YOUR FRUIT IN A JUICER DOESN'T MAKE IT HEALTHIER.

As brilliantly explained by Laura (see Drinks, pages 76–103), when you juice fruit as opposed to eating it whole, the sugars, which are normally bound in cells, are released and therefore count as "free". Kristen Crothers explains that when you bite into an apple your body has to break down the fruit sugar (or fructose) inside the plant cells before it is released into your system, meaning you don't get the same increase in blood sugar as you would if it was juiced. It's these spikes in blood sugar that, according to some scientists, can increase the risk of obesity.

The moral of the story? Eat sugar, enjoy birthday cake, devour plenty of Cadbury Creme Eggs and definitely dine on beans on toast at least once a month. Save your hard-earned pennies from the blind robbery of a green juice, collect the monies and spend them on therapy instead. A far more healthful investment that involves less mint stuck between your teeth and unpredictable bowel movements. Everyone's a winner.

LAURA'S TALES OF THE TUCK SHOP

From cinema sweets to your parents bribing you with chocolate in order to get you to wash the dishes, it seems that all of us have poignant memories of our youth sweetened by the presence of our favourite treats from the tuck shop. Through digging up past memories of our own, and those of our parents, we realized that many family relationships seem to be held together by the sticky remnants of sat-on bonbons and arguments solved with sickly sugary cola bottles. Although you can't buy love with a candy-striped paper bag full of extortionately priced goodies (apparently), it seems we all have a weakness for sweets, even as we age.

My own memories of a "tuck shop" in school came thanks to a boy in my class – taller than everyone in the school, teachers included – who shiftily doled out small hand-packaged bags of Haribo giant strawberries and blue bonbons to swarms of salivating children, like bags of meth to junkies. He was quite the entrepreneur, and made a fortune from his 50p sandwich-bag-sized snacks, capitalizing on the youth's need for sugar and a cultural climate in which Jamie Oliver was trying to nick all the sugar from the school cafeteria. In my own experience, the more you deprive a young person of sugar, or sweets, or chocolate, or crisps – all the so-called "naughty" things – the more they will want them; prophetic of my adulthood experiences, as I went on to embark upon multiple diets and eating disorders.

In fact, let's change that: the more you deprive anyone, at any age, of anything, the more they will want it.

When I first became obsessed with restricting my diet in college, naive to the enormous cravings starving yourself can cause, I found myself confused at how obsessed with sugar I had become and how much my pulsating, snaggly sweet tooth had grown out of my dieting, sealed mouth. During this time, I could've eaten chocolate cake for breakfast, lunch and dinner, and would have still bitten your hand off for the empty plate from which I could lick up any leftover crumbs.

(Apologies if I ever did that IRL, btw. It was a difficult time and very much within the capabilities of a seasoned binge eater.)

At college I always had a Caffè Nero loyalty card on the go, and whenever it came to receiving my free hot drink, I'd go all out, as it was one of the only rare treats I'd allow myself so that I'd continue to get skinnier. I'd swap my usual Earl Grey tea with skimmed milk for a full-fat chai latte – hold the cinnamon – and a slice of triple chocolate cheesecake (that was my idea of all out at the time...). I'd guzzle it all within minutes, feeling suitably sick and guilty by the end of my splurge. It wasn't unusual for me to regret this binge immediately and end up throwing up my only fortnightly indulgence. This guilt-ridden treat – something I could have eaten previously without a second thought – highlighted how deep I was involved in restriction, therefore intensifying a previously quiet urge to binge to compensate my ravenous body.

This obsession with sugar signalled the beginnings of my binge eating disorder, and soon spread to any kind of junk food, not just chai lattes and chocolate cheesecakes. Today, I'd be more inclined to view a slice of cheesecake as a chore, only because I've matured a savoury tongue instead. My short-lived sugar addiction is fuzzy for me, as binges often are. Binges were ritualistic, yet evolved along with the intensity of my cravings. When I left college and the comfort of a corner in a familiar Caffè Nero, that's when my eating disorder became more unruly and unpredictable. A bar of chocolate became three Galaxy Cookie Crumble sharing bars and chai lattes evolved into an entire carrot cake. I think this phase in my life of eating enough sugar to feed a small village for a year was enough to put me off sweet treats for life. There's something extra revolting about throwing up hot, half-digested chocolate. I won't go into detail, but the colour of the stuff dribbling down the bowl of a toilet...eew.

This disturbing image probably explains why I now always choose chips over chocolate. Give me crisps, chips and pork scratchings...but Jaffa Cakes and Fruit Pastilles? That's just not me any more. I'm just not that kind of girl, not since giving those eating disorders the boot.

My friends say I have the diet of a man in a pub. I quite like that title.

EVE'S TALES OF THE TUCK SHOP

At the age of about ten, I would often have Maryland Cookies for breakfast. Not because my parents were neglectful anarchists, but because it was about this age that I reached the dizzying heights of the cupboard of dreams, where teatime deliciousness lay patiently waiting. At 8am every morning, I would pitter-patter down the stairs and snake on to the lino floor of the kitchen, careful not to wake my brother for fear of the discovery of my sacred ritual. With all the might my five feet could muster, I'd flex to my tippiest toes and crack open Pandora's box. And by Pandora, I mean my poor, responsible mother, who had absolutely no idea that her sneaky child was pinching her favourite biscuits while she was sleeping. Sorry, Mum.

I'd skilfully tease down a packet (although on many occasions didn't quite manage it; cue the avalanche of cherry Bakewells on small child's head) and scurry off to nibble through them during my regular morning episode of cult classic *Bear in the Big Blue House*. I'd brush off the crumbs (onto the carpet, as every respectful child does) before placing a bowl and spoon on the drying rack to stage that a) I'd had an "acceptable" breakfast and b) I'd beaten my brother in brownie points for washing up well. Then, one day aforementioned avalanche woke the entire household up. My parents – expecting to find a child-catching burglar – instead rushed down the stairs to discover their child flat-backed on the kitchen lino, surrounded by a sandstorm of chocolate digestives. Eating a Maryland Cookie. I soon reverted to Coco Pops, or – if I was really lucky – those amazing little crunchy wheat shells encasing a thick, lava of molten chocolate.

The sweet tooth continued through my secondary school years when my best friend Grace and I would bookend a shopping excursion with a trip to the nearest pick 'n' mix facility. One particular favoured sweet station was The Nut Hut – a dried fruit and chocolate-covered nut stall that stood within the lavish storeys of Watford's Harlequin Centre. It took two bus rides to get back to my house in Whetstone, north London, which we'd while away, exchanging yogurt-covered banana chips for spongy apple rings, sharing a single set of earphones belting out McFly's latest corker. It was the longest bus journey in the history of the world, and really we would have been much better off getting the train. But as we rejoiced over the discovery of a chocolate-covered toffee, high off the bargain prices of Primark, we disembarked the bus regretfully.

The freeing thrill of a pick 'n' mix situation continued to entice me throughout my teens and into early adulthood. The undisturbed pleasure of creating a bespoke bag of sugary nuggets of enjoyment was a process not to be taken lightly. The skill of selecting your favourites (fried eggs, chocolate raisins, jelly babies fyi) while ensuring the weight of the bag was light enough not to bankrupt you wasn't always easy, and sometimes I'd inevitably be forced to substitute a fizzy strawberry for a subpar but lighter milk bottle. At some point during our mid-teens, Grace and I discovered the wonderment of Woolworths and, with that, £2 cups ready for you to cram full of all the sweeties your heart desired. With the weigh-and-pay obstacle now obsolete, we'd go to town on those cardboard cones. Having crammed in (via nifty fist work) 500g worth of gelatine delights – and a handful straight in the pocket – we'd saunter back to Grace's house where we'd inhale our goodies while bingeing on *OC* box sets. We were definitely supposed to be at school.

Oddly, when I became ill sweets were the only thing that seemed to remain on my "safe" list, when everything else had been senselessly culled. I'd be damned if I'd go within an inch of a Snickers bar, but a 300g pack of Haribo Tangfastics was no problem. The sugary fizz was an invisibility cloak; the so-called "empty" calories slipping into my digestive tract unnoticed. Perhaps it was the subconscious power of my sweet tooth, or perhaps it was easier to imagine the sugar crystals evaporating into nothingness. Chocolate, of course, would melt directly into my fat cells and cause them to spread across my hips and thighs like cancer. Ridiculous.

These days, I part with more than 60 of my precious pounds every month in fees to an wanky east London membership club purely on the justification that said club provides a fantastic selection of "free" pick 'n' mix to all members. Air quotes are necessary because, given that I don't use any of the other club facilities (the gym, for instance), the complementary cola bottles are actually pricey AF. Needless to say I get a fair bang for my buck. At every opportunity, fistfuls of sweeties are subtly-not-subtly pummelled into my pockets, and I average at least one jelly baby spillage every day. Sure, it's embarrassing when your boss questions the trail of liquorice allsorts that prelude your desk, but on the Uber ride home from a night out – I think we know who's winning.

HOW TO BATTLE A RESTRICTIVE CYCLE

Eve explores the durable cycle of restriction and offers up some psychologically sound methods to obstruct the wheel of self-sabotage.

It wasn't until I got to university that it ever occurred to me to deny myself anything edible. My genetic privilege was such that I'd enjoy a gargantuan chocolate chip cookie and post-supper Rolo yogurt every day and never stray too far up from a UK size 8. My friends' envy baffled me; being thin wasn't *everything*. Little did I know that four years later I'd be cooped up in a hospital bed – a result of that very "ideal".

When I succumbed to peer pressure, aged 21, and first decided I ought to make "healthier" choices, it was an uncomfortable transition. At the time, I thought I was merely dabbling in the typical world of the twenty-something – every girl tries to keep in shape, right? Perhaps, but what is clear to me now – armed with the microscope that is hindsight – is the seeds of restriction which were slyly planted inside my head. Back then I could temporarily halt the germination of ED by driving back to London and demolishing a banoffee cheesecake with my best friends. Once at home, surrounded by the comfort of Mum's cooking, I very quickly realized that soup without bread was silly, and tortellini actually tasted really good. Yet, I'd return to the land of the high-waisted shorts and crop tops and suddenly, the only carb acceptable was bulgur wheat. Meanwhile, I'd still hammer a Pizza Hut buffet and thoroughly enjoyed thrice-weekly trips to McDonald's drive-through. Hence my speckles of restrictive eating didn't really register.

I guess if I'm honest, my prohibitive inner voice grew louder from University onward. It was a subtle increase in decibels but it seeped into my subconscious all the same. So, when I embarked on a habit of not eating much at all two years later, I shouldn't have been so surprised.

All eating disorders will, at some point or other, focus on severe restriction of food. Even in binge eating disorder and bulimia – which involve cycles of eating large quantities of food – periods of restriction and fasting, purging or self-punishment are recognized by eating disorder charity Beat as defining characteristics.

Although bulimia and anorexia are the only eating disorders for which restrictive behaviours are necessary for diagnosis, the undercurrent of self-hatred and denial of something pleasurable is common in all eating disorders. Having suffered with anorexia, I'm only able to comment in this capacity, but hope that these steps will go some way to help others caught in a cycle of self-discipline.

1. ESTABLISH A ROUTINE

Neurological studies show that once the body is malnourished, activity in the areas of the brain implicated with self-regulation and rigidity is heightened as it enters survival mode. This means that – certainly at the beginning of breaking a restrictive cycle – a structured routine of eating will keep your nervous mind satisfied enough for you to get through your dinner.

All models of eating disorder treatment include a structured meal plan. According to Professor Janet Treasure, psychiatrist and pioneer of the Maudsley Model of eating disorder treatment whom we spoke to earlier in the book, making structured plans can be a powerful way to ease the transition from not eating anything at all to re-establishing a regular food pattern.

This is as important physically (especially for those in need of refeeding) as it is mentally. After attempting to go it alone with my recovery, and failing miserably, it became clear that feeding myself sporadically was a vehicle for my anorexia to manipulate into starvation without me even noticing. Ultimately, I was only able to effectively break the cycle when the decision-making was done for me and I was robbed of the freedom to wiggle out of eating enough.

It's not easy, but the best way to redirect your arsehole of a brain is to iron out a set of clear, strict instructions and follow them...to a tee. Starting with breakfast, write a detailed menu of everything you will eat, every day, for the next seven days. Specify portion sizes and measurements if you know you have a tendency to skimp on your servings. If you need to, measure out quantities to make sure you're getting exactly the amount you need. It may seem counterintuitive but by committing to eating a certain amount every day, the eating disorder's control begins to diminish.

Try to make each meal as healthy, balanced and regular in portion size as you possibly can – and make it something you enjoy! Try and stick to the same – or very similar – three basic meals every day. Stick your menu on the back of a cupboard, and give a copy to someone you live with or a close friend – they are your cheerleaders. Keep mealtimes consistent in terms of environment, timings and company. Once you know exactly what is coming, there is less for your mind to be scared about and the restrictive cycle feels less necessary.

For one week only, try and do everything you can to stick to this plan – even if it means rearranging plans or preparing Tupperwares of baked chicken in advance. It's a painstaking commitment, but one week of your life is worth sacrificing for the sweet taste of freedom.

2. EXPERIMENT AND CHALLENGE YOURSELF

Professor Treasure says, "There is a subsection of ED patients who are very rigid, inflexible in their thinking and perfectionistic. They're not very good at seeing the 'bigger picture' and tend to hone in on details." Thinking bigger picture about the minutiae of life is tough, and us ED kids often have ways of doing things that we rarely steer away from. To add insult to injury, the effect of starvation on the brain only serves to compound these problems.

Cognitive remediation therapy, pioneered by researchers at the Maudsley Hospital in London, has been seen to be effective for challenging a cycle of restrictive eating[4]. The beauty of it is that the exercises involved have very little to do with food itself. It's about encouraging people to take a few risks and shift habits.

The theory works on the basis that, by challenging non-food-related thought patterns or habits, brain plasticity is increased, thus allowing you to loosen the restrictive, rigid thought patterns and behaviours when it comes to food. The full treatment is lengthy and involves several sophisticated cognitive tasks (which I am not clever enough to make sense of) but there are some things that you can easily apply to your daily routine.

The Maudsley suggests doing as many of the following "behavioural interventions" each week, making sure to note down how it felt.

- Choose brands that are different to your favourite staples when shopping
- Change around a small item of furniture in your room

- Shop for a different item (not related to food or eating) that you're not used to buying, perhaps a type of plant or a lamp
- Change your mode of transport or journey to work, walking on the opposite side of the road
- Wear less or no make-up

Challenging your brain's go-to conclusions about seemingly mundane tasks will lessen the cognitive load when you come to break out of a practised cycle of restricted eating.

Another method, which draws on similar cognitive concepts, is to perform so-called "behavioural experiments", whereby you challenge yourself to try something either alien or scary. This approach stems from the basis of a treatment called Exposure and Response Prevention[5], which tackles the eating disorder by facing the fear head-on.

It's important to first honestly assess how daring an experiment you are able to manage – start with small, incremental changes and gradually increase to foods, or situations, that elicit a real fear. It's a good idea to plan the experiment; tell a loved one about it, and – if possible – have them by your side for support.

This can literally be as simple as having lunch (and I don't just mean a handful of sad leaves drizzled with balsamic vinegar) when you otherwise may skip it. I still practise this method if ever I can feel food worries bubbling under the surface. If there's something on the menu that makes me feel sick to my stomach with anxiety – providing I'm feeling brave enough – I'll eat it.

It's easy for me to say now, but trust me: the remedy for your pasta-related anxiety is, unfortunately, a bowl of steaming, silky spaghetti. And the minute you get through the third bite, that nonsensical fear fucks right off.

3. WRITE A LETTER AND READ IT TO SOMEONE

Letters are often used throughout eating disorder treatment –

in various capacities. One particularly helpful revelation for me came halfway through my eight therapy sessions when I wrote, and read aloud, my stream of consciousness at just about every mealtime. Needless to say, it was pretty fucked up; a depressing prose full of self-disgust, despair and sheer terror. However, reading my spiderweb of thoughts to a separate, detached entity made them suddenly all the more...mental. And sad. As my very brilliant therapist (I was extraordinarily lucky) challenged me on some of my preconceived ideas (namely, that putting on weight would make me unlovable), I began to question the helpfulness of such thought patterns and, eventually, they became less powerful. If you see a therapist, suggest this as a possible intervention exercise. If not, pick one person you trust and love unquestioningly and ask if they'd mind dedicating 20 minutes of their life to your ridiculous thoughts. They won't. Chances are they've probably had exactly the same thoughts too.

4. WRITE DOWN YOUR LONG-TERM GOALS

Of the aforementioned letters, a second memorable one came close to the end of my therapy. I still had a fair bit of weight to gain and, for a reason I could never quite put my finger on, there was a significant lack of motivation to push through the last, laborious hurdle. My health was fine(ish), I could eat with enough freedom to no longer be classified by friends as, "weird about food", and I was just about able to wear high-waisted skirts without having to call on an army of safety pins. The need to gain weight was less about survival, and more about investing in my long-term health. Something which I couldn't quite pluck up enough self-interest to do...yet.

Mustering up the motivation to reach the next step is a hard axe to grind. According to Professor Treasure, one useful method is to encourage that bigger picture thinking.

I won't say this exercise magicked away my fear of fatness, but what I will say is this: it fired up the flickering spark of motivation to get well for good. My therapist asked me to write down everything I would do if I had a year to live.

I spent all week thinking about my answer and in the following week's therapy session, I read it aloud.

It's easy to pretend that you'd make the most of every day if the end was in sight – but how do we even know what makes us truly happy?

I like to think that it's the simple things that complete my total happiness and, ultimately, ensure total relaxation.

Although I don't have much of an inclination to bungee jump, take a load of heroin or go to China (maybe Japan though), I'd kinda like to do the things I know make me happy.

I'd go out to dinner with Mum and Sam and order a big pasta dish; I'd rewatch the OC (for the 100,000th time) with Grace and our beloved Ben & Jerry's. I'd cram in as many dinners/drinks with friends and possible – every single friend I have. One room, smoked salmon bagels, plenty of pick 'n' mix.

I'd book the most luxurious all-inclusive for me and Will. Hot and interesting would be my only requisites. We'd lie by the pool all day and eat tuna club sandwiches. I'd be sun-kissed and he'd have a burned nose, but we'd look healthy, happy and very much in love in our holiday pictures. I'd wear the silky summer dressing gown he likes when I come out the shower. We'd have great sex. And breakfast buffets.

Mum and I would go to Israel. We'd explore the old city together and discover new things about our ancient history we never thought about. Together. We'd go back to the Accadia Hotel (where I holidayed as a child) and reminisce about the blissful trips that now only exist in another life. We'd wander the street markets and I'd eat falafel from the stalls. Mum would show me where she lived and tell me endless stories of the impeccable detail of Dad's Hebrew, how she always felt safe when he was walking beside her through the streets of Tel Aviv.

I would write. Maybe a book, maybe just letters. I'd want those I love to know how wonderful they are. I'd learn a language (or maybe just brush up on my French), I'd learn to ride a bike PROPERLY and finally learn to swim WITH my head under water. I'd go to Sushisamba, I'd buy a Vera Wang wedding dress and wear it every day.

It may appear trite, but "bigger picture" imagery can provide serious motivation for getting you through the shitness. Attempting to pull a 180 on a restrictive mindset is one of the most arduous tasks you will ever have to face and to *want* to do it, you're gonna need a pretty great reason. Write this letter, keep it close to you, and you'll have a constant reminder of at least one crucial reason at your very fingertips.

5. DO SOMETHING FUN

The inevitable thought patterns of "I don't deserve anything good...ever" are a sure-fire route to perpetuating a habit of restrictive eating. In restrictive eating disorders, such internal dialogue – related to food – provides the path on which starvation sidles up to you before eventually gripping hold. DO NOT LET IT. You are as worthy, wonderful and valuable as every other person on this planet and, having battled an *illness*, you are definitely due a share of good times.

Many of those now recovered from an eating disorder will tout the importance of "self-care" (not in an Instagram hashtag way) for establishing a kinder relationship with yourself, therefore granting your body and mind permission to eat.

Sure, you can do all the textbook activities such as soaking in a flowery bubble bath or painting your nails glittery pink, but this guidance also applies to *actual* fun stuff too.

Arrange a night out with your gal pals and drink enough gin to make you flirty, but not floozy. Watch your favourite childhood musical and belt out the songs as you would if you were ten-year-old you. Go to the cinema and watch a god-awful chick flick or a cringey slasher movie – and pick the perfect person to join you in your overemotional response to either of the above. Go shopping for a stupid present for a friend...or something non-stupid for yourself. Listen to a fascinating podcast; buy a posh coffee from a wanky shop; have a good old swipe on Tinder; HAVE SEX!

You DO have a fundamental right to enjoy all of these things and you bloody well should do. Try at least one and see how you feel about eating afterwards. Nice things feel nice...and food is nice too.

6. FOOD IS YOUR MEDICINE

At the risk of sounding reductionist (clearly recovery isn't as simple as "I know I need to eat for my health...so I do"), there were times throughout my recovery when thinking of food as if it were a medicine helped fight the external pressures kindly offered up by the diet industry. The analogy became particularly poignant when the true state of my health hit home – as the effects of starvation are far too often underplayed.

Starvation – and maybe coeliac disease – are the only medical circumstances in which I feel comfortable referring to food as a "cure". When malnourished, the reintroduction of food in the body is a pretty remarkable thing to watch. It quite literally lifts the curtain of cloud from your eyes. As if you needed convincing, here is a list of eating disorder-related ills that can be fixed up by food.

- Brittle bones, leaving you at high risk of osteoporosis or osteopenia

- Severe acid reflux which, in the long term, can lead to oesophageal cancer
- Freezing cold extremities
- Kidney and liver damage due to mineral deficiencies
- Arrhythmia
- Tooth decay and staining from purging
- Severe constipation
- Hair loss
- Oesophageal ulcers or bleeding in the oesophagus (from purging)
- Severe, enduring ear infections
- Anaemia
- Insomnia
- Infertility
- Haemorrhoids (resulting from constipation)
- Bruising to bony areas of the body
- Sudden fainting
- Sudden death....

While the evidence isn't wholly clear as to why, it is well known that it takes a significant calorie increase to reverse the effects of malnutrition. Yes, emotional regulation and cognitive support is key for empowering you to be able to put grain to mouth, but ultimately, your key to survival is calories, which is why medical professionals will prescribe a calorie-rich diet to heal both body and brain from the psychological and physical catastrophes that come from starvation.

Write a list of all the ailments or negative consequences you suffer as a result of your eating disorder – both psychological and physical. Try and imagine you were a (good) doctor and were tasked with treating a child for the symptoms you've highlighted on the piece of paper. Would you deny them their medicine? No, because you're not a sadistic prick. Try to come back to this analogy when you feel challenged or tempted to restrict yourself – there is only one way out of this, and I am afraid it may involve salted caramel brownies.

7. GET HELP

Admitting the need for professional support is daunting, nerve-racking and not in the least bit pleasant. If you're anything like me, you'll do everything you can to deny the glaringly obvious fact that you are unable to get well on your own until somebody gives you no choice. Learn from my mistakes; act fast. These illnesses are just that; illnesses, and no one should be expected to be able to nurse themselves back to health without medical assistance. Although they may not always be as helpful as you'd hope for, the first port of call is your GP. Print out one of Beat's clear and extremely helpful guides from their website. It is specifically designed to guide naive GPs through the referral process and is your best chance of getting the specialized mental and physical health support that you absolutely need. If the GP fails to refer you to the local eating disorder service, keep nagging until they find appropriate professionals. Visit beateatingdisorders.org.uk or call their helpline if you are finding it complicated. Unfortunately there are very few experts who really get this stuff, but the ones that do are goddam brilliant. Don't you dare settle for second best.

SWEET TREATS WITH CHAMPION BAKER CANDICE BROWN

A particularly thrilling part of my job as a journalist is the opportunity to speak, in depth, to my utmost heroes. One such interview was with *Great British Bake Off* winner Candice Brown. The 2016 champion baker told the tale of her grandfather's Alzheimer's disease, honouring me with a unique window into the home of her doting family.

Although the interview was predominantly about the health of Candice's grandad – as was the piece I was writing – somehow the conversation couldn't help but veer toward food. Scattered throughout the tale of her family life were essential, edible details. From the taste of fruit cake that withstood her grandad's dementia, via the corned beef sandwiches that the family took to his nursing home, to the drop of Scotch that would "bring him back to life", food was a consistent light, shining in the darkest of times.

When I told Candice of Not Plant Based and our "live to eat" philosophy, I barely had to explain myself – she got there instantly. "Life is short, and I don't want any regrets," she told me. "I'll definitely enjoy a slice of cake – just like Grandad did."

CANDICE BROWN'S PEANUT BUTTER AND MARSHMALLOW BLONDIES

The brownie's blonde best mate! This is actually my best friend Anna – she's the blondie and I'm the brownie. Don't be tempted to overbake these or they will lose that gooey centre. The marshmallows on top are sticky, stretchy and sweet, a perfect match to the crunchy and ever so slightly salty peanut butter.

Cuts into 12

175g unsalted butter, melted
300g light soft brown sugar
200g crunchy peanut butter
2 large eggs
1 tsp vanilla bean paste
200g plain flour
1 tsp baking powder
pinch of salt
150g dark chocolate (minimum 70% cocoa solids), cut into rough chunks
200g pink and white marshmallows

Preheat the oven to 180°C (fan 160°C), Gas Mark 4. Line a 20-cm square baking tin with greaseproof paper.

Mix together the melted butter and sugar until the sugar has dissolved. Add the peanut butter and stir until combined. Beat in the eggs and vanilla bean paste.

Sift the flour, baking powder and salt into the bowl and fold to combine. Stir through the chunks of chocolate. Pour the mixture into the lined tin. Place the marshmallows in rows on top of the mix.

Bake for 50–60 minutes until risen. The marshmallows will have toasted golden and melted so will be very sticky. Remove from the oven and leave to cool fully in the tin. Once cold, lift out of the tin, using the paper to help, and cut into squares.

"Raw foods make you beautiful"

– bodyandsoul.com.au

DIETS DEBUNKED

THE TRUTH ABOUT FAD DIETS

From Raw Till 4, to Keto, Paleo and even the 5:2, Eve cuts through the BS to decipher if any of the world's most popular diets stand to achieve anything other than the reinforcement of self-hatred. Spoiler alert: they don't.

RAW TILL 4

In 2017, vegan blogger Henya Perez did her rounds on the social media circuit after embarking on a diet of only raw fruits and vegetables – until 4pm daily – in a bid to treat her yeast infection. (**Exhales**). Unsurprisingly, Henya's "mono-meals" (2,000 calories' worth of a single vegetable or fruit) didn't do her health any favours and the twenty-something social media starlet ended up with both a bout of severe IBS and a brain full of obsessive orthorexic thoughts. It also didn't cure her yeast infection. Existing on uncooked (flavourless, miserable) plant-based food is a rising trend among health-conscious types. Dairy, meat and fish are a no-go and, predictably, all grain-based carbohydrates are shunned too. Based mainly on the pseudoscientific babblings of American evangelical homeopaths, the lifestyle claims to provide the solution to all manner of health problems and conditions including diabetes, cancer and autism. Although there is one "doctor" advocating the theory, his exact credentials seem to be missing from the internet – including from his own website[1]. Advocates claim that by eating "unprocessed" food that hasn't been heated to 46°C, the food remains at a nutritional optimum, with all nutrients, vitamins and minerals intact. Eating "live" plant enzymes, they say, is great for cell regeneration in the body.

First of all, the 46°C nutritional "optimum" line is a total lie, but I'll let a qualified dietitian explain that shortly. Secondly, while fruit and veg will indeed up your levels of vital vitamins A, B, C, K and folic acid, it's a miniscule benefit when compared to the risks of depriving yourself of the ingredients necessary for you to be ALIVE. Calcium, protein (three cups of spinach = just 3g), vitamin B12, iron, zinc, vitamin D and, well, energy. What's more, it's unlikely that most of the vitamins in the fruit will even be absorbed by the body as many (A, D, E and K) need a helping of fat for absorption. Plus, sourcing all 2,000 calories from fruit and vegetables takes some serious work, not to mention the overconsumption of loose stool-inducing fibre. It's this soluble fibre (that dissolves into water) that is likely responsible for dehydration.

Oh and you know that whole no-carb thing? Well, more fool you, Freelee the Banana Girl (not her christened name, I expect), because science says that fructose – the sugar in fruit – is in fact a monosaccharide or, in other words, a simple form of carbohydrate. Also, a diet so high in sugar (yes, fructose is still a form of sugar) is in many ways a straight train to diabetes; spikes in blood sugar can affect insulin regulation, hence increasing your risk of the very illness the diet professes to treat. Dietitian and former president of the British Dietetic Association Luci Daniels has something to say, too. "The bioavailability of nutrients in some foods is better when those foods are cooked – such as lycopene in cooked tomatoes, or betacarotene in carrots. Is there any evidence that the bioavailability of iron in spinach is increased if you eat it raw? Not that I am aware of. The thing to bear in mind with all these diets is the question of what success means to you. If success means weight loss then, yes, you will absolutely lose weight by just eating raw fruits and vegetables. But are you going to maintain that for the rest of your life? Does it make you feel guilty when you have a sandwich at lunch? Probably – and therefore, it's not sustainable. In terms of nutrition, it's not adequate. Yes, it's good to eat more fruit and vegetables, but you need to eat other foods with it to ensure a nutritionally adequate diet long-term."

THE ATKINS DIET (AKA LOW-CARB)

Hopefully, with the help of both the brilliant Alan Levinovitz and The Angry Chef in earlier chapters, you now have a fair grasp of the illogical roots of the low-carb fad and why it is non-scientific, diet-culture spin. It's a crying shame that something as delicious, simple and sustaining as a carbohydrate-based meal has been vilified; purely driven by the resounding Western desire to be thin. It's especially odd given that, gram for gram, there are exactly the same number of calories in carbohydrates as there are in protein (4, to be precise).

Carbohydrates are defined as one of the three macronutrients found in food that form a large part of our diet – the others being fat and protein. There are three different types of carbohydrates found in food: sugar, starch and fibre[2].

Sugar is found naturally in some foods such as fruit, honey, milk (in the form of lactose) and vegetables. Other forms of sugar can be added to food or drink – such as sweets, chocolates, biscuits or soft drinks. Starch is made up of sugar units bonded together and comes from plants – it includes bread, rice, potatoes and pasta. These provide a slow and steady release of energy throughout the day. Carbohydrates are a source of fibre – the range of compounds in the cell walls of food that comes from plants. Fibre is an important part of a healthy, balanced diet as it can promote bowel health and reduce cholesterol levels, and high-fibre diets have been shown to reduce the risk of cardiovascular disease, type 2 diabetes and bowel cancer.

Foods high in fibre are vegetables, pulses, whole grain varieties of starchy foods (wholemeal bread, brown rice, bulgur wheat) and potatoes eaten with their skins on.

Carbohydrates are broken down into glucose (sugar) before being absorbed into the bloodstream. From there, glucose enters the body's cells with the help of insulin. Glucose is used by your body for energy; unused glucose can be converted to glycogen and stored in the liver and muscles. If more glucose is consumed than can be stored as glycogen, it is converted to fat and stored for long-term energy. Hence, if you're dodging carbs, you are probably depriving yourself of plenty of protective nutrients as well as an easily accessible macronutrient that will keep you fuller for longer. While the low-carb versus high-carb debate is still active with regards to type 2 diabetes, there is a significant amount of evidence to suggest that long-term, low-carbohydrate diets are no better at shifting excess weight than any other diet[3]. And given what we know about restrictive dieters and their heightened risk of further weight gain and other metabolic conditions[4], it's probably not gonna deliver that "perfect" lean body (which doesn't exist) either. Or, may I add, do anything positive for your health in the long term.

Luci says: "I don't think a diet without carbohydrates is healthy long-term. You need about 80g of carbohydrates (about one portion of rice, uncooked) just for your brain to function every day.

I question the long-term effect on both cardiovascular health and gut health – you often get a lot of constipation with low-carbers because of the lack of fibre. It's especially harmful if you suffer with constipation-predominant IBS symptoms. Many people on low-carbohydrate diets also find it difficult to exercise because they are running low on energy. It doesn't have an evidence base, many of the doctors peddling it have been struck off from the medical community and, to be honest, I wouldn't advise it."

KETO

Luci may have effectively outlined the case for inclusion of carbohydrates in the diet, but among the sea of evidence floats globules of skewed "information" that seem to justify the low-carb lovers and, worryingly, is supported by medics.

Many (some who are credible) have challenged the common approach to weight loss interventions with the notion of high-fat, low-carb diets. The case for high-fat diets in the fight against type 2 diabetes and morbid obesity has picked up steam over the past few years and has been packaged neatly into a highly commercial, aesthetically pleasing "lifestyle" complete with KetoDiet hashtag and Kim Kardashian as cover girl.

The diet revolves around the metabolic state of ketosis, in which the body burns fat for energy in the absence of available carbohydrates. Burning fat instead of carbohydrates in turn produces an energy source known as ketones – hence the name. Advocates argue that the body can be pushed into ketosis by restricting the amount of carbohydrates in the diet and liberally enjoying fats in foods such as fish, meat, dairy and nuts. Apparently the diet helps to regulate blood glucose levels, hence lowering the body's demand for insulin – especially important for those at risk of type 1 or type 2 diabetes (lower levels of insulin allow the body to effectively burn fat). Sounds vaguely scientific, but what do the experts say?

"I haven't seen enough evidence to sustain that high-fat is better in these incidences than low-fat," says Luci. "Again, it's a short-term gain and a long-term ill effect. There is a weight of evidence from the entire academic diabetic community that shows the risks of a diet high in saturated fat. When we've seen enough evidence that if you are on a high-fat diet for ten years it won't affect your cardiovascular health, I'll be interested to see. It is true that, after a while, your body can start changing fat into carbohydrates, but eventually you will hit a wall. Many of these low-carb diets advocate restricting fruit intake; but that denies you important antioxidants. The ketones that are produced makes your breath absolutely stink!"

INTERMITTENT FASTING

Even years into my recovery, there's no chance I could get away with living off the recommended calorie intake for a ten-year-old child for two days a week without spiralling into another anorexic episode. But I understand that not everyone is exactly like me, and some may not be plagued by the dogged clench of anorexia. It's true that there are some who are advised to lose weight for health reasons and perhaps this seemingly simple method could prove helpful?

According to the NHS, most of the available evidence in support of fasting diets (eating 600–800 calories on two days of the week) for their potential to increase the lifespan and slow cognitive decline in an ageing, demented brain is limited to animal studies. Clearly, the food choices made by a monkey are vastly different (and less complicated) to that of a complex human being, and despite the illusion of some men you meet in nightclub cloakrooms, the same goes for rats, too. Both rats and monkeys live considerably shorter lives than humans. Some rodents in fact only live for about two years. There's probably a fair few things that occurs in the following 80 years that may impact a person's health. The only conclusive evidence relates to the mechanism that may prove protective against Alzheimer's and dementia. This cellular process, which sees the natural regeneration of cells, is called autophagy and in 2016 Japanese scientist Yoshinori Ohsumi was awarded the Nobel Prize for his work in understanding these potentially protective mechanisms. Take note: said Nobel Prize winner did, at no point, claim that intermittent fasting would stimulate this regeneration. In some rat studies, fasting appeared to trigger a genetic switch which "switched on" the process of regeneration, but both Oshumi and genetics professors at the Dementia Research Institute exercise caution: although fasting may turn on this process in rats, we have no idea how this translates to human beings, nor are we aware of the potential effects on the rest of the human body. The research showed that in rats, just 24 hours of fasting triggered autophagy, but given that rats are about a millionth of the size of a fully grown human (okay, that's a slight exaggeration), the therapeutic timescale for us is still unknown.

While some of the research does show via laboratory experiments that fasting could be linked to biological markers associated with diseases such as cancer – insulin-growth factor is one example – this doesn't necessarily guarantee outcomes in the real world[5]. But despite the barely there evidence, and the experts saying that it can't yet be transferred in real life, a collection of celebrities and health "gurus" have run with it, and are now laughing all the way to the bank.

Luci says, "Have I ever recommended it? Never. Most people who do this diet are merely managing their relationship with food – on the days when you are not fasting you will end up eating more than you would do otherwise. Especially for people who need to lose weight to control diabetes, most of the research shows that after a year you're in about the same place as you were when you started. Crucially, we have to minimize the number of failures of a diet because the research shows that failed diets can have a detrimental effect on both our mental and physical health."

PALEO

Also known as the caveman diet, this preagricultural way of eating has been around since the 1960s in some shape or form. Yet buffed-up, blonde personal trainers and celebs such as...er...Jack Osbourne have recently jumped on the primal eating bandwagon, hailing a diet free from the "toxicity" of dairy and spared the sacrilegious grains of processed carbohydrates. Hunter-gatherers, they argue, existed on foraged berries and vegetables, nuts, seeds, animals (even the guts and brains) along with animal fat. Modern day paleos aren't so much about chasing and spearing chickens, but collecting their prey, neatly packaged in vacuum-packed plastic from their local branch of Whole Foods instead. Naturally they don't eat "processed" postmodern nasties like carrot cake, packaged bread, Oreos or jelly beans, and they steer clear of legumes such as lentils, peas and beans. Honey and sweet potatoes are fine. White potatoes are not.

Aside from being about 70 per cent illogical, the paleo diet falters due to one crucial point: the life expectancy of humans in the Paleolithic period was around 30; today, in the Western world, it's around 80. This is largely because our digestive tract has evolved over the past 7,000 years in order to consume dairy; as a result, the majority of children don't die immediately after birth. Just about all of the food we consume – in terms of ingredients – has also adapted over the past two million years and so no longer represents the prehistoric state that paleos hold as golden. As for clogged arteries and heart disease being modern diseases, tell that to researchers at the Mid America Heart Institute who discovered atherosclerosis (arteries clogged with fats and cholesterol) in 47 of the 137 Paleolithic mummies examined[6]. Paleo stinks of yet another restrictive diet, ultimately resulting in weight loss, which – despite the disguise – is what many equate to success. Given that making like a caveman involves cutting major sources of energy out of your diet (dairy, sugar, most carbohydrates), it's no wonder you drop a couple of stone.

Luci says: "Most people in the West are living longer than ever before, and aren't eating a caveman diet – how do you explain that? The diet is worrying as we are now seeing lots of young women being diagnosed with osteoporosis because they are avoiding milk and therefore lacking in calcium. And why? Just because someone wrote a book about it? Does that mean women should feel guilty for having a milky coffee? No. We need calcium for our bones and we are lucky that milk – a great source – is so widely available these days. There are plenty of people who live until they are 100 and eat a cheese sandwich every day for lunch." There is a sea of other nonsensical diets that I could quite easily destroy with a couple of paragraphs but I've contained myself to just five. Mostly because they are not worth your time, or my word count. Now turn the page, have a Hobnob and redirect your attention to far greater issues – like literally anything else.

LAURA'S PRACTICAL TIPS FOR SHUNNING ELITIST DIET CULTURE

It hadn't occurred to me, when I first ventured into the dieting world at a young age, that I was seeking help (for my supposed "fatness" and low self-esteem) from an industry that didn't care about me; that was puppeted by the elitist middle class and built upon the foundations of making you feel shit about yourself. And for me, it worked a treat.

Think this is too bold a statement? Think again. Check your Instagram feed. Check those diet books gathering dust on your shelves since you realized you couldn't stick to such impossibly rigid plans. Are these people who are telling you which foods to eat and which to avoid in order to best fuel your body all young, by any chance? Are they all attractive? Rich?

I bet the answer to all of these questions is, probably.

When wellness bloggers first started to get cookbook deals,

I bought them all. I'd dream of one day being like these beautiful, slim women with their inexplicably shiny hair and the clinically white teeth. I'd Wikipedia these "authors", after deciding that they were real-life angels, in the hopes that I too could perhaps follow in their career paths one day, and myself be inexplicably shiny and white-toothed.

Unfortunately for me, that didn't happen. All I got was a lighter wallet and a heightened sense of failure.

I soon realized that most of these women were, in fact, the faces behind carefully mastered, manipulative marketing schemes. You know the story: woman has hard life eating badly, then transforms herself with trendy new diet plan. Diet culture is fundamentally arrogant, and unattainable standards are set for the average consumer in order to keep them forking out their money – and fork I did. By telling us that a few more expensive foods are "super" and some are not, wellness alienates people who are poor. I had entered a world that was telling me health was only afforded to me if I could afford the price tag, and I certainly could not. This is one sure way to rapidly worsen an eating disorder and batter the confidence of a young girl to a green smoothie pulp.

Having come out the other side, here are my tips for avoiding elitist diet culture.

1. STOP GIVING WEALTHY PEOPLE YOUR MONEY

Step one is to stop buying diet books. Does this person really need your money? Wouldn't you rather spend it getting pissed up with your friends instead? Life is about balance, and you don't need a book with a shiny cover to tell you that...except this book, with the shiny cover. (We aren't wealthy though, so it's okay.)

2. TELL YOUR FRIENDS TO BE QUIET

I have a friend who is really in love with her boyfriend, and I hate her for it. I mean, how dare you be happy? And how dare you continually tell me about it? Ugh! Selfish.

Her insistence on bringing her boyfriend up every time we see each other prompted me to make her a bae jar, which meant putting money in said jar every time she spoke about him. It didn't stop her...but my point here is that your friends shouldn't bore you to death with things you aren't interested in hearing about. If you are a struggling disordered eater, your friends shouldn't be telling you about the latest fad diet they are trying, or the weight loss shake a Kardashian told them about on Instagram.

Talk about holidays, talk about hair, talk about dogs...but tell your friends to STFU about dieting.

3. UNFOLLOW ALL ACCOUNTS THAT MAKE YOU FEEL BAD ABOUT YOURSELF

Have an Instagram and Twitter cull, where you unfollow all those accounts that make your heart sink every time you see their latest posts. You know the ones: the girl with the washboard abs, the guy with the flawless skin. Nobody is that perfect in real life, and if following these accounts is making you feel sad, unfollow them. I did. You will feel so much better for it.

4. STOP READING THE NEWS

Okay, let's not be too dramatic here. If you enjoy reading about Donald Trump and his Twitter rampages, by all means go ahead. But if all the latest fearmongering news about which food will "kill" you next makes you want to restrict your diet, don't read those articles. As a journalist, I will say that a lot of them aren't based on much science anyway and are often overhyped in order to get clicks. I should know...I used to write them, so I wouldn't pay them much attention from that perspective.

Since moving away from London, I try my best to avoid the news, because it makes me feel low. If it does the same for you, avoid it too, and don't let anyone make you feel bad about it, either. You aren't doing this to be ignorant, you are protecting your health.

5. BE KIND TO YOUR CRAVINGS

Often when you are craving a certain food, there is a reason for it. Usually you are just hungry. Allow yourself permission to eat, despite the fact you once read that you shouldn't eat after 6pm... Everything you have been taught through the internet is likely bollocks, and if your body wants a jacket potato, your body probably needs it.

6. TELL GUILT WHERE TO GO

Women (and men...but mostly women) are programmed to feel bad about themselves or to feel guilty for disobeying the food rules brought to them by bloggers with no nutritional backgrounds. That's why so many of us end up spending the rest of our lives on diets and unhappy with our bodies.

Don't listen to feelings of guilt. You deserve to eat. We all deserve to eat.

7. DO YOUR RESEARCH

As mentioned above, most bloggers telling you what to eat don't have any nutritional background. How mad is that? Honestly. Would you ask someone to give you a filling just because they had nice teeth? Despite having no dental qualifications? No you would not.

If you read something about dieting that sounds like it's too good to be true, it probably is. Look into the backgrounds of these "professionals". What evidence are they basing their claims on? None, probably.

8. LOVE YOURSELF

Because we love you, whatever your size!

"An ultra low-fat diet can improve several risk factors for heart disease, including high blood pressure and high cholesterol."

– healthline.com

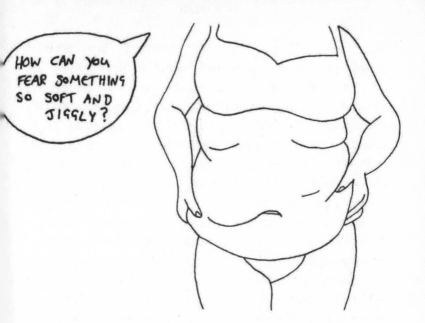

FAT

EVE EXPLAINS THAT YOU CAN BE HEALTHY AND FAT

In the past five to seven years, something wonderful has happened to the content of our conversations about women's bodies. What began as the long-unspoken truths of a handful of brave women with beautifully diverse body types transformed into the best thing to happen on the internet, like, ever. Never before has the online world felt more inclusive, with the widespread power of young, fresh, diverse individuals sharing their stories to the masses and being celebrated by social media – and mainstream media – for doing so. Bodies of different ethnicities; fat bodies; gay and lesbian bodies; non-binary bodies; trans bodies; bodies of varying ability – too long have the marginalized been repressed. Their voices are increasingly louder, and, to quote *Transparent*, "You better get into the whirlpool, or get the fuck out." (I added the fuck bit).

As a naturally thin, cis, white, able-bodied woman, I am deeply aware of my privilege. My anorexia triggered alarm bells at my GP surgery, not because it's a serious mental illness, but because I was thin. Too thin. While I'd never claim to be able to understand the plight of those without my privilege – and I am sure their experience of this world is a far heftier battle – my health has also suffered as a result of body conformity.

Because I am not fat, medical professionals assume I am healthy. Because I am not fat, friends and family assume I am well. Because I am not overly fat, or overly thin, doctors ignore the fact that my periods are missing, and that I may well become infertile. When I suggest, as I have been advised by a gynaecologist, that I eat as much as I can until my periods return, doctors become jittery, and nervous. "Don't go overboard," they say, "you look well. Your weight is healthy." Because god forbid I ever become fat.

As a health journalist, a relentless part of my day job is sifting through the countless press releases that warn (usually in unnecessary capital letters) of the perils of fatness. Links to heart disease, diabetes, bone diseases and various types of cancer clog my inbox like toxic cement. The causal link – they say – is apparently clear-cut. Fat equals disease. Fat equals a sickness of slothfulness, overindulgence of the very worst degree. Never do I witness such tirades of vitriolic, judgemental poison as I do when it comes to opinionated folk talking about fat people. The last prejudice that is still deemed acceptable, I've borne witness to friends, relatives and colleagues talk about bigger people in a manner that, if it were about other subsets of society, we'd be horrified. Yet, with fat people, it's okay. Because "it's for the good of their health". My response to these "concerned" folk is always a) since when was another person's health any of your business, and b) does being fat make a person any less worthy of respect? If their answer to the latter is yes, I have to strongly resist the urge to punch them in the face and run off quicker than you can say diabetes. Joking...ish.

This attitude means that much of the research in the area of obesity and health is biased, given that medical and health professionals are consistently taught to view fat as a feared crisis. This bias often prevents patients from accessing the right treatment (I've heard many tales of patients being told their BMI is the reason for an unrelated rash or mental health problem) and colours the way medical research into the health of fat people is conducted. There are plenty of studies[1] to show that the stress of fatism and body-related stigma directly affects heart health; the body-hatred cycle encourages further binge eating patterns, increasing the risk of obesity. Yet, time and time again, the link between bigger bodies and physical health problems is presented as clear-cut. Studies fail to control or account for the impact of body-related prejudice that may be resulting in health implications, and the research ends up promulgating the same old rhetoric: fat equals illness[2].

Dietitian Lucy Aphramor and author and health professor at the University of California Dr Linda Bacon are interesting researchers in this field. Both practised and trained as dietitians and nutritionists for several years while growing increasingly frustrated at the weight bias installed in healthcare provisions both in the UK and in the US. I spoke with Lucy a year ago for background on an article I was writing for our website. It was an eye-opening conversation and one that armed me with the knowledge to challenge holier than thou wellness wankers who claim that fat people are a drain on our NHS. One particularly fascinating piece of information she shared was that, in spite of plenty of research showing the effects of being an ethnic minority on cardiovascular health due to stigma and racist attitudes, the assumption is that South Asian men get heart disease because they are fat.

Linda Bacon is the author of the book *Health at Every Size*, and her philosophy is one that I would love to see introduced into our healthcare system. Her theory presents a socially inclusive way of dealing with public health issues such as obesity. Bacon – who formulated much of the founding principles of HAES (see healthateverysize.org.uk) – argues that "fighting" fat for the past 30+ years has got us precisely nowhere, and has resulted in extensive collateral damage along the way (eating disorders, self-hatred, mental and physical health problems). Wouldn't it be better, she poses, to create a world in which every body is accepted for its natural form and, instead, we focused on improving HEALTH rather than WEIGHT?

I can't begin to imagine the hostility felt by those in a bigger body. As a spindly, weedy Jew, I wasn't designed to be big and strong. I am all too aware of this privilege and, although I know my voice is still valuable, I would never use it to speak of the fat experience. And marginalized fat women (and men) often experience a secondary layer of oppression, making it even more important for them to have a voice. People of ethnic minorities, LGBTQ+ people, those who are disabled, scarred or suffering with an illness – these are all people for whom the bigger body offers a unique experience. In order to make public health policies useful for everyone, representation of these underserved populations is essential.

BUSTING FAT MYTHS WITH LAURA

"Fat" is probably the scariest word in the disordered eater's dictionary. It's defined as the gummy stuff that sticks to your thighs and is blamed for hiding your "real" beauty. It's the poison in your food that translates to the hang over your favourite jeans, doubling your bum and thickening your ankles. It's the curse that weighs around your neck, announcing to the general public that you are just as "ill-willed" and "lazy" as they'd expected you to be. It's the reason you can't get a job, a boyfriend or a break in this life.

At least, that's what I used to believe (and I'm sure a lot of you still do at the moment).

When it comes to the discussion of "fat" in food, the thing that is most frequently mentioned when discussing the fat we eat is "good" and "bad" fats. Registered associate nutritionist Oonagh Trehin reveals the truth: "Fat is just fat. We can categorize different types of fat based on their chemical structure, for example saturated (mostly from animal sources) and unsaturated (mostly from plant sources) fats. However, using 'good' or 'bad' to describe a nutrient isn't very helpful, and we must remember that fat is a nutrient."

Fat fundamentally is a very important part of our diets, as it's one of the macronutrients that we eat in large amounts, along with carbohydrates and protein[3]. These three macronutrients all provide our body with vital energy, so it is obviously super-important that we include a variety of these in our diet. Some fats are essential, meaning the body can't produce them, so we must get them through food. There are two important essential fatty acids: alpha-linolenic acid (ALA), or omega-3 fatty acid, is an essential fat found in fish, rapeseed, flaxseed, some nuts and green leafy vegetables. Linoleic acid, or omega-6 fatty acid, is found mostly in vegetable, seed and nut oils. These fats are used by the body to produce longer-chain fatty acids, which play a role in cholesterol metabolism, brain development and much more. They should feature in every diet. You hear that? No more fat-free yogurts please.

Trans fats are fats present in small amounts in a wide range of foods. Health concerns about these fats has recently led to many manufacturers reducing the amounts of trans fats in foods. For example, until the 1980s margarines contained 10–20 per cent trans fats. However, since then, production methods for margarines and spreads have changed due to concerns about a link between trans fats and the risk of coronary heart disease. This has led to the reformulation of many margarines and spreads to make them much lower in (and virtually free from) trans fats.

The big and scary trans fats are worth a mention here, as they've received a lot of stick over the years; like most saturated fats, trans fats can raise blood cholesterol levels and can also reduce the "good" HDL cholesterol, as well as increase levels of another form of blood fat called triglycerides, which can raise your risk of coronary heart disease (CHD). Gram for gram, trans fats appear to increase the risk of CHD more than saturated fats, and so are potentially worse for our health. However, before you panic and throw out the contents of your fridge, know that most people in the UK don't eat a lot of trans fats. On average, we eat about half the recommended maximum, which is 5g a day, so you shouldn't worry. Most of the supermarkets in the UK have removed hydrogenated vegetable oil from all their own-brand products. The British Dietetic Association recommends that as part of a healthy diet, you should aim to keep both the amount of saturated and trans fats to a minimum[4]. In general, trans fats are found in cakes, biscuits, hard margarines, takeaways, pastry, pies and fried foods...all the good stuff basically. Note that we're not told to cut them out entirely. That would be totally unrealistic.

Frighteningly, throughout my dieting years, rather than listen to medical experts I chose to listen to celebrities who were getting paid hefty book advances to tell me to swap my usual olive oils for fat-free alternatives. I had no idea of the impact this could have on my long-term health, nor did I care so long as I could lose weight and quickly. Oonagh says, "Cutting out whole nutrients and groups of food is not advisable. Gram for gram, fat provides more energy than carbohydrates and protein, so removing that source of energy may result in us feeling more hungry than usual. It is also important to note that nutrients do not occur in isolation – if you remove all sources of fat from the diet, you will also remove the essential fatty acids, as well as some vitamins and minerals that we commonly get from fatty foods. For example, steak contains some saturated fat, but it also contains protein, iron, zinc, vitamin B12 and other nutrients."

On the subject of fat-free products, although they sometimes contain fewer calories than other products (which I'm sure was an important thing for you at one stage, if not right now), they are not necessarily healthier. Fat satisfies us. Without fat, other things would need to be added to our food in order to make it tasty and filling, and usually, that thing is more sugar. Without fat, some of these products don't actually satisfy us and this can lead to overeating, which means that your fat-free diet might not even help you lose weight anyway. For example, if you eat a real deal chocolate brownie made with butter, one is probably enough to satisfy you. To be healthy, it is important to include a range of foods in our diet, and to allow ourselves to eat the food we want and when we want it.

There is a reason behind every craving, whether it is hunger, anxiety and wanting to be comforted, or because your body needs a certain nutrient. When we restrict and ignore our cravings, the likelihood is that we are going to end up bingeing and developing an unhealthy relationship with our food and bodies in the long term. The enjoyment of food is just as important as the nutritional value of food; as we have emphasized throughout this book, you should listen to your body and eat with attitude. In other words, don't allow anyone to sway you into eating fat-free because it "worked" for them.

If there's one positive to come from our eating disorders, it's a better knowledge of the ingredients that make up the food we love. We now know that a cheesecake with low-fat cream cheese makes for a weird, watery milk-cake that won't set – despite leaving it in the fridge for 48 hours. We are armed with the knowledge that a slow-roasted joint of lean meat will deliver a dry and disgusting roast dinner, and offering work colleagues sugar-free biscuits made with nuts and not much else won't get you extra mates in the office. Don't insult food chemistry by playing with it to appease your freakish eating habits. If something ain't broke, don't fix it – just eat it straight from the pan, preferably with your hands.

Oonagh concludes with some science: "When we eat food, our digestive system works to break it down into smaller pieces that it can move around more easily to provide energy to our cells – fat becomes fatty acids and glycerol, protein becomes amino acids and carbohydrates become glucose. Glycerol and amino acids can be broken down further to provide glucose, the body's preferred energy source. If we have enough energy, excess fatty acids and glycerol are turned into triglycerides, as is any excess glucose. These triglycerides are largely stored in adipocytes. Adipocytes form adipose tissue in the body. Adipose tissue is important as it forms a protective layer around our organs and acts as an energy store. When we consume a high intake of energy that is more than our body requires, our adipocytes expand to store the extra energy and this is what we commonly term fat. This fat is excess energy, not dietary fat."

You hear that? Your body is a machine clever enough to reserve energy rather than flush it down the toilet. To be fat does not mean your life is over. To be fat is not necessarily to be unhealthy, and to not eat your fat is to be stupid. I realize that in writing these last few pages I am unlikely to have reversed years of fearing fat and being fat for you, the reader, but I am hopeful that I have begun to gently massage in the idea that fat might not be the evil thing that diet culture has led us to believe.

FAT IS (STILL) A FEMINIST ISSUE, BUT IT AFFECTS BOYS TOO

Eve interviews Susie Orbach, the original advocate of body positivity and author of world-famous bodies bible **Fat Is a Feminist Issue**, *to find out if society is more accepting of our bodies in 2019.*

In 1978, the release of a seminal book stirred up conversation concerning the societal obsession with thinness. It was titled *Fat Is a Feminist Issue* and it was written by a psychotherapist inundated with patients desperately afraid of being fat. Susie Orbach was her name, and it was one I would become vaguely familiar with throughout childhood as I passed the paperback copy on my mum's bookshelf time and time again. The catchiness of the title clearly stuck as, at the age of 22, after becoming ill with anorexia, I asked mum if I could borrow it. It was the first book in her collection of feminist literature that I'd shown an interest in (I cruelly rejected her offer of a dally with Simone de Beauvoir at the age of 12 because...well, I was 12) and she was so thrilled I thought she may cry.

With the ingestion of only the first couple of chapters, all the seemingly illogical and nonsensical thoughts that were driving my eating disorder suddenly started to make sense. Up until this point, I'd worked on my underlying issues and understood that I controlled my body and my food because I couldn't exert control over external factors in my life, and this gave me a sense of comfort. But what I still couldn't get my head around was why fat delivered such an intense and powerful fear. At many points before, during and even after my eating disorder, I would have much rather been diagnosed with a bone-wasting disease than be fat. The prospect of seeking out a size 12 or 14 ("fat" in my disordered mind) in a clothes shop was horrifying. And why was such an eventuality so terrifying? I had absolutely no idea.

Fat Is a Feminist Issue (or *FIFI* as it's known to fans) posed a few likely explanations. Susie taught me that my aversion to a bigger self was little to do with a personal narcissistic oddity, and more to do with the society in which I, my mother and my mother's mother lived. Most women in Western societies have a fucked-up relationship with food, she argued, largely as a result of patriarchal, capitalist ideals that have filtered down the generations to oppress women (and, increasingly, men) and make money for companies that thrive off such oppression. Never before had the question of why women eat when they are not hungry been examined in such depth, and never before had the reader been exposed to the complexities of eating. Through her accounts of one-to-one therapy sessions with women who have struggled with body image and food issues for the majority of their lives, Susie showed me that this was a problem far bigger than my own anxious mind. Though it might manifest in different guises from person to person, the fundamental belief remains the same: if I am fat, I am unworthy. Some 40 years after the initial release of *FIFI* (it was republished with a new introduction in 2006) many of the themes discussed and lessons about our relationship with fatness still ring true. It's a depressing state of affairs, with the author repeatedly claiming in interviews that, despite our postmodern knowledge of womanhood, the explosion of body positivity and #MeToo, our relationships with our bodies are even more toxic than they were back then. I couldn't bear to accept that we, as a society, have regressed. If the original godmother of body confidence didn't have hope for the future, then that doesn't instil faith for the rest of us. And if we are all well and truly fucked, is there any point in trying our best to fight it? There was only one way to find out – I picked up the phone to Susie Orbach.

EVE: *Hello Susie. You are my hero. Please explain to me why I and so many others like me are petrified of being fat?*
SUSIE O: It's a relatively recent phenomenon. If you think about the courtesans in the nineteenth century – considered the archetype of beauty – there were fat ones, thin ones, a whole range. And the focus of bodies wasn't extended to all women. It's only since the democratization of beauty came about that [the pressure] has been applied to all women. This idea that we all can be beautiful and we all *must* be beautiful is a recent phenomenon. It started with Hollywood at the turn of the last century and then it was driven by industries:

diet, exercise and food industries that make huge profits from the collective desire we have to change our bodies. Then the women in Hollywood weren't enough; it started affecting younger and younger, and older and older women.

EVE: *Wow. That is bleak. So it's all fuelled by money-hungry bosses who spotted a clever way to make a quick buck?*

SUSIE O: Capitalism is a very cruel system. It's driven by individualism, the idea that you need to know who you are based on your body, rather than your contribution. It's destructive for everybody, but the margins are huge. If they can make everybody feel as rubbish about their bodies as women do, there's a lot of profit to be made.

EVE: *But my next-door neighbour hates fat people. And she ain't making cash money...I don't think...*

SUSIE O: People project the things they hate most about themselves on to fat people, all their perceived greed, desires and inability to control themselves. They think, "Well, at least I'm not like that. I'm not on that side of the track", so they separate themselves from it. It's similar to how we project negativity on to people of the countries we've invaded to make them feel as though they are less. Fat people have now been designated the place of all uncontrolled being.

If you have an obsession with thinness you will have a prejudice against people who either organically go that way [bigger] or turn out that way.

EVE: *This stuff is really terrible, but it doesn't cause eating disorders, right?*

SUSIE O: Well, not on it's own, no. But of course most people who have problems eating aren't anorexic or incredibly obese. Most of them are a regular size. Of course if we saw a whole range of sizes all the time, and everything from size 8 to 20 was deemed to be just as glamorous, then of course it would change the ground on which [eating disorders] are formed. There wouldn't be a monoculture in which there is only one way to be.

EVE: *People tell me that if we celebrated people who were a size 20 we'd be glamorizing obesity...*
SUSIE O: Yes, severe obesity isn't healthy, but the figures have been exaggerated. The category of obesity as a disease didn't even exist before 1995 when the World Health Organization reclassified it. Then they came up with this ridiculous thing called the BMI and all of a sudden millions of people were classed as overweight. Everyone with a BMI of 25–30 was considered overweight, when there is absolutely no evidence to suggest that this is unhealthy.

EVE: *That is shocking. Do people know about this and the effect it has on people with disordered eating?*
SUSIE O: I put all of this to an obesity enquiry 15 years ago and guess what? It didn't make it in. It was led by people in industries. People don't care unless you're anorexic or very, very fat, but nobody measures the scale of eating problems for people who don't show it physically.

EVE: *Earlier in the interview you mentioned the food industry. How are they to blame?*
SUSIE O: They produce all these foods that are high in fat, sugar and salt – non-foods – which make it much harder for people to feel hungry for what they actually want and not get frightened. Some of these foods are designed to keep us eating more and more and more of them. It's a major point in terms of distortion of appetite and is a recent change to the situation, which is really concerning me at the moment.

EVE: *Once you pop you can't stop. It's a thing. But what about chia seeds and spirulina? They're not real food either, surely?*

SUSIE O: Yes, there are now many different ways people manipulate the way they eat. They say it's healthy but it's not. It's really about avoiding eating and avoiding being fat. People are now afraid of their appetites.

EVE: *That doesn't bode well for us millennials. Please tell me things have improved since you first wrote* FIFI?

SUSIE O: I think it's more dangerous now. There's a lot more body fascism now. It's not just for women any more – also for boys. The beauty industry, the cosmetic industry and the social media industry are all very powerful. Instead of putting on your make-up, you now have to create yourself especially for social media. It's a desperate search to find something that is acceptable.

EVE: *But...body positivity? The increase in diverse bodies on Instagram? GIVE ME SOMETHING POSITIVE, SUSIE!*

SUSIE O: Everything that is on the side of the so-called angels is obviously good. But it's not easy to feel body positive. There is a difference between proclaiming it and actually owning it – you have to be able to risk feeling okay with your body. You can only really achieve that if we as a culture change things. We can only change things individually if we – as a social movement – are also doing something.

EVE: *So we're all a bit screwed. Is there anything we can do about it?*

SUSIE O: Ask how big is this industry? What has been put into this weird, herbal thing that I'm being sold? Why are nutritionists pushing stuff that the dietitians think is rubbish? There's a million questions to ask.

EVE: *And what about the questions we can ask ourselves?*

SUSIE O: One is this: if I wasn't obsessing about my body, wanting to transform it all the time or discipline it – what would I be able to do?

EVE: *What like, become a mega-rich lawyer and buy a yacht?*

SUSIE O: NO! Not those things. I mean, what contribution would you be able to make? If you just took your body for granted and trusted it. What are the difficulties that you would encounter and what advantages would it bring? You might feel less insecure.

EVE: *Wow, that's deep. Any other gems?*

SUSIE O: Look back at a picture of yourself in which you think you look great. Then think about how you felt about the way you looked when the picture was taken. I bet you didn't feel you looked great at the time. It's worth knowing.

So there you have it – orders from the Queen herself. Gather arms with your fellow warriors and charge – with full force – at those at the top of the pyramid, those who are counting your money as we speak. Ask yourself a few important questions, learn to trust your body and probably read all of Susie's books.

HOW TO BATTLE A BINGE EATING CYCLE WITH LAURA

The most miserable and lonely I have ever felt in my life was when I had tried to go cold turkey from purging my food, having accepted that I had a serious problem with bulimia. I then had to battle through a binge eating problem that I didn't fully realize I had. Although these two eating disorders vary by definition, they centre around the same problem: an inability to control the volume of food going in.

You might think that bulimia is more troublesome for a person in physical terms, due to the damage it can cause to your throat, teeth, skin, digestive system and heart. But from a mental health point of view, from a "I don't know what I'll do if I carry on piling this weight on when all I want is to be skinny" point of view, at least bulimia allowed me to release the effects of my binge eating by throwing the calories down the toilet instead of allowing my body to digest them fully. Bulimia kept me somewhat slim, but binge eating left me vulnerable to what I feared most: getting fat. There was relief, with bulimia, but with binge eating I couldn't stop filling my body with food until I felt I could pop. Bulimia somewhat masked how truly hooked on bingeing I was. I couldn't get through a day without uncontrollably stuffing my body with food until I felt sick and useless. Every day, all day.

When your main goal in life is to be skinny, there's nothing to make you feel more like an eternally slobbish failure than an addiction to binge eating and, worse, not really understanding why you are doing it. Was I addicted to food? Or just stupid? I try not to think about my binge eating experiences in detail as it's difficult for me to revisit the depression and anxiety that accompanied my illness during this time; my memories of the years I spent relentlessly binge eating have all sort of blurred together in a heavy fog of regret. I do vaguely recall, however, eating out of bins, off the plates of people I didn't know (waitress life), eating food that was out of date and food that didn't belong to me – upsetting flatmates, friends, colleagues and family members. I could never tell them, though. They'd never understand that I couldn't stop myself, and I certainly couldn't deal with that embarrassment. To be consumed by binge eating disorder is to feel totally helpless. It caused me to lose friends (eating their food didn't help), feel low, feel worthless, spend all my money, gain weight, feel like I was constantly swollen – the list was endless.

I mention gain weight toward the end of that list, implying that this side effect of binge eating had less of a hold over me than it actually did – but let me assure you that this was not the case. I grew up believing skinnier people were more attractive, more successful in their careers, less ridiculed, more likely to find love – essentially all the things I wanted for myself one day. As a hugely insecure child and teenager, I saw myself as an ugly duckling, hoping that if I could achieve consistent skinniness I would one day be the women from the magazines I'd envy-plastered over my walls and prove everyone wrong: that I was no Plain Jane. Comments from women I admired throughout my life influenced my fatphobic thinking. "Beyoncé has thick legs", "Be careful with your portions, that metabolism won't last forever!" "Hasn't so-and-so has put on weight? Eesh...". Here's a tip: don't talk ill of powerful women in front of easily influenced youngsters, even if it's only stemming from your own jealousies.

My recovery weight gain, and current comfort at being bigger than I ever was during my binge eating days, has led me to analyse what I had been running away from throughout those years. I recognize now that it was an intrinsic fear of being fat, and therefore unlovable. I honestly believed that people who judged my appearance were worth having in my life. I honestly believed that if I was fat, I might as well not exist. Can you believe that? You probably can. It's perfectly normal thinking for a human being. You know, with our inbuilt instinct to want to shag etc.

(Can I just add, before we move on, that by no means am I "fat" now...I am simply trying to talk from the point of view of younger me with the eating disorder riddled brain.)

A reason for my settling with my body today is partly because there was a difference between the weight that I had gained during hurried binge eating bouts and that gained slowly throughout my recovery. During binges, what I was gaining overnight wasn't fat (well, maybe a touch), it was mostly water and the heavy burden on my digestive system, hence my puffy face, sore stomach and need to nap every hour. Binge eating is a form of self-destruction, which the human body isn't able to cope with on a daily basis. This leads me to my next point – defining what the disorder actually is.

There's a difference between overeating and binge eating – let's just clear this up first of all. The first step in battling a binge eating cycle is to identify what one is. With diet culture, we've been taught to regret almost everything we eat: carbs, fat, eggs, cheese, dairy (or anything that comes from a cow), fruit, cake, chocolate, anything remotely tasty. So it's no wonder that we all struggle to distinguish whether we have actually had a "binge" or whether we are just eating perfectly normally. During my battle with binge eating disorder, I sat down for meals with friends who could "relate" to my struggles, because they couldn't help but order chips with their salads. Please note that this is NOT, by any stretch of the imagination, binge eating disorder. UK charity Beat defines binge eating disorder (also known as BED, making it sound far more kushy) as a serious mental illness where people experience a loss of control and eat large quantities of food on a regular basis. It can affect anyone of any age, gender or background. People with binge eating disorder eat large quantities of food over a short period of time. BED is not about choosing to eat extra-large portions, nor are people who suffer from it just "overindulging" – far from being enjoyable, binges are very distressing. Sufferers find it difficult to stop during a binge even if they want to, and some people with binge eating disorder have described feeling disconnected from what they're doing during a binge, or even struggling to remember what they've eaten afterwards. Binges are usually planned and can involve the person buying "special" binge foods. Binge eating usually takes place in private, though the person may eat regular meals outside their binges. Sound familiar?

After identifying that you might have a problem, the second step toward battling binge eating is to get some professional help. I would say that this will be your hardest fight, as medical professionals (unless specialist or paid for) don't tend to take people who are fat or who look "normal" seriously when they say they have an eating disorder. This is what prevented me from getting help when I needed it most, because I didn't feel I was skinny enough to be struggling.

Don't be like me. Demand the help you deserve. Don't accept the "maybe lose some weight and see how you feel" answer. Complain, stamp your feet, ask to see another specialist. I have a friend who is currently going through the shitstorm that it is to get help for binge eating disorder, and after seeing three different GPs, she is finally being listened to. I am not suggesting you waste NHS resources, but binge eating disorder is a serious mental illness. Do not let anyone belittle your condition because you look a certain way. Binge eating can lead to high blood pressure, high cholesterol, type 2 diabetes and heart disease. Binge eaters will also have low self-esteem and lack of confidence, depression and anxiety. You deserve help.

For the third step: while waiting for professional treatment, there are things you can do to help ease the stress of the illness.

1. REMIND YOURSELF THAT EVERYTHING'S GOING TO BE OKAY

Because it will be. You are not your last binge. You are not your eating disorder. You are wonderful, please be my friend.

2. RIDE OUT A BINGE

Or at least, try to. I know, this seems impossible when you have an eating disorder, but when the urge to binge rises, try to sit through it as it peaks, then eventually watch as it plateaus. This will become easier and easier to do over time. It's not the end of the world if you are unable to do this – that's why you're waiting for the professional help.

3. DISTRACT YOURSELF

Keep your hands and mind busy as you try to ride out the binge. Read a book, watch a series of your favourite TV show, draw a picture, knit – whatever your pleasure, do that. Try to replace a negative emotion with positive behaviour.

4. SPEAK TO SOMEONE

This could be your distraction. Urges to binge eat usually emanate from feelings of anger, loneliness, boredom or simply because you are tired. Whatever it is, tell someone. If you don't feel comfortable telling them about your eating disorder, tell them about your feelings or worries instead. It will help, trust me. And if you have nobody to tell, tell a journal or set up an anonymous blog. The internet can be your friend and is full of people just like you.

5. INDULGE IN SELF-CARE

So you've binged. So you couldn't ride out the urge. What of it? You're only human. Rather than beat yourself up over it, take care of yourself. Rub your swollen stomach, have a bath, do a face mask, paint your nails. You are worthy of care, even with an eating disorder.

6. HAVE A NAP

Again, self-care. Often when you eat too much, you can become drowsy as your body attempts to digest all that food you've just eaten. Listen to your body. If you need to sleep, sleep. It doesn't matter that you only woke up an hour ago. You'll likely feel better when you wake up – less sick, guilty and groggy.

7. DO NOT WEIGH YOURSELF AFTER A BINGE

Please! Don't! Do! This! This is probably the worst thing you can do after a binge as you'll only feel terrible about yourself. It isn't "actual" weight and is a total waste of your time and tears. Don't measure yourself either...I know what you're like.

8. DO NOT PLAN TO RESTRICT

After a binge, the logical step for a binge eater is to plan to starve themselves the next day (or week) as compensation, or to go for a really long run or something. Don't. You are unwell. You don't deserve to beat yourself up. Swap your long run for a short walk.

Plan to eat more vegetables in addition to what you normally eat. But don't restrict. It will only make you want to binge even more, because guess what? You'll be hungry.

9. TRY TO IMAGINE YOURSELF EATING BEFORE YOUR NEXT BINGE

Yes, you probably will binge again. I'm sorry, but it's true. It's not that I don't have faith in you, it's because I've been there, and mental illnesses do not vanish overnight. Recovery is a long process and can take years. Take it one step at a time. The next time you feel an urge to binge, try to imagine yourself eating the food you want to eat before you binge on it. Do you really want it? Will it make you feel sick if you eat it? How will you feel after? These thoughts will hopefully slow things down a little for you, and help you panic a little less, therefore calming those urges down.

10. GIVE YOURSELF A BREAK

This is not your fault. None of this is your fault. Repeat, repeat, repeat, repeat.

"WHO ATE ALL THE PIES?" WITH THE HAIRY BIKERS

Thanks to much-loved Hairy Bikers Si and Dave, we can offer you their lip-smacking chicken and mushroom pie recipe, complete with buttery, flaky rough puff pastry. Wild mushrooms not crucial (you can use chestnut or button). Butter essential.

THE HAIRY BIKERS' CHICKEN AND WILD MUSHROOM PIE

Serves 4–6

For the rough puff pastry

225g strong white bread flour
pinch of salt
185g cold butter, cut into cubes
2 teaspoons fresh lemon juice
125ml cold water
beaten egg, to glaze

For the filling
25g butter
2 tablespoons sunflower oil
300g mixed wild mushrooms, halved or sliced if large
3 tablespoons plain flour
2 tablespoons finely chopped fresh parsley
2 long shallots, finely chopped
2 garlic cloves, crushed
4 skinless chicken breasts, each cut into 6
2 teaspoons finely chopped fresh thyme leaves
100ml white wine
150ml chicken stock
150ml double cream
sea salt flakes and freshly ground black pepper

First make the pastry. Put the flour and salt into a large bowl. Add the butter and then, using a round-bladed knife, gently cut the butter down to mix it into the flour. Keep cutting the butter into smaller and smaller pieces, tossing them in the flour until lightly covered.

Add the lemon juice to the water and pour into the bowl. Keep working the mixture with your knife until the water is all combined and the bowl is clean. Tip the dough out on to a floured surface and use a floured rolling pin to roll out the dough to a rectangle that is three times longer than it is wide.

With a short end facing you, fold down the top third of the pastry, then fold up the bottom third and press the edges with a rolling pin. Give the pastry a quarter turn and then use the rolling pin to make three shallow depressions across the pastry – this helps to keep the pastry straight. Roll into a rectangle again.

Repeat five times, each time rolling the pastry into a rectangle, folding the ends into the middle, pressing and making a quarter turn. Wrap the pastry in clingfilm and chill for at least an hour or overnight. Allow to come up to room temperature before rolling.

Melt half the butter with a tablespoon of the oil in a nonstick frying pan. Fry the mushrooms for 2–3 minutes until they are golden but not too soft. Put them in a bowl and toss with the flour and parsley.

Return the pan to the heat and add the remaining butter and oil. Gently fry the shallots and garlic for 5 minutes until softened, stirring regularly. Meanwhile, season the chicken pieces with the thyme and plenty of salt and pepper.

Turn the heat up a little, add the chicken and cook for 2 minutes, turning occasionally until browned on all sides. Add the wine and leave to bubble for a minute. Stir in the mushrooms, plus any excess flour in the bowl and cook for about a minute, stirring until the sauce thickens. Adjust the seasoning, turn into your pie dish and leave to cool.

Roll out the pastry until it is about 5mm thick. Cut some strips – about 1cm wider than the rim of the dish, from around the edge. Brush the rim of the pie dish with beaten egg and fix the strips in place, overlapping a bit where necessary, then brush with a little more egg. Nudge a pie funnel into the centre of the dish.

Before adding the pastry lid, cut a small cross in the centre of the pastry – to form flaps that will fit over the funnel. Gently fit the pastry lid over the pie funnel and press the edges firmly to seal around the neck. Trim the excess pastry from the sides of the dish and then knock up the edges of the pastry.

Preheat the oven to 220°C (fan 200°C), Gas Mark 7. Brush the pie with the remaining beaten egg and place it on a baking tray. Bake for 30–40 minutes until the pastry is puffed up, golden and piping hot.

"Why you should NEVER eat past 7pm"

– Good Housekeeping

MIDNIGHT MUNCHIES

LAURA PUTS SLEEP AND FOOD MYTHS TO BED

If you've ever dieted, you'll know the discomfort of going to bed on an empty stomach. When you go to bed hungry the cramps, pains, lightheaded haze and angry belly grumbles hamper your ability to get in the hours you need to ensure you aren't a zombie at work the next day. When the most important thing to you is how much you weigh, it may seem like an impossibility to drag yourself out of bed when the munchies set in late at night, as every diet-related article we've ever read seems to think that eating late at night automatically converts celery sticks into deep-fried sticks of lard.

There is an overwhelming number of arguments against eating late at night and a quick google reveals why we're so scared of catching those midnight munchies. We, of course, love to call bullshit on wobbly-science-based articles, and are more than willing to disagree, instead letting you know that you are allowed that midnight snack you've been craving. The *Telegraph*, for example, published an article titled: "Why you shouldn't eat late at night, according to science"[1]. It reported that a study had suggested that snacking late at night could increase your risk of diabetes and heart disease. Researchers from the Perelman School of Medicine at the University of Pennsylvania claimed that eating late at night raised glucose and insulin levels, both of which are causes of type 2 diabetes, and they also found evidence that poor timing of meals can affect cholesterol levels, which can increase the risk of heart disease or heart attack. Oh...and worst of all, it makes you fat! However, the researchers only asked nine adults of a healthy weight to take part in the study, and only monitored them for eight weeks. Nine people! Are they serious? How are we supposed to gather reliable data from only nine people for only eight weeks, when there are over seven billion on the planet right now? We know that publications are probably going to continue to post unreliable health claims until the internet explodes and we all have a communal existential crisis...but at least try and conceal the smell of your bullshit a little bit.

Despite claims all over the big wide web scaring us into believing that if we eat a slice of cake late at night we'll put on three stone by the morning, that doesn't seem to bother our hero Nigella Lawson. She's a woman after our own hearts for many reasons: she promotes the idea that thin doesn't always mean healthy, she unabashedly eats what and when she wants, and she loves waffles. But what has wellness bloggers worldwide waking up in a cold sweat is the sight of Nigella continuing to saunter downstairs in a silky dressing gown, glamorous, confident and hungry, years into her TV career. Nigella's late-night pantry raids have been a theme throughout her TV shows, and nothing is off limits, even when the clock passes midnight.

When the late-night cravings hit, we, like Nigella, are certainly not about telling you that fillet steaks aren't to be cooked at 3am in the morning, or that cheese toasties can't be eaten right before bed. More often than not, if your body is craving food, you're probably just hungry. Maybe you've done more exercise over the past few days than usual, or you could have eaten less yesterday than your body required because you weren't feeling great. Registered nutritionist Rebecca Jennings agrees with us, and explains that science actually says that there's no set formula to when you should feed your body. "If you are getting up in the middle of the night for a snack, it might be to do with your calorie intake throughout the day. Trying to restrict calories during the day, but then waking up to eat is our body's way of telling us it needs food."

If you have a habit of restriction, and are therefore snacking late at night, this could, in fact, be causing you more bother than you think, as the disruption of sleep can impact your eating behaviour the next day, as well as your mood and cognitive functioning. Some research has discovered that lack of sleep or poor sleep quality could increase calorie consumption the next day, which I'm sure you'll understand if you've been waking up at 6am every day for work and are now on your second breakfast.

Some believe that eating late at night will not only make you fat (which we know isn't true), but it will cause you difficulty when trying to get to sleep. Due to the amount of variables that go into sleep quality, this is a tricky myth to bust. A few studies have looked at calorie restriction and sleep quality and didn't find any difference in quality of sleep when comparing the two, which suggests that a lot more research is needed, especially regarding different calorie intakes, macronutrient composition and densities of meals. What we would suggest, as we always have done, is to try listening to the rhythms of your own hunger, and not to the findings of studies with only nine participants (*cough cough*).

Although we certainly aren't opposed to eating late at night if you are hungry, nor are we suggesting that you can stuff yourself with lots of food, sleep it off and wake up with washboard abs. This won't be the case, and could be a dangerous mindset for those who struggle with binge eating. Your body works hard to digest food whether you're awake after eating or whether you decide to go to sleep. Sleeping after a heavy meal in no way means that the calories don't count. The reason why we often feel sleepy after a meal, according to an article written by Dr Angus Stewart, senior lecturer in nutrition and dietetics at Edith Cowan University, is because as we're digesting our food, more of our blood is sent to the stomach and gut, to carry away the absorbed newly digested metabolites[2]. "This leaves less blood for the rest of the body and can cause some people to feel a bit 'lightheaded' or 'tired'." Dr Stewart goes on to say that it isn't necessarily the volume of food that can cause this drowsiness, but what we eat, too. "We've known for many years that meals with an imbalance of nutrients – that are rich in either fats or carbohydrates – are associated with feeling sleepy. But this is not the case when nutrients are balanced or the meal is rich in protein." Binge eaters I'm sure will be able to relate to this. Dr Stewart explains that scientists in Germany have documented that meals high in carbohydrates that also have a high glycaemic index cause an increase in the hormone insulin. "Insulin promotes the absorption and use of glucose from the bloodstream after a meal. But it also allows the entry of a special amino acid (we get these from the digestion of proteins), called tryptophan, into the brain. This is important as tryptophan is converted into another chemical in the brain called serotonin, a signalling chemical or neurotransmitter that can be associated with calmness and drowsiness, especially in children." Going to bed hungry isn't good for you, but neither is eating a loaf of bread every night with a view to sleep away the calories. I ask Rebecca if there is any food and drink that will actually help you get to sleep, if insomnia is something that you might struggle with. "This is an interesting question, as there is a lot of research out there looking at certain nutrients and sleep quality. We have a naturally occurring hormone called melatonin that regulates our 'sleepiness' and helps us to remain asleep. We make it in the brain by converting tryptophan into serotonin and then to melatonin. Tryptophan has therefore been used in the treatment of sleep disorders and has shown improvements in sleep. There's lots of foods that have been looked at which are high in tryptophan, such as foods high in calcium – cheese/milk for example, tuna, chicken, turkey, peanuts and chocolate."

Like Dr Stewart said before, carbs can make us sleepy, but that isn't always a bad thing. We all need to sleep, don't we? There have been some recent studies on the effects of carbohydrate ingestion on sleep quality, and their results have indicated that a meal high in carbohydrates, if consumed an hour before bedtime, may improve sleep quality. High GI meals have also been proven to significantly reduce the time it takes you to get to sleep, so white rice, pasta, bread *should* be included in the evening meal.

It would be impossible to end a chapter on food and sleep myths without addressing the old wives' tale that cheese gives you nightmares. According to Rebecca, the British Cheese Board actually did a study on this one! "They gave 100 males and 100 females 20g of cheese 30 minutes before bed and found that not one recalled having a nightmare. Obviously, this is one study and there haven't been too many others – but science would suggest the opposite of a nightmare. Cheese (produced with milk) is high in the amino acid tryptophan, which helps to release our sleep hormone melatonin, which helps to regulate our sleepiness. So cheese before bed actually might be more beneficial than detrimental!"

No harm in using a ball of mozzarella as a pillow, after all!

SNACK WARS: ADVICE FROM THE FOOD HEROES

Unsure of which edible delight is going to suitably scratch that hungry itch? Could it be a steaming bowl of stringy macaroni cheese? Perhaps it's a supermarket cookie dotted imperfectly with Smarties, or maybe it's just an apple? (It's definitely not an apple.) Eve asks professional cooks and eaters to inspire you to put your finger on exactly what it is you fancy.

I've never been much of a decision maker, especially when it comes to food. Even prior to my eating disorder, placing my order at a restaurant made for my own – slightly pathetic – form of Russian roulette. Usually, after sufficiently irritating everyone around the table with incessant jabs for their opinion on whether the fish was fresh, the pasta sauce rich or the lasagne "probably similar to the one I make at home", I'd resort to a risky, snap decision. This almost always resulted in me further irritating my friends and family by staring at their meals with envy, while I begrudgingly chomped down a bowl of pasta that, yes, I probably could have made myself at home. Until I met Will.

The son of a farmer, with the immune system of a bionic ox, Will has only two exemptions from his food repertoire: mushrooms and hot fruit. Still, if mushrooms are fried to oblivion and buried in a bowl of beef pho he's unphased, and he will dutifully down a bowl of my homemade crumble as long as it's coupled with ice cream. Within a few months of the beginning of our relationship, I'd eaten pigeon, pork belly and kidneys (and lots of other foods, of course). I no longer needed a life coaching session every time I went out for dinner and my menu choices were based on a sense of adventure and excitement. One Christmas, Will's mum bought us a collection of vouchers for various Michelin-starred meals all over London (or middle-class food stamps, as we called them) and together Will and I embarked on an 18-mile tour for the taste buds. I was now the master of the menu, choosing the dish that would provide a new, thrilling experience for my mouth and my mind, and I never again suffered the regret of a poor dish decision. Some of my most treasured food memories were created in our four-month culinary jaunt. The deep gratification of seeing Will's face beaming with delight after I'd shoved a forkful of my perfectly spiced lamb in his mouth, or insisted he watch me crack the top of a perfectly caramelized crème brûlée, was similar to having really great sex. The connected sense of shared pleasure that makes you feel as though everyone else but you two has disappeared. By the time the last voucher was spent I was both gastronomically satisfied, and head over heels in love.

When my eating disorder hit a year later I began to gradually restrict the new taste sensations that I would allow my body. As long as a dessert was 80 per cent fruit and a starter was a lightly dressed salad (and I could subtly discard whatever protein came as a topping), I could still enjoy a fancy dinner. For the first few months, anyway. Eventually, main courses were an intellectual minefield – wasn't duck full of fat? How much butter was the fish fried in? And does it come with a side of vegetables that I can eat instead? Of course, as soon as this line of thinking robbed my rationality, my physical health deteriorated too. And soon enough date nights consisted of tap water, a plate of dry vegetables and a side order of screaming and shouting. We stopped going out for dinner soon afterwards.

To this day, that euphoric sense of food freedom and bewildering excitement is yet to return. I pick what I fancy, but I'm not salivating at the thought of my incoming pudding. Nor can I ever quite pluck up the courage to order something totally obscure, on the off chance that I might like it. These days, it's just not worth the risk. To those who relate to the screaming sense of enchantment that food choices illicit, I beg you: harness it, cherish it and choose unwisely – with your eyes, stomach and whichever part of your body is intrigued by what garlic-basted snails may taste like.

For those who – like me – are still working out what on earth you want to order, follow my lead and take instruction and inspiration from those who know best. The foodies.

For the most part, as the advice would suggest, eating according to your bodily cues is preferable. But after a lifetime of having your hunger signals hijacked by Slimming World adverts, heartbreak and multipacks of Oreos, listening to your body is rewarded with eerie silence and a heap of confusion. In the interest of sparking excitement around food, I've found a (slightly unhealthy) near-obsession with chefs and cooks to act as a gentle push toward unknown flavours. Let's be honest, if it's good enough for Selasi off *Bake Off*, it's definitely good enough for you.

As the Not Plant Based website evolved and we were fortunate enough to be granted contact with some of the most influential names on the food scene, we asked some of them one simple question: "What is your favourite thing to munch?"

Safe to say that, so far, I haven't been disappointed by these instructions and, more importantly, none of these plates/snacks/puddings/eateries have been half as scary as I'd imagined. When you're ready, try ticking off each one. Remember, they come with expert recommendation.

MARK HIX

"Something really simple like crab, freshly caught from the harbour near where I'm from in Dorset. Served with a hunk of fresh sourdough bread and some fresh ripe tomatoes. Either that or really good fish and chips."

GIZZI ERSKINE

"I'm all for bringing back the buffet. I love a great charcuterie board with meat, cheeses, fresh bread and delicious flavoursome salads. But I also love a good roast dinner so long as there's really good gravy with a depth of flavour. I like a big, slow-roasted joint like lamb shoulder, or a ham hock."

CANDICE BROWN (WINNER, *THE GREAT BRITISH BAKE OFF*, 2016)

"A couple of well baked, crusty sourdough rolls with some fresh butter and a cup of tea. You can't beat it – I just love bread."

SELASI GBORMITTAH (FINALIST, *THE GREAT BRITISH BAKE OFF*, 2016)

"The food I fancy depends on the mood I am in. Sometimes it can be a big, moist chocolate cake. Other times, it's a meaty, spicy pizza with a thin crust, or a joint of slow-cooked meat such as a hog roast...if I'm feeling especially greedy."

RUBY TANDOH (FOOD WRITER AND FINALIST, *THE GREAT BRITISH BAKE OFF*, 2013)

"I can't settle on anything. Sometimes I think that I'd have three courses of dessert: cherry pie with ice cream, a bowl of thick, spiced rice pudding and a cone of coffee ice cream. But other times, I feel a pang for something salty and punchy – like pasta with anchovies and olives, or – oooooh – deep-fried anchovy-stuffed sage leaves."

MARINA O'LOUGHLIN (RESTAURANT CRITIC, THE *GUARDIAN*)

"[If you ever get the chance, go to] Joe Beef in Montreal, Majore in Chiaramonte Gulfi (Sicily) or Bistrot Paul Bert in Paris."

NEIL RANKIN (HEAD CHEF, TEMPER RESTAURANT IN LONDON)

"A good steak tartare and fries – and I love barbecue. We've been cooking it for almost a million years now. It's part of our DNA."

MICHAEL ZEE (FOUNDER OF @SYMMETRYBREAKFAST)

"I love a pink wafer, the ones you get in a family tin of biscuits. I once said in an interview on The Food Network that they were like a Utopian vision of the future."

IZY HOSSACK (FOOD BLOGGER AT *TOP WITH CINNAMON* AND AUTHOR OF *THE SAVVY COOK*)

"French toast made with super cinnamony batter with maple syrup and blueberries! Sweet brunch dishes are my FAVE."

ANTONIO CARLUCCIO

"Osso bucco. I like that a lot."

EVE SIMMONS

"*A varied selection of supermarket antipasti: grilled artichokes, sun-dried tomatoes, herb-drenched olives, salty anchovies. Accompanied by a colourful array of dips – hummus, baba ganoush, tzatziki – with a mountain of doughy flatbreads for dipping capabilities. Followed by a packet of Jelly Babies.*"

LAURA DENNISON

"*When asked for my favourite thing to munch on, I couldn't not mention leftover new potatoes, straight from the fridge and sprinkled with salt. It's my go-to for when I come in steaming drunk, as it takes little prep and is always something we seem to have in the fridge – #irishfamily.*"

HOW TO GET SOME REST

Eve looks back on the sleepless nights she endured during hospital treatment for anorexia and recalls the techniques that actually worked in helping her to drift off. Warning: it's a heavy one.

So, being on a psychiatric ward is weird. Let's just get it out there; I, Eve Simmons, was once deemed too incapacitated to fend for my own physical and emotional needs by the UK National Health Service. At a weight so low that I'd rather not refer to it, at the risk of triggering others, and after failing for a number of weeks to regain the pounds crucial to keep my organs functioning, I was shipped off and locked up. Although, as there was no sectioning involved, officially speaking, I had "voluntarily" signed myself up for eight weeks of captive psychological torture. I won't trouble you with the full story of how I and every other vulnerable young patient were treated like drug-dependent prisoners by the nursing staff and denied any adequate psychological help for our PSYCHOLOGICAL illness...but I will offer a sliver of insight into the ordeal.

Hospital was everything I thought it would be and worse. Much, much worse. In the six-and-a-half weeks I spent cooped up in that corridor in London, there was one activity that saved me from attacking the ward manager with a box of freshly sharpened colouring pencils (razor blades were forbidden, obviously). It may not surprise you to know that this activity was writing.

I documented my daily activities (or lack thereof) in a daily journal, retreating to the secluded comfort of my laptop the moment I felt uneasy in my highly uneasy surroundings. Never was this activity more pertinent than at night. The slowed footsteps of night staff nurses and slovenly hum of the ancient heating system kept me alert until at least 2am most nights. When I'd finally managed to calm myself with seven episodes of *Sex and the City*, I'd just about nod off before waking again an hour later thanks to the glare of nurses' torches permeating my window. Sometimes they'd flippantly open the door and shine the thing straight at your bed, as if checking for open windows before they popped out for a pint of milk.

Sunday and Wednesday nights were by far the worst; I'd be lucky to get more than an hour's worth of shut-eye. Sleeping meant waking up to the dread that awaited you at 6am on Monday and Thursday mornings: the weigh-in.

At 5.45am, the bedroom door would swing open to the bellowed instructions: "Wake up. Empty your bowels. It's weighing time." Through 12 weigh-ins, I never once was able to successfully empty my bowels at 5.45 in the morning. I must lack the gene or something.

A collection of bones, half-hidden in childhood blankets and fluffy dressing gowns, would teeter into the lounge area, waiting to be called into the box of a clinic room where our fate would be sealed. Anything other than a gain would elicit a disapproving look from the measuring nurse, who would tut, turn her back to you, then scribble something down in her red book. You were then free to go back to bed until 8am, when you'd be called for breakfast. It was during these sleepless nights that I proved most productive with my writing, documenting whatever this-can't-actually-be-happening moment I'd experienced that day.

I'll save you from my extensive collection of night-time mind workings (buy the next book) but, because you've stayed with me for an impressive number of pages, I present you with a brief snippet.

DAY 3: 7/10/2015. MONOSODIUM GLUTAMATE

164cm. For the millionth time, I am 164cm tall. There is no need to wake me from my first full night's sleep in six months to confirm this. To be fair, I was already half-awake from Will's early morning farewell phone call. He's going to Portugal with his parents for a few days, which I think will be good for him. I love it when he knows exactly the right thing to say.

The vomiting woman opposite had a rough night. How do I know? BECAUSE SHE WOULDN'T STOP BANGING HER STUPID PIXIE CROP AGAINST THE WALL. I couldn't work out if it was intended as some sort of protest; if so, what on earth was she protesting about? If only she could eat that egg mayo sandwich like the rest of us are forced to. And why does she feel the need to wretch like Ernie (my cat) used to?

A girl with bug eyes and sickly, yellow skin just walked past my room carrying a plastic bag (unbranded) and a pot plant which contained a single wilted stem that was once some sort of tulip. It's literally the saddest image I've ever seen.

New favourite nurse: E. Never mind the consultants, I swear to god that these Nigerian women have saved my life. E has a son. He's ten, but she'd quite like to have a little girl at some point. She's not sure what to write for her dissertation – she's keen on fertility but isn't quite sure which area to specialize in. When I'm at my lowest, thinnest, weakest and most anxious, it's not the therapists that heal my tortured brain. It's the collection of mothers (or soon-to-be mothers; one is just about ready to pop) who came all the way from West Africa to fatten me up and fix me. I will cherish each and every one of them forever. Even if E did say one day that I look like Amy Winehouse – we have a similar nose, apparently. E told me how, in Nigeria, it's customary to massage a newborn's nose to encourage the shape into a "point". Apparently, they also do this with newborns' bottoms to make sure that they're nice and plump and juicy.

I demolished my sweet-and-sour chicken and boiled white rice. The chicken was rubbery and the rice should have been introduced to a little something called seasoning. I was still teary from my ward round meeting when lunchtime came around – apparently my only chance of making a full recovery is to stick through the full admission programme which is no shorter than SIX MONTHS. In other words, unless your BMI is 17.5 or more, you ain't going nowhere. Oh, and I cried hysterically and begged to see my mum in front of a room of 15 staff members, most of whom I had never seen before in my life. During my first ever dietician appointment with Luci, we agreed "no explosives" during or just before a meal as the added emotion leads to an anxious anorexic performance. So that's going well.

Anyway, back to E. She told me her husband cheated. She found out via text messages from his co-worker that filled the inbox on his Nokia 3310 (his "cover-up phone").

"Now, I just don't love him like I used to," she explained. "I love and I want to be in love with someone so much that I want to spend every minute with them and be around them all the time." Her fuchsia eyeshadow twinkled at me as she closed her eyes in passionate thought.

Two weeks ago, a plate of sweet-and-sour chicken, complete with gloopy, translucent paste and plain boiled rice, would have made me close to hysterical. Most likely, I would have tried my utmost to meticulously scrape off the sauce from the chicken and, if I was feeling really brave, I may have attempted a dessertspoon or two of rice. Today, I ate it all. And a side salad. And a vanilla Activia yogurt. And an apple. Don't get me wrong, my heart has migrated to my jaw and my stomach looks like something out of the film Alien, but I did it. And as E filled me in on the joys of working at KFC between mouthfuls of monosodium glutamate goo, I found myself actually enjoying it.

"They tell us not to say well done to the girls here when they finish a meal," she said, "but I think I should say it to you now. Well done, Eve."

I think I'll have the same again next week.

Troubled sleeping isn't just reserved for life on a psychiatric ward, unfortunately. All throughout my late teens and early twenties I have trudged through times of tossing and turning, sometimes going a full week with barely a wink of sleep.

If you're prone to a fair amount of catastrophic worrying (like me), night-time darkness is a sudden reminder of that terminal illness you might get, which there'll be absolutely nothing you can do about. Sleep is just one of many obstacles that provokes my bastard of a brain to engage in a *Question Time*-esque debate, calling on its trusted weapons fear and anxiety to "protect" me from the very worst scenario.

Here's a list of the non-worries that automatically swim around my head within seconds of burying myself under the duvet:

1. I have £1,000 in my bank account. That has to last me three whole weeks.
2. I had £1,300 last week. I'm definitely being robbed.
3. If they can get into my bank account, do they know where I live?
4. Mum has a hospital appointment today – she says it's a check-up but what if it's not?
5. OMG, I can't believe my mum is dying!
6. I can't afford a funeral.

7. Why haven't I got cancer yet?
8. OMG, THAT MOLE HAS CHANGED.
9. AND IT HURTS.
10. How do you know if you have schizophrenia?

And the list goes on...

Add a diagnosis of anorexia nervosa to this concoction and what you have, my friend, is an inconsolable, frightened and incredibly hungry individual.

Catastrophic worrying is usually triggered by a disturbing external event or prospect, causing my mind to ruminate to the point where my heart is in my mouth and I'm shakily awaiting the midnight rapist who is almost definitely going to climb up my drainpipe and burst through the window. But when you've spent every night for six weeks confined to a hospital bed, crippled with suffocating anxiety (and with no access to unlimited sleeping pills and/or another person to cuddle your fears away), girl's gotta find a way to deal.

I collected a toolbox of psychological utensils during my outpatient treatment, which came in handy. While some methods are well suited to sleepytime, others can be used habitually at any point in the day and, generally speaking, the more you practise them, the more likely you'll notice a reduction in your anxiety levels.

The psychological skills I now harbour are precious and, in some cases, lifesaving. Simple, quick and free, these practical anxiety-busting tips shouldn't just be available to those who are sick enough to need them. Hence why I am now passing them on to you.

1. DISTRACTION

A wonderful tool, designed to bridge the gap between a heightened emotional state and logical thought. You'll be surprised how easy it is to trick anxiety symptoms with the help of a few subtle "Hey, look at that!" techniques. If you're feeling generally a little on edge, try distracting yourself with your surroundings. Not ideal when you're tucked up in bed, I know, but practising such things during the day may lead to an all-round relaxed state. Trying a new experience or visiting an undiscovered area should force your mind to focus on acclimatizing to your new surroundings – the further out of your comfort zone, the better.

2. STOPP (STOP, THINK, OBSERVE, PLAN, PROCEED)

This excellent method of distraction can easily be done inside your own head (to stop your fellow train passengers thinking you've escaped from somewhere). As soon as you feel anxious thoughts or feelings building, immediately stop your body from physically moving and name the following: five things you can see, four things you can hear, three things you can touch (reach out and touch them if you can), two things you can smell. Finish the exercise with one long, slow, deep breath, then proceed with your day.

3. REMEMBER

Connecting with memories is an effective way of transporting your mind relatively quickly. Pick something you remember fondly and try to retrace a part of the experience. Sometimes it's a simple as remembering the lyrics to a childhood song or the name of all your high school teachers. Replay your first kiss, or the first time you had sex.

Although, if you're anything like me, you'd rather forget it.

4. EXPERIMENT

Behavioural experiments went from being my most feared form of therapy to my most lauded in a matter of months. They are particularly effective in the treatment of phobias and anxiety disorders as, nine times out of ten, the thing you're most afraid of is fear itself. A particularly valuable behavioural experiment of mine, for instance, centred around something most people wouldn't even consider a "thing": a tablespoon of mayonnaise. I didn't like mayonnaise. Heaven forbid there was a speckle of mayo on my tuna sandwich, regardless of the fact that I would happily smother my chips in the stuff pre-eating disorder. One day, a nurse enquired as to my aversion to it and all I could muster was, "It's...er...fatty." Interested as to whether I actually disliked the taste, the nurse proposed I take a risk and try it.

Presented as a behavioural experiment, it didn't seem all that bad. Needless to say, I experimented and quickly realized that a) my aversion was almost completely governed by unfounded fear and b) tuna melts are SO much tastier with a big dollop of mayo. In the interest of sticking two fingers up to Mr Anxiety, I continue flirting with behavioural experiments to this very day. Be curious about your fears and you'll find them a whole lot less scary.

5. NEVER MIND THE NOSY NEIGHBOURS

If someone could transcribe my thoughts, this book would be a walk in the bloody park. Unfortunately, iPhones aren't quite there yet and alas, my never-ending internal soliloquy exists only to make me unable to watch complicated films and keep me awake at night. However, with a little bit of understanding and extra thought, we can soften the razor-sharp edges of thought patterns. Ask yourself this important question: are the things/events I am worrying about based on FACT or OPINION? In other words, are your anxieties based on what actually happened or what you think happened or what may happen in the future? I like to think of my pain-in-the-ass anxieties as nothing more than nosy neighbours. They like to pop in occasionally, take a look around and have their say. Sooner or later, though, they'll get lost and knock on someone else's door.

6. USE YOUR BODY

Not in a weird way. In my most anxious states I have often longed for a sudden attack of appendicitis to distract me from the terror inside my mind. Instead of hoping to be struck with an agonizing illness, it seems there are other (less extreme) physical sensations that will provoke a similar effect. Try putting ice cubes on your wrists or splashing your face with ice-cold water. Or, if you're that way inclined, book an appointment for a wax. The intense physical sensation will force your mind to concentrate on breathing. Even if it's only for a couple of minutes, it's worth it for light relief from a vicious mind.

7. LISTEN UP When I first learned about the concept of "mindful listening", my response was, "But I can't hear anything." I couldn't understand how playing close attention to the heavy breathing of the balding dude sat next to me on the bus was supposed to alleviate my stresses. Until I discovered the right sound. If you are able to find inner peace via the hum of the washing machine or the screech of a police siren, then good on you, but for the rest of us, music offers an ear-friendly solution. Aggressive, punchy rock can be useful for some (preferably at a loud volume), although concentrating on the lyrics of the story in a soulful ballad can be a soothing distraction too. Failing that, crack out the Justin Bieber classics and just try and get to the end of the album without singing along...

8. TRY MINDFULNESS

Continuing the theme of mindful practices, it's worth allocating at least a few minutes of your day – if you can spare them – for some sort of mindful experience.

Traditionally, mindfulness is paying attention, on purpose,

in the present moment, non-judgementally[3]. This state of awareness can be achieved through all sorts of meditation – and, no, you don't have to sit cross-legged and download a sounds of the ocean playlist. The easiest way to get into mindfulness is to make like millions of others across 150 countries and download the Headspace app. Plug yourself in for 10 minutes wherever and whenever you want and learn to watch your worried thoughts go by like passing traffic. It takes a while to get the hang of it, but once disassociating from your thoughts is possible, the rest of the day seems a lot easier to deal with.

9. DESTROY THE SHOULDS

The so-called "tyranny of the shoulds" was first coined in 1937 by Freudian psychoanalyst Dr Karen Horney[4]. The theory has since been developed and further explored by several influential figures in the psychology world. Consider how many times, each day, you think of the words should or shouldn't. I shouldn't have another slice of cake; I should go for a run, for example. It's probably quite a few, right? Then think about whose rule book you're adhering to – who or what says you should or shouldn't do something? Now, no one's suggesting that you must break every societal rule in order to achieve true fulfilment, but I am encouraging you to be aware of where such pressures come from. Are they self-inflicted? Do you actually, really want to go for a run? Nah, me neither.

10. BE THANKFUL

Sounds like a cringey Christmas card, but bear with me. When times are especially shitty, I find a unique comfort in making a mental list of all the elements of my life which aren't. I don't believe that thinking about how lucky you are in comparison to others is necessarily helpful when you feel like the world and its big brother is out to get you, but a careful consideration of your present situation and things that you value is often a little lifter-upper. It should at least help you to muster a smile.

PRIORITIZING PLEASURE WITH NICOLA MILLBANK

In late 2016 – the early days of Not Plant Based – Eve was approached by a young, effervescent woman who she sort of recognized off the TV show *Silent Witness*. Nicola Millbank, or Milly as her social media army know her, is a part-time actress, part-time sensational cook. Having built up somewhat of a cult following on social media, Nicola had begun to notice disturbing conversations bubbling up among her followers, something she felt Eve may be able to help make sense of / share her irritations. They met over flat whites in a coffee shop near London Bridge station, wiping away milk moustaches and bonding over the ridiculousness of brownies made out of vegetables.

A self-taught home cook with a joyous attitude to *all* food, Nicola just couldn't fathom the current trend of the food world; why would a person voluntarily deny themselves the food they love? It was only when the question was posed by Nicola – with her infectious food fanaticism – that Eve clearly heard the absurdity of it. There's something about the company of a free-eating woman that grants you permission to entertain the idea that sometimes, your pleasure is a priority. We'd encourage anyone on an escape route from disordered eating to surround themselves with as many powerful, unrestricted, female eaters as possible. Women can eat whatever the fuck we want; just you watch us.

NICOLA MILLBANK'S CHAI SPICED AND CLEMENTINE POPCORN

1 tablespoon vegetable oil

50g popcorn kernels
50g unsalted butter
75g light muscovado sugar
2 tablespoons golden syrup
¼ teaspoon ground cinnamon
¼ teaspoon ground ginger
¼ teaspoon ground allspice
zest of 2 clementines

Line a large baking sheet with some baking parchment. Heat the oil in a large saucepan over a medium-high heat. Tip in the popcorn kernels, cover with a lid and cook until the popping stops, about 5 minutes, shaking the pan frequently throughout.

In another saucepan, melt the butter, sugar, golden syrup, spices and clementine zest. Heat very gently until the sugar has dissolved then turn up the heat and let the syrup bubble for 4–5 minutes until darkened to a rich caramel colour.

Pour the syrup over the popcorn and stir until combined. Tip out on to the parchment paper and spread in a thin layer. Leave for a few minutes to set and serve when completely cooled.

Milly's Real Food is published by HarperCollins.

"30 Foods You Should Never Eat After Age 30"

– eatthis.com

THE NEW FOOD RULES, ACCORDING TO THE EXPERTS

Life on Earth is full of rules. Don't run by the side of the swimming pool, don't drive through a red light, don't punch the woman in front of you in the supermarket queue because she is being rude to the cashier. It is therefore understandable that us humans freeze like deer caught in the headlights when it comes to having free licence to make our own decisions, and that is certainly true when it comes to what we eat.

Wellness gurus have made careers from our vulnerabilities and our desire for a set of instructions to follow, peddling books crammed with rule after rule regarding how and when we eat. But guess what? No matter how many of these we buy, we are still just as unhappy with our bodies. We still can't listen to our own hunger cues without feeling guilty for eating a proper meal instead of the green juice we had planned. That is because most of these food rules are in fact not based on science. According to dietitian Ursula Philpot the fewer rules you have the better – a mantra that sums our book up pretty neatly.

We too were just like you, trawling the web for the next "perfect" set of guidelines which would transform our lives. But that never happened, and our relationships with food remained just as twisted as before. You too, huh?

The *Eat It Anyway* new food rules are different. They don't say you should eat before 4pm, and they don't say you should cut anything out of your diet. For most people it's not helpful to cut things out of your diet, especially if you've had a history of disordered eating. Interestingly, when anyone changes their diet, or when they cut something out of their diet, in about 90 per cent of cases they will report some positive outcome – initially. BUT, over time, this plateaus and then the temptation arises to cut something else out, to get that same effect. So, please, let's put an end to dodgy food rules and diets, and trust the experts instead.

WHEN TO EAT

When you google "don't eat after", you get the following results in the suggested searches: 2pm, 5pm, 6pm and 8pm. It's no longer enough for fad dieters to simply not eat after dinner time...but now Google suggests – thanks to a plague of mostly ill-informed "news" articles and blog posts – that we have to skip the evening meal entirely? The sheer enormity of different and confusing rules on when to eat dinner signals that we have a much bigger beast to tame when it comes to figuring out when the hell we should be eating than we first thought. The publication of this book presents an exciting opportunity to convince you lot that such food rules are a bunch of twaddle, and that we should all just chill out and have a bag of crisps.

We clicked on the "don't eat after 2pm" search – just out of passive-aggressive curiosity – and found it troubling to read that medical professionals have put their names to such articles, one titled: "Want to lose weight? Stop eating after 2pm!"[1] Well, no shit Sherlock, of course stopping eating at 2pm will likely reduce your calorie intake and therefore make you lose weight...but does anyone consider the ethics of publishing such harmful crash-diet theories?

If you're reading this, you anxious eater, you, you'll likely have tried skipping dinner before and will know that you'll wake up so hungry as this is unnatural to your body's natural eating rhythm – as it would be for most of us. It's horrible, isn't it? Going hungry. Well, that's because biology has created a system whereby our bodies makes us feel very uncomfortable when it needs food to continue functioning. It's a design that has kept us humans alive for millennia, and yet the internet and a desire for unrealistic body types is ready to throw that all out of whack. Imagine having binge eating disorder or bulimia and reading an article telling you that not eating after 2pm will be the answer to your slimming dreams. Restrictive dieting with either of these eating disorders will increase urges to binge, and perpetuate the cycle. Now, imagine having anorexia and reading that article...it's scary to think of the damage telling someone not to eat could have on a person's health. We know from personal experience, and it's scary to think about.

In this book, as you know already, we advocate eating to the beat of your own stomach. We understand that everyone is different, and that some function better on an early dinner, whereas some prefer a late one, but what we do know for sure, regardless of the time you prefer to fill your stomach, is that you need to eat to survive. There simply isn't the evidence-based clarity to justify printing articles about when to eat in such general terms.

The expression to "breakfast like a king, lunch like a prince and dine like a pauper" had been championed in recent times across publications such as the *Daily Mirror*[2] and the *Daily Telegraph*, following a study carried out by researchers from Imperial College London, Nestlé Research Center, the University of Thessaly, King's College London and VU University Amsterdam. The articles claim that in order to fight obesity, we should eat our biggest meal of the day at breakfast, but both fail to mention that Nestlé produces breakfast cereals...and that they were involved in the study, and so more than likely would have had an interest in promoting such self-indulgent findings. Hmm. Registered nutritionist Rebecca Jennings says that, in reality, there is no real yes or no answer when it comes to whether we should eat our biggest meal first thing or at dinnertime. "The most important aspect when considering food intake is ensuring that the overall calorie needs of the individual are met to ensure optimum health. For some people that might mean eating more of their calories in the morning, and for some it might mean in the evening. Yet the distribution of calorie intake needs a lot further research. The research in favour of limiting food intake in the evening appears to be supported by fluctuations in glucose tolerance, gastric emptying, energy expenditure and the thermic response to meals being lower in the evening. It also suggests that meal satiety is higher in the morning than the evening, therefore when we consume the food in the evening, we're less satisfied by it so our calorie consumption becomes higher. However, while some studies have found having more calories in the evening is associated with increased weight gain, lots of other studies disagree."

The Nestlé example gives a scary glimpse into the reality that brands have been wooing science into producing "evidence" to make their products seem healthier for the consumer, as how healthy a product is seems to be what we're all worried about nowadays. It is therefore important to approach every food rule you have ever come across with caution. The reason most people research when to eat is because they are concerned about their weight, but the science just isn't there to back up the claim that you should only be eating crumbs in the evening in order to stay slim. In fact, there are very few human studies looking at meal timing specifically. There have been a few studies to suggest that eating after 8pm led to a higher BMI due to a greater calorie intake, however, the self-reporting in these studies can be highly inaccurate, and there are so many other factors to consider as to why calorie intake at night is higher. You might just be one of those people who are hungrier in the evening. The best time to eat is when your biological hunger cues have indicated you're hungry and also when you're able to make something or buy something to eat, given the constraints of your lifestyle. Go on, read that last sentence again.

Second to weight gain, another concern for wellness and so-called nutritional experts seems to be bloating. We bet most of you never even noticed it was a thing until various Instagram stars told you to look down and poke at your belly to compare it to their bloatless own. Bloating is something that most of us experience after we eat, and is a perfectly normal response to digestion[3]. However, for some people bloating is more than an occasional inconvenience and, in these circumstances, it should be explored with the help of a doctor. So long as we try to consume fruit and veg daily and eat in a fairly balanced way, most of us don't have to worry about bloating.

There is a myth circulating that eating late in the day can worsen bloating...for reasons that science appears to be unaware of. Rebecca Jennings adds that we can bloat at any time of the day depending on what we have eaten, how much we have eaten, how quickly we have eaten and how long gastric emptying takes. There isn't sufficient evidence to suggest that we are more predisposed to bloat in the evening. However, some research suggests that, because we often eat our largest meal in the evening, this could lead to more of a bloating feeling than at other meals. The idea that we are more bloated in the evening because we have eaten more makes far more sense than simply because the sun has moved to a different spot in the sky.

If you want to eat like a pauper in the evening and a king at breakfast – if that is what works for you and your body – carry on. But, equally, if you feel that your body functions best eating cereal late at night and nothing in the morning, who are we to say otherwise? We're supporters of science, and the science here says that there isn't the evidence to promote a formulaic schedule of when and what to eat throughout the day. We are all different. We are all allowed to eat differently. Don't listen to studies influenced by breakfast brands.

HOW TO EAT

For this question, there is only one logical answer: in whichever way you please. Perhaps you're at a family barbecue and your sister has a particular penchant for the crinkled, crisped skin that hangs off of a tender thigh of chicken. You eat the meat, but save the skin for your sister as part of a carnivorous family ritual. When you're forced to go to lunch with a colleague with whom you have nothing other than the subpar supply of coloured highlighters to discuss, you opt for a grab-and-go meal to save you sitting across the table from them for the longest hour of your life. If you're on a date with a man or woman and they describe Barack Obama as overrated, you definitely don't want dessert. But if the restaurant just to happens to be next to a Krispy Kreme, then you definitely do. The point is that food, for much of history, has never been just food. The objective of eating is never simply to fill a nutritional hole. Eating does not exist in isolation and every diet expert worth their salt will incorporate the messiness of life into any proposed understanding about the way in which we eat.

Renee McGregor, the sports and eating disorder dietitian we met earlier in the book, explains this perfectly: "Food is so much more than fuel; it's about wellbeing, belonging and happiness. While we all know that food provides us with nutrients, it also feeds our soul and helps us build relationships. When you are sat around a table with friends, eating and drinking, the focus is not on what you are being served but on what you are discussing and how those conversations impact and shape you. Nutritional intake doesn't always have to be about getting it 'right'; a balanced approach to food and eating means a balanced attitude to living, where rest and restoration with friends and family are equal in parts to working hard to pay the bills."

Human beings, by their very nature, are social animals – we could not have flourished as the dominant race by way of individualistic mentality. The vehicle through which we were able to reach our sociable tentacles out to others was food. As far back as the Stone Age, early man quickly realized that storing – and eating – food alone, purely for energy, was a short-sighted idea. Inevitably, food became spoiled quickly, forcing tribes to unite and share their stash while generating healthy competition using increasingly sophisticated hunting methods[4]. Culturally, food can be eaten symbolically, strengthening a spiritual connection between people, their community and a divine entity. In China, for instance, new parents aren't sent eggs dyed crimson red for a boost of post-natal protein, but rather for well-wishing, symbolizing a new, exciting start in life. Jews don't eat unleavened matzo crackers for part of the year because bread makes them bloated, but to commemorate the ancient Israelites' hastened escape from captivity in Egypt. The dinner table is a training ground for childrens' wider socialization in the world; studies show that family-style meals are where they learn cultural niceties such as pleases and thank yous, and passing bowls of food to others teaches sharing and self-nurturing[5]. In China, breakfast isn't only intended for eating, but also for important business meetings and exchanging professional information[6]. Even if we wanted to eat for nutritional purposes only, it's unlikely anyone would be able to. Studies consistently show that all manner of social and emotional situations manipulate what – and how – we eat. If we're told as children not to eat something, we're far more likely to eat it in excess[7]. We tend to eat more if others eat more, or if we're in large groups of people. If you're on a date with someone you fancy, you'll eat less than you would if you weren't that into him/her[8]. And if you're feeling miserable, you're much more likely to dine out at Maccy's than you are to eat a rainbow and whizz up a concoction of vegetables and healthy fats in your Nutribullet. A review published in the *American Journal of Public Health* of the Health At Every Size model of intervention (as discussed in the previous chapter) provides compelling evidence to justify my arrival at the following conclusion: people are most healthy when they stop thinking about food. Studies have found that this approach improves blood pressure, blood lipids, cardiovascular fitness, mental health, susceptibility to extreme hunger and body satisfaction. Once individuals who are shameful of both their eating and their bodies are taken out of their own heads and put back into their bodies, the external and internal stress is lessened.

As dietitian Ursula Philpot puts it: "We over-intellectualize food and apply too many rules. What you need to go with is your first instinct. It's about gradually tuning in to what your body is saying." Easier said than done, I know, but once you begin to drown out the circulating noise with your own rule (there are no rules) your decision is pretty much made for you.

EAT WITH YOUR MEMORIES

By now we know that food isn't just about eating. It's a method of transport that carries you through the memories and experiences of life. Many of our most precious moments wouldn't have existed if it weren't for the tastes that accompanied them. Here are just two examples...

SMOKED SALMON BAGELS AND EGG MAYO SANDWICHES

How munching her way through her memories aided Eve's escape from anorexia.

Have you ever taken a picnic to the cinema? No? Didn't think so. I have, and although it may save you from taking out a mortgage to pay for a box of popcorn, I wouldn't recommend it. I'd advise you to be especially cautious if your family are Jewish and therefore define picnic food as a gloriously stinking selection of gefilte fish balls, pickled cucumbers, egg mayonnaise sandwiches and chopped liver pâté. If the cinema of choice is in a predominantly Jewish area such as Stamford Hill in London, or Borough Park in Brooklyn, perhaps your Tupperware of preserved fish and mashed-up egg will go unnoticed. But it's probably not a good idea do it in the central Bournemouth branch of Odeon, at two o'clock in the afternoon. Slap bang in the middle of the school summer holidays.

I was 13 and my brother Sam was 15; we were visiting my beloved auntie and uncle in Bournemouth the summer after my dad died. As we sat in the cinema foyer (!) tucking into our pre-*Spy Kids* snack, lovingly prepared by my auntie Shoshi, the gangs of Bournemouth (teenagers in trainers) descended on our sophisticated spread. They stared, they sniffed, they sniggered. Sam and I winced, willing the attackers to just disappear into their screening of *Dude, Where's My Car?* Yet, despite the jibes, taunting and disdainful inhalations, neither Sam nor I could quite bring ourselves to...put the fish balls down. They were simply too delicious. Through shared determination, we stayed strong and carried on eating, right to the carp-breath end. Rather than shovelling handfuls of overpriced, buttered cardboard into our faces, we dined on a (semi) balanced meal while Uncle Lenny told stories of Dad's hidden acting talents or family trips to Weymouth. Fitting into the culinary box of the British countryside wasn't important; we fitted in to our box, our family.

It wasn't until a few years ago that Sam and I remembered the fateful eggy cinema day and doubled over in laughter at the astonishingly mental nature of the scenario, and how we must have looked to an onlooking gentile; spreading egg paste on to our kosher-for-Passover matzo crackers and divvying out literal balls of fish. Perhaps it slipped our memories because it was an enjoyable meal which had kept us nice and satisfied all the way through *Spy Kids*. Until later that afternoon when, if we were lucky, we'd be granted a packet of Bamba or Bissli (Israeli crisps now available in Tesco's, fyi).

My brother now lives in Los Angeles and when he comes home for a fleeting visit between film editing jobs, my mum's frantic concern is annoyingly true to the stereotype: "What shall I give him to eat?!"

"Just tell her to get me the usual," he texts, "fish balls, bagels, chopped liver, egg mayo..."

Let it be said that my mother is the most incredible cook. I know it's clichéd, and of course I *would* say that, but seriously: her effortless foodie talents know no bounds.

Even at the age of 22 (yep still living at home because it's London and I'm not a gazillionaire), the subtle scent of Mum's crispy roast chicken wafting from the kitchen was a source of childish excitement.

Until the age of about nine, Mum would spend the morning of every one of my birthdays intricately crafting my birthday cake. I'd find her leaning over the kitchen worktop, bundled up in her scruffy dressing gown, rolling hot-pink sheet icing into a rectangular mass, which she'd then drape over her perfectly moist Victoria sponge. Then, she'd mould the remaining icing into two plump balls and sandwich them on top of each other, before adding ears and drawing on eyes with black food colouring. It was christened The Piggy Cake. This routine continued throughout my dad's illness (he was diagnosed with cancer when I was nine), with an adaptation on the piggies according to my level of maturity. One year it was red in honour of Arsenal football team. I was going through a phase.

I'm aware that I've painted my mother as quite the yummy mummy housewife who whiles away the hours inventing farmyard-themed baked goods. In fact, my mum was much too busy "reclaiming the night" on feminist marches, fighting for better maternity leave deals at the publishers she worked for and collecting offensive satirical comic illustrations of Margaret Thatcher. It was only after a suggestion from my dad that she ever considered the possibility she'd have children. Yet, once my brother and I arrived on the scene, she'd cook dinner every evening and she'd bake a piggy cake on every birthday. At Christmas and on Jewish holidays she'd prepare a three-course meal for all ten members of our extended family, and she became devoted to my grandma and her care when she was diagnosed with dementia. (When Mum was just 13 years old my grandma had thrown all her clothes out the window and ordered her to sleep elsewhere. Grandma was a "difficult" woman. Nevertheless, Mum persisted with unconditional love and kindness.) It must also be said that my darling mother achieved all of the above while editing a successful women's magazine, writing four books, completing an MA in gender studies (what else?) and producing one fantastic and awe-inspiring daughter. And a son...I guess.

The dinnertime requests made by my brother and I are rarely for Mum's buttery fish pies, delicate meatballs or even her doughy-yet-fruity apple cake; scrumptious as they all may be. Instead, we present a shopping list that reads much like the one that was used for our cinema picnic. With the addition of Waitrose's finest bagels, of course.

When I first returned to the comforting arms of chewy white bread AA (after anorexia, duh), it was tough to adjust to a world in which one of my fundamental purposes in life was no longer the avoidance of white carbs. Even white sourdough still evoked some trepidation when the complementary bread basket arrived in a restaurant. But bagels (or beigels as my grandmother called them) weren't nearly as unnerving. I knew they contained a lot of sugar (another ingredient I was on the rocks with) and they were far from the artisanal, hand-baked variety I'd grown so attached to. These were made in a factory (!) But it didn't matter. Warmed in the oven until spongy, with little nodules of bumpy, terracotta outer skin; charred from mum's overzealous reheating (sorry, Mum) – they are quite literally irresistible. As are the bagels' smelly bedfellows, in all their socially unacceptable glory.

I'm not advocating a long-term safe/unsafe categorization of foods; if you're still classing some foods as "unsafe", I'm afraid you still have an active eating disorder. However, recovery is tough and going from nought to sixty for breakfast, lunch and dinner can be hugely anxiety-inducing. Most eating disorder treatment will encourage you to face your so-called fear foods one at a time, gradually building up the skills and confidence to conquer one, and then move on to the next. If the familiar pull of a nostalgic connection helps the peace process, then immerse yourself in memories to your heart's content, I say.

As I've always suspected when it comes to eating disorders, the condition has very little to do with the ingredients in food itself. The same can be said for recovery; the innate, enveloping desire to harness and nurture important relationships is a useful tool. In desperate times throughout my recovery, my commitment to societal norms or fulfilling the expectations of loved ones has carried me through unexpected three-course dinners or the odd surprise office delivery of cupcakes. Challenging the crucifying brain-voice is a hurdle that can only be jumped at a certain point in recovery – it's important to say. Unfortunately, eating disorders are an illness, the neurological and psychological nature of which makes them stronger than any amount of emotional currency. But anything's worth a try, right?

"Using nostalgia during recovery is quite a beautiful thing," says psychologist Kimberley Wilson. "It does exactly the opposite of what eating disorders do, which is disconnect you from your desires and ability to think. Connecting with your memories could enable you to reconnect with part of yourself and to when things felt better. Food can be an anchor to those times and places."

There is one caveat, however. Revisiting your childhood is comforting, providing you felt safe there. Let's be honest, it's a sad fact that this often isn't the case.

Eating with memories is in fact used within treatment for eating disorders, based on the principles of building one's food repertoire from scratch. According to dietitian Ursula Philpot, who works primarily with people with eating disorders, nostalgia is useful at weeding out the genuine likes from the blogger-told-me-to-eat-quinoa forced preferences.

It might not be Christmas dinner (having a dead dad doesn't lend itself to a joyful festive season) and your most cherished memories might exist as far away from your family as possible. Maybe it's the tub of Ben & Jerry's ice cream favoured by your teenage gang, or the supermarket pizza you'd share with your university hook-up after a night of boozing and deeply unsatisfactory sex. It's the soothing spaghetti Bolognese cooked by your best friend when *that* dude randomly stops texting you back. It's the first childhood sampling of a frappuccino in all its slushy, decadent, ice-cool glory. It's crunchy, milkily soft fish and finger-sized chips eaten to the soundtrack of lapping waves as fresh sea air fills your lungs and you manically avoid seagulls shitting on your hair. It's birthday cake. Not necessarily because dry-ish vanilla sponge, claggy supermarket jam and sickly sweet sheet icing does it for you, but because someone you love has taken the time to create or buy something intricate and beautiful, especially for you.

"BAD" FOOD, GOOD MEMORIES

Laura uses her memories to compartmentalize the different stages throughouther life, and analyse how "bad" food was instrumental in shaping the person she is proud to be today.

Before I moved to London for work, I used to believe that good food came in a pale shade of beige and could be warmed up in under two minutes in a microwave. Eating well, to me, always meant (and still does, I suppose) being able to feed myself quickly, and for that food to be very carb-heavy. Since moving home, I've noticed that the conversation around food here differs greatly to that further south. My Londoner mates would snarl for sure if I told them tales of enjoying cold, claggy Cantonese food left over from the night before, while curled up in bed in the morning – even without a hangover – because eating like a pauper sure doesn't sound too appealing to them, not when avocado on handmade soda bread and flat whites for over a tenner exist. It's not that I enjoy separating myself from this snobbery in a bid to preserve a down-to-earth vibe...it's just that all of my most treasured memories – the good, the bad and the seriously ugly – centre around cheap, highly processed "garbage".

One happy memory involving my brother is when he won £20 in a bag of Walkers salt and vinegar crisps. Remember when Walkers gave out money in their crisps? I can think of no better marketing ploy than to offer children both food and cold, hard cash. Salt and vinegar crisps have been my favourite since a young age, in spite of the betrayal of gifting my sibling with money and not me. He spat out crisps as he unearthed the small, black plastic casing of treasure. He knew exactly what this was – we all did – and of the rare, glorious opportunity it would provide to gloat in my face. My brother was manic with glee, jumping around the living room as everyone laughed in juvenile jealousy. Twenty pounds to a child is a fortune, so I left the room, walking past every few minutes to yell "Stupid!" at him, each time causing him to erupt into fits of cackles. He was so happy, and although I couldn't have admitted it at the time, it was impossible for me not to be happy for him too.

Birthday cakes in our family always used to be a big thing, and offered yearly opportunities for the whole family to get together and begrudgingly sing happy birthday to each other, safe in the knowledge that there would be a sweet treat for each of us once the candles were blown out. Myself and my two brothers would fight to blow out each other's candles, and it would end in tears more often than not. These birthday cakes, I've noticed as I recently celebrated my 25th, have been a timely reflection the descent of our family's finances and a lack of effort since we're all now adults. Elaborately iced cakes in the shape of puppies when I was a tot have today become those £1 Victoria sponge cakes from Asda, half-eaten by the time I get home from work. I'm not complaining, really. As I explained before, my sweet tooth has become less sharp as I've gotten older. Perhaps I only enjoyed those moments anyway for the routine of it and family celebration – who knows.

Food memories from before my eating disorder seem very romantic. Willowy, and soft, and warm-bellied. I fondly remember having weekly swimming lessons before the age of ten, and enjoying a guilt-free Happy Meal at McDonald's each time afterward, arguing with my friends over who got luckiest with their toy and who could colour in the neatest with the free crayons provided by the fast food chain. (It was me, always.) "Healthy" outings – like doctors' appointments and activity days – were often followed up with a food-related treat to keep us kids quiet on the way home. After our biannual check-ups at the dentist, we'd earn a chocolate bar each, and I'd always choose the limited edition Snowflake (a Flake with a web of white chocolate down its middle) until they stopped selling them, for reasons I still haven't forgiven Cadbury for to this day. They say that it's dangerous territory to use food as a reward system, and that might be true, but this parenting style did contribute to a lot of delicious moments for me.

I have some very gleeful memories of the primary school lunch hall, aside from the time I was told to stand at the front for talking through prayer and turned bright red. I remained a goody-two-shoes after that to avoid further mortification. Our year was small, and we were all close friends who seemed to share the same taste buds. None of us were disappointed when a different variety of turkey twizzler or chicken nuggets was served on plastic trays with Smash and a dessert. The only two desserts I remember were chocolate concrete cake or a cube of vanilla sponge with icing, sprinkles and custard; I adored them both.

High school, however, was an awkward time for me, as I struggled to fit in and be comfortable with who I was and how I looked. I've always been introverted, melancholic and deeply thoughtful, which unfortunately aren't qualities school children admire when being popular is the most important thing you can be. Regular break times for food offered a much needed respite for me and were some of the only memories from high school in which I'm not fizzing with anxiety. Baked beans and Cheddar cheese in a white flour wrap, heated in the microwave to a tongue-scalding temperature, was one of our cafeteria's specialities. I'd have one of these during first break, then a pot of penne pasta covered with too much tomato sauce and not enough grated cheese. My friend once threw a full pasta pot over someone's head during a scrap.

My highly processed, fairly ordinary diet graduated to eating very little when I moved away to college. I couldn't bear the thought of spending any more time at my high school's sixth form, sharing a bubble with other people who didn't pay much attention to me, so I moved to a liberal, intelligent college where I could experiment with dyeing my hair horrible colours, losing my virginity and getting a septum piercing. This experimenting extended to manipulating the shape of my body, which had recently developed a few curves. Bananas with a cup of tea and skimmed milk became comfort food, and when my body rejected this new stupid diet plan (of course, because I was hungry), I began instead eating everything, as everything sure seemed more impossible to resist than bananas. I can safely say that during all the years that I had an eating disorder, I was not able to enjoy a meal. I was not able to enjoy a meal because I could not get through a meal without feeling like a bad person deserving of such guilt.

After fucking up my education, thanks to the heavy weight of some mental health problems and dropping out of university twice, I thankfully was lucky enough to land a pretty impressive first job in journalism within a leading news agency. This job was the reason I moved to London, and why I was able to experience "finer" dining, and momentarily stray from my favourite working-class foods. I had the opportunity to try oysters, fresh truffle and Prunier caviar; to have lunch prepared by a private chef on a yacht in the middle of the Mediterranean Sea on one of numerous press trips with this company, which I will never forget. I'm not denying that this was beautiful living, and that eating gourmet food has opened my eyes to a world I would never have the budget to experience normally, but this dabbling hasn't put me off the food I grew up with and that I associate with so many happy memories.

This, for me, exactly demonstrates the importance of nostalgia when it comes to how we eat. I could eat a dog-rotten plastic tube of yogurt and prefer it to a £500 steak, because it reminds me of the time I sat with my childhood friend Francesca and accidentally squirted yogurt in my eye and we both peed ourselves with laughter.

What I have grown to realize, throughout all the shit that I went through with food, is that it will always be there, and I'll never be far away from my next memory, which I'll be able to recall in years to come because of what I was eating at the time. I realize this as I sit here eating cheesy nachos with sour cream and half a pint of Coors Light; when I think back to how many hours we put into writing this book, I'll think, "Yeah, nachos are great, aren't they?" Although it's impossible to only play back the good things when it comes to the showreel of your life, I know that, for me, "rubbish" food is the string to which my memory Polaroid bunting hangs, and the reason why I'd choose packaged Scotch eggs over quail's, any day.

NOW PUT IT INTO PRACTICE: LAURA'S 11 CHEAP FEASTS THAT PLAY BY THE NEW RULES

I am the queen of depressing dinners. You might think that this is a title that I shouldn't champion with pride, and for a long time I didn't, but I've grown to accept my impatience and to love dishes with (more often than not) no more than two ingredients. I imagine this is largely due to the food nostalgia that I've just explained.

When I first tried to unlearn all the nonsense food rules I had abided by for years of disordered eating, I found myself hurriedly ploughing my way through meals that I loved when I was younger, and which I had deprived myself of since. This created a pattern of speed cooking in order to satiate my confused palate, and this has continued to suit my sluggish lifestyle pretty well.

I've tried not to be a lazy shit. Honestly, I have. But when I am hungry, I am hungry, and I don't have time to wait for over an hour for a jacket potato or a lasagne to cook, else I'm going to hangrily bite the nearest person's head off. I am not one of those people who basks in spending hours in the kitchen and creating spectacular feasts. I want cheap, I want cheerful and I want to speedily dribble it down my chin as I watch The US *Office* season four for the seventh time.

Despite dropping out of university (twice) and not totally gaining the whole experience, I've been able to adopt a student-style diet, meaning that most of the meals I prepare myself are both quick and cheap. This method of cooking suits my frantic, anxious, freelance lifestyle, as well as my lack of time, which is inevitably the case. I do not have a consistent income and am often worrying about when my next pay cheque is coming in, so to eat in this way, for me, is essential.

Cheap-as-chips meals are underrated, and if, like me, you are a modern mess, you'll appreciate this list of my top speedy feasts for pennies that are actually nutritional heroes.

1. BEANS ON TOAST

I'm a big fan of toast at all times of the day, not just for breakfast. There's nothing more comforting than a slice of wholemeal with a healthy serving of melting butter spread across it. Add half a tin of baked beans, and you're on to a winner. Not only are baked beans delicious and naturally low in fat (if you're into that), but baked beans are also packed with fibre and protein.

As a money-saving tip, try freezing your bread for toasting. This especially helps if you are cooking for one. The number of times I've bought loaves of bread and have had to chuck half of it away because it's turned blue by the time I get around to eating it is criminal.

2. BUBBLE AND SQUEAK

Traditionally, bubble and squeak is cooked cabbage fried with cooked potatoes and often served with meat, but in my family, it's dry-frying any leftover vegetables and potatoes that are sitting in the fridge. Dry-frying means without oil, which helps to keep down any additional fats. Season well and serve up piping hot.

3. "WHATEVER'S IN THE FRIDGE" SANDWICH

Again, I come from a family who are big on leftovers. Dita Von Teese once said that she didn't trust anyone who didn't eat leftovers... and, girl, I'm with you.

Sandwiches are totally underrated in terms of their nutritional value. In health mags, sandwiches are always being made over, with the bread replaced with cauliflower steaks, Portobello mushrooms and other nonsense. But sandwiches can actually act as a building block for a healthy diet.

Sandwiches offer the perfect breaded platform on which to stack your daily protein, vegetables and dairy, all in one sitting. My sandwich of choice is avocado, Brie and prosciutto, but a cheaper option could be tuna, sweetcorn and spinach leaves. The possibilities are endless, really. See what you have in the fridge and get going.

Try to have wholemeal or wholegrain bread (same goes for rice and pasta) where you can, as fibre is great for your digestive health and can prevent nasty things like bowel cancer.

4. MICROWAVED BAKED POTATO

I only say microwaved here because, as I mentioned before, I am a totally bone idle cook. Potatoes are less calorie-dense than most other starchy foods and are also high in fibre, potassium, vitamin C, vitamin B6 and folate.

Like the sandwich, you can stuff a baked potato with whatever you wish; just try to involve some veg, a little fat and some protein. My favourite is a baked potato with beef chilli, a dollop of sour cream and some broccoli.

Oh, and don't forget to eat the skin for even more fibre.

5. PASTA AND PESTO

Pasta and pesto is the ultimate student meal, isn't it? It's quick, cheap and pretty good for your body. Starchy foods are a good source of energy and the main source of a range of nutrients in our diet[9]. As well as fibre – which we know can help keep our bowels healthy and help us feel full – they contain calcium, iron and B vitamins. I opt for shop-bought pesto (we know by now that I am lazy) but, if you want to make your own, even better. Add some veg to this feast to make it even better for you. Try cherry tomatoes and olives (olives in jars are cheaper, just fyi).

Let's not forget to mention that dried pasta can be a budgeter's lifesaver, as it typically has a long shelf life...so you can buy it in bulk and stash it in your cupboard if you wish.

6. RICE, SALMON AND FROZEN VEG

It's recommended that a healthy diet should include at least two portions of fish a week, including one of oily fish. Oily fish, such as mackerel or salmon, is high in omega-3 fatty acids, which help to keep your heart healthy[10]. A plate of rice, salmon and frozen veg (not frozen when on the plate, obviously) is a well-rounded meal containing all the elements needed for a balanced diet.

When buying salmon, it's worth doing your research into sustainability if you're concerned about the future of our seas, but it's also worth noting that frozen salmon is sometimes cheaper, if you're on a budget. The freezer is your friend!

7. SHOP-BOUGHT STIR-FRY

Ready-prepared packets of stir-fry veg are great, because they are cheap and a great way to get a variety of veg on your plate without spending a lot of cash. I used to hate cooking just for myself, as you often end up spending a lot of money on individual ingredients, but this method solves that problem.

Stir-fries allow for artistic licence. Try adding prawns and chicken to your veg and serving with noodles and soy sauce.

8. THE HUMBLE OMELETTE

Despite not being a huge fan of the taste of eggs, I can appreciate their versatility and low price tag. They are also a great source of protein (you knew that already through Instagram... didn't you?). But did you know that they also contain vitamin D, vitamin A, vitamin B2, vitamin B12, folate and iodine[11]? No, you probably didn't. Omelettes are a great feast for when you're in a hurry. Or so I'm told anyway...yuck.

9. SPEEDY CHICKEN CURRY

Experts agree that we shouldn't eat too much red meat, and certainly not every day, so chicken is a great protein alternative. Plus it can be frozen for those on a budget.

If you're not someone who has a cupboard stocked with spices you can always use shop-bought spice pastes or sauces – but do watch out for the salt content. Try adding mushrooms, onion, spinach and lentils to your curry to add extra fibre.

10. THE REDUCED AISLE SCURRY

Right, my cheap-as-chips feasters! I'm sure I don't have to explain to you what a reduced aisle in a supermarket is. I'm sure you know what time your local one begins to fill theirs, too. If you're lucky, you might strike gold and find something glorious like a steak for your evening meal. Red meat – when eaten in small doses – provides us with iron and vitamin B12. Make your own chips and serve with garden peas and English mustard.

If you're not so lucky, you might end up with a smashed-up barely in-date sausage roll and a bag of wilted lettuce. Better luck next time in that case.

11. THE SLEEPOVER BANQUET

When I was in my teens, and of the age when I had enough pals to pack the floor of my bedroom with friend-filled sleeping bags, we'd spend the days leading up to the sleepover (we'd need at least two weeks of planning) discussing what films we might watch and the snacks we'd have.

Snacks are integral to every sleepover. Mine never broke the bank of my parents, as everything we ever wanted could be found in the nearest Asda. Doritos, olives, cheese, chocolate, more chocolate and of course ice cream were all on the menu, and we all loved it. Never did we wake up regretful of our "binge" the next day because, as kids, you know that happiness is an important part of life, and that sweet treats and triangle crisp indulgences make for lots of happiness indeed.

My last cheap feast idea suggestion is to enjoy the occasional splurge on all the foods you want with your mates, without labelling it a "cheat day". Life is too short to allow those old food rules to prevent you from having a cheese platter with your best girls and washing it all down with way too much rosé.

WHEN FOOD IS CULTURE

Fried rice is a special though simple dish. I think it reminds us how to eat; it's a warm comforting dish for most Chinese in Asia and every home will have their version. This dish is a typical yin/yang dish – yin qualities are cooling, so mostly come from the use of vegetables, while yang qualities are warming, so come from the use of pungent aromatics like garlic and ginger. Prawns are yin, eggs are yang... you get the picture. Overall this is a balanced dish and is a great metaphor for eating in general, reminding us to eat with balance – fresh vegetables, yes, but a little bit of whatever you fancy thrown in. It's the perfect dish to use up any leftovers too.

CHING HE HUANG'S SPECIAL FRIED RICE

Serves 2–4

4 teaspoons rapeseed oil
2 medium free-range eggs, beaten
2 garlic cloves, finely chopped
1 tablespoon fresh root ginger, peeled and grated

2 spring onions, sliced into 1-cm rounds
150g cooked shelled prawns, defrosted if frozen
½ red pepper, diced
50g cooked garden peas, drained
400g steamed jasmine rice, cooled
2 tablespoons light soy sauce
1 tablespoon oyster sauce
1 teaspoon sriracha (optional)
½ teaspoon freshly ground white or black pepper
1 teaspoon sesame oil

Place a wok over a medium heat and add 1 tablespoon rapeseed oil. Swirl the oil in the wok, then pour in the beaten eggs. Stir the eggs to scramble them, cooking for about 30 seconds until they are golden and fluffy. Transfer the eggs to a small plate and set aside.

Wipe out the wok with a piece of kitchen paper and then place back over a high heat; pour in the remaining rapeseed oil. Add the garlic, ginger and spring onions and stir-fry for 10 seconds, then add the prawns and stir-fry for a further 20 seconds.

Add the diced pepper, peas and scrambled eggs and mix well before adding the cooked rice. Mix well to combine, stir-frying for about 1 minute, or until everything is heated through.

Add the soy sauce, oyster sauce, sriracha, pepper and sesame oil and toss together well for 1 minute. Serve at once.

www.chinghehuang.com

"Can we have that in a doggy bag?"

– notplantbased.com

TAKEAWAYS

21 REASONS TO STAY RECOVERED

The pages of this book have equipped you with a very potent weapon: knowledge. Hopefully, you will go forth and use this weapon to the benefit of your peace of mind (and McDonald's cravings). But beware: for every nugget of sound information, there are millions of nutjobs ready and waiting to suck the truth right out of you.

Education is only half the battle. You're now faced with the task of navigating a world in which going to the gym or the supermarket is a competitive sport. It's not going to be easy, and perhaps there'll be periods of hopelessness. Inevitably, a broken heart, toxic friendship or unexpected redundancy will pop an emotional cork, allowing feelings of inadequacy and unworthiness to filter through. The temptation will, of course, be to turn to your familiar method of control; a perfect distraction from the terror of feeling not quite good enough. BUT... if you can manage it, try not to. There is an alternative route to control which grants you Queen Bey levels of power.

When you win (which you will) – you can break away from anxious eating and finally be granted a sweet freedom you never even knew existed. Free from the heartbreak of peeling yourself out of too-tight skinny jeans. Free from having one slice of banoffee cheesecake, when you really wanted two. Free from the wagging finger of calories listed on the back of Coco Pops. Free from the hollow emptiness that follows when someone says you look "healthy". Free from constant, exhausting social comparison and Instagram black holes. Free from pizza with a stupid salad in the middle of it.

There will come a point, not too far from now, when all the things you believed to be most important will suddenly fade into nothingness, leaving people, memories and genuine contentment in their place. It's a utopia that leaves little room for diet and weight loss companies to continue to score killer profits, and doesn't work in favour of personal trainers. You'll have to challenge just about every advert you come across – be it magazine, film, TV, billboard or radio – and the battle can be tiresome and appear never-ending at times. Therefore, the occasional trite motivational Instagram quote can actually be useful for peeling you out of bed. Although the word "motivation" is pop-psych and corny, so we like to think of our snippets of encouragement as "rocket fuel". Or, more specifically, "Reasons to eat. Properly."

EVE

1. YOU ARE HUNGRY

The body is complicated and mysterious but isn't backward about coming forward. For generations past every one of the sixteen billion+ individuals on the planet have relied on their hunger to keep them alive. And this was way before Weight Watchers points. You are no exception.

2. YOU GET SHIT DONE

You will be amazed at how much brain space suddenly becomes available when you are no longer consumed with thoughts of how many calories you burn in a Pilates class. You could write books (er, case in point...), build a house, learn to code, write impassioned letters to government, provide the exact combination of words that a best friend needs to hear...the list goes on. Even more exciting, you can do nothing while thinking about nothing. Bliss.

3. PEOPLE LOVE YOU

They do. Trust me. I don't believe anyone should "get better" or improve their health for the sake of others – the most meaningful push comes from a desire to do right by yourself. Having said that, I have always found an unexpected text from a close friend or an invitation to a do from a trusted colleague a helpful reminder that there are plenty of people who value my company – despite what my brain tells me. If you're lucky the only thing your friends will care about is your happiness, health and ability to reach your full, varied potential. Nobody who really and truly cares about you could give a single shit about what you look like. Or what you eat.

4. THINK OF THE POOS

When I began eating properly again, the best result – physically

– was the effect on my bowel function. No longer did I need to dedicate 20 minutes of every other day to the toilet seat. Excreting a poo became a fleeting non-moment among the day's events, like sneezing or tweeting. Forget the gut health brigade with its probiotic supplements and fermented cabbage; there is one very simple rule: eat enough food, and you will poo. Fibre-heavy food helps, providing it's in moderation (dinner party guests with a runny tummy aren't fun for anyone).

5. EVERYTHING YOU'VE BEEN TAUGHT IS BULLSHIT

Well, almost everything. All those Instagram posts, magazine photoshoots or even Facebook profile pictures you see of other humans showcasing washboard stomachs, ample racks and perfectly coiffed hair (without those straggly, frizzy bits poking out the side) are NOT REAL LIFE. At best, they are the one picture in 100 in which – thanks to camera trickery and lighting – a body shape appears in a certain way. And remember that for many of these people it's literally their job to look that way. If a smidge of flesh appears in the least bit lumpy, or they haven't plucked their eyebrows in a week, they won't get paid. Feel sorry for them, poor little rich, stupid people.

6. YOU CAN HELP OTHERS LIKE YOU

When Not Plant Based was nothing more than a germ of genius in the brain of Laura Dennison, I was on the other side of London, nervously navigating all-you-can-eat buffets and willing editors to pay me for a heartfelt written account of my eating disorder. I was figuring my shit out – sandwich by sandwich – but I still wasn't quite there yet. Then, I met Laura, launched the website and very quickly became immersed in a world of wonderful, similarly messy people who "got it". With every post in which I took a spectacular emotional dump all over the Internet, I was gifted notes of empathy and gratitude from young people who'd found comfort in my words. The knowledge that, by simply being honest, I could soften the blow of this bewildering illness was game-changing. It was a relief greater than any I felt by skilfully dodging the bread basket or squeezing into size 6 skinny jeans. Suddenly, the world was wider than my anxieties and insecurities; my most meaningful question was no longer "What if I get fat", but rather "What can I do to help these people?" Obviously it took a lot more than a load of lovely fan mail to escape the entrapment of my eating disorder, but it certainly kick-started the process. Now, as a stronger, healthier and happier person who has free space in her mind to think about disordered thoughts objectively, I can deliver something of immeasurable value. I can harness my personal insight to provide a safety net for thousands who are going through exactly the same battle that I did. I can be the knowing hug that I needed but never discovered. And you can too.

7. BABIES, CAREERS AND GROWN-UP SHIT

Two of these things are in no way necessary to forge a path to recovery, by the way. But, for those who are that way inclined, it's a reality worth flagging. For as long as I can remember, I have wanted children. Call that the poisonous residue of an oppressive patriarchal society or whatever, it is what it is. And it's real. At the time of writing, I haven't had a period for three years. Doctors say that menstrual cycles need a little extra weight to regenerate, which isn't helped by the fact I was on the pill from the age of 18. Whatever the reason, each month I am terrified by my bloodless knickers. Of course, the ability to conceive is not *the* reason to recover, and for many a house full of screaming children and food-smeared upholstery is a hellish prospect. But as I attempt to go above and beyond my "healthy" weight target and actively gain kilos to the point of too-tight jeans, the bigger picture of my future family is a useful motivational tool. Even if I decide against it in a few years' time, at least my options are open and not restricted by a redundant, destructive fear.

And it's not just about babies; being locked in the rumination of disordered thoughts makes it tough to get through a working day, let alone further a career. In the height of my eating disorder I was the worst employee imaginable. I may have turned up an hour early every day and taken on five freelance writing jobs to overfill my evenings and weekends, but rest assured, every paragraph I produced was an illegible load of bollocks. No amount of hours spent sacrificing my social life would nourish my brain enough to make up for the nouns missing from my sentences. The preoccupation with an upcoming lunchtime would make a 300-word news story a five-hour-long operation. Fast-forward four years and, although my residual anxieties haven't disappeared, I manage pretty well at co-producing eight pages of a national newspaper every week, while writing articles for a website and devouring a book every couple of months on my tube rides to work. Oh, and I wrote a book – which (I hope) is of far better quality than the slapdash jitterings of my mid-ED articles. But I guess you'll be the judge of that.

8. LIFE IS OVER SOON

Let's be clear: this isn't my way of saying, "At least you don't have cancer!" One source of pain, be it physical or emotional, is not more or less than another, it's simply different. Unfortunately, we live in a society that values physical health over and above mental health, meaning if your diagnosis doesn't definitely end in death, people have limited sympathy. Even if your eating disorder isn't going to kill you, something else will. You are only gifted to the world for a finite period of time and, guys, the universe deserves to bask in your company. You have people's lives to inspire, experiences to celebrate, frogs to kiss, ice cream flavours to sample and karaoke nights to embarrass yourself at – it's a lot to fit in. Life is unpredictable. It's a terrifying truth, but it's also exciting. Live it while you can, as best you can, and don't waste it staring cluelessly at the ingredients list of cereal boxes.

9. SANDWICHES

There are so many. And they are all SO GREAT. The clean rip of an opened supermarket sandwich is a thrill that I endeavour to grant myself at least twice a week. Eating a poolside club sandwich while dollops of mayonnaise land on my sticky, sun-creamed skin is, for me, ultimate contentment. Boxing Day turkey sandwiches with a layer of sharp cranberry sauce, a cheese and ham toastie on fried bread that cracks with the first bite, leaving an itchy trail of crumbs in the crevice of my cleavage. Wraps! Pitta pockets! Burgers! Fajitas! Quesadillas! You get my point.

10. YOU SAVE £££ ON CLOTHES

As a devout clothes worshipper, I average about two sartorial purchases per week. This habit didn't disappear when I became "disordered"; in fact, it got worse. As I struggled to make sense of my new, pint-sized body, I housed it in fabrics and patterns that I thought would make my reflection more palatable. I settled into a uniform of shapeless dresses and oversized jumpers – I was the girl who was *so* into fashion, she looked like something out of a magazine. Underweight fashionista was my new tribe – so what if I had to buy another packet of safety pins or my fortieth pair of culottes...that's just what everyone does, right? Wrong. Underweight fashionista is not a tribe or an identity. It's a disorder and, in my case, a fatal illness. As soon as I was formally diagnosed I stopped buying clothes to fit my temporary body. I began to recognize the unsuitability of my beloved wardrobe as a fault with me, rather than the fault of the collection of garms that saw me through the best years of my healthy, happy life. Oddly, the new outfit high hit harder when I slotted back into my old clothes than it ever did when I ripped open the plastic of a new ASOS purchase.

It was as if I'd treated myself to an entirely new wardrobe – every item already loaded with emotional meaning. I rediscovered elasticated skirts I'd discarded when I realized I needed a waist-belt to keep them hoisted up. They looked miles better nestled on my hips as was intended without the excess material bunched around my middle. I rewore minidresses that saw me through my first and second dates with Will, and felt just as girly and giggly in them. I binned all the toddler-sized jeans and swamping jumpers that I'd come to rely upon. Shedding my anorexic armour was the first step toward committing to a new, healthy body. It seems shallow, but it's a symbolic step that's not to be sniffed at. These days I am still discovering outfits I'd pushed to the back of my wardrobe for fear of them slipping off me. I try them on and rejoice when they don't hang but fit snugly on my squeezable hips and cling to the folds under my buttocks. And that is a sentence I never, ever thought I would say...

LAURA

11. HAPPINESS

Bet you never thought this was a real, achievable thing after a troubled relationship with food, huh? Well, I'm here to tell you that it is, and I'm going to use the happiness I have felt throughout my recovery as evidence. Of course I have low days, when I feel unconfident and useless, but overall I live a contented life, which day to day is not hugely different to how I lived when I was ill – aside from the whole making myself sick and dieting to exhaustion malarkey.

I truly believe that happiness comes from having balanced mental health and accepting what you have at this moment in time – not money, boyfriends or that next promotion at work. Let me explain with a story...

I've recently started doing some PR work – the anti-diet variety, of course – for a couple of large companies. At one of these jobs, I was sitting with one of the leading directors and, toward the end of my shift, he began chatting about how he'd love to win the lottery so that he could pack it all in and focus on a work project that he was honestly passionate about.

This guy, might I add, is already extremely wealthy, with enough money to never have to work again, and yet he was still on the wheel, chasing after the next sum that would pay for his happiness.

This forced me to look at my own situation and recognize my own happiness, regardless of my financial situation. I have been able to come out of a terrible time with a mental illness. I quit my unscrupulous, mundane journalism job at a news agency to set up a blog that I was truly passionate about while not jeopardizing my morals by having to write about diet products. I am now extending these same morals into PR work.

I never do the lottery, as I never feel the need – I know, I'm that guy now. Money, I understand, makes life easier, but it has become clear to me that happiness is not something that can be bought. It begins with appreciating what you have right now, and being kind to yourself through not comparing yourself to others and by doing what feels right for you.

Staying recovered will certainly help.

12. DATING

For a long time, I believed that to be caught with a belly that slightly hangs over when you lie on your side in bed with a guy was the worst thing in the world – yep, worse than terrorism. Needless to say, if you live your life like this you can miss out on a lot of the fun that comes along with dating, or being in a relationship. I'm not saying that you need to date in order to be happy, but I am saying that when I had an eating disorder, I prevented myself from doing so, as I didn't think I was good enough to. Let me tell you that you are.

13. BODY APPRECIATION

They say that you always want what you don't have. For me, I always wanted a thigh gap and straight hair. I don't have either of those things naturally, especially not today (it's hair wash day), and I haven't died yet. There are always going to be things about yourself that you wish you could change, but you will dramatically decrease your quality of life should you live wishing you had someone else's body.

This is not to say I am anti plastic surgery or wanting to look your "best" – please, do whatever the fuck you want – but I am saying that one man's trash is another's treasure, and what you think sucks about your body someone else will wish they had.

14. NURTURING THE RELATIONSHIPS YOU THOUGHT YOU LOST

I have a wonderful friend called Lucy, who I went to college with and who witnessed the (physical) worst of my eating disorder. For years, I felt embarrassed to reconnect with her, even though we got on so well, because she was present in my life during a very negative time and I didn't want her to view me now with that imprint of me from my past. Despite this fear, I asked her to meet up with me anyway, and we now see each other weekly. She made me a birthday card thanking me for getting back in touch. She drew a cake on the front. It was fabulous.

15. PASTA

The expression "beauty comes in all shapes and sizes" is especially true when it comes to pasta. Penne, spaghetti, stuffed, rigatoni, linguine, pappardelle, fusilli – whatever your pleasure, you can for sure find it in pasta.

Imagine all the platefuls of pasta you missed out on during that carb-free phase? I can't even begin to...

16. CHEESE

(*Cries for ten minutes imagining a world without cheese.*)

17. EXERCISING FOR BANTS

Remember that episode in *Friends* where Phoebe runs like a nutter and Rachel is all embarrassed? Well, Phoebe was on to a good thing here. When I exercised during my eating disorder, it was totally joyless. I'd spend over an hour at the gym most days, then staring at my reflection in a sports bra, wondering if it was all worth it.

It wasn't.

Nowadays, you're more likely to find me in the weekly Aquafit class at my gym, flailing around in the pool with 40 middle-aged women, all shaking their bingo wings to Michael

Jackson. It's such a laugh, I love it.

18. CONFIDENCE

Confidence has always been something I've had to battle with, until recently. To avoid reading aloud in class – and therefore revealing to my peers that I was a shaking, babbling mess – I would have rather not gone to school. I grew up feeling ugly in comparison to the women I saw in magazines, and I always felt my opinions weren't worthy of being heard. Instead, I'd suppress my voice and harm my body through bulimia and too many piercings. Rattling self-doubt and youth were a dangerous combination that led to years of an eating disorder.

But fast-forward to a time when Not Plant Based exists, and although I still experience wobbles of anxiety, for the most part I am confident within the person I am today, my opinions, the work I have done, the morals I have and the choices I make. I very much have recovery to thank for that.

19. BETTER HEALTH

One great thing about recovery is that you are less likely to end up killing yourself. Sounds dramatic, yes, but let's not sugar-coat the fact that eating disorders are mental illnesses that kill people and that anorexia has the highest mortality rate of all the mental illnesses.

As a result of my bulimia, I have caused irreversible damage to my teeth, to my ears (they pop a lot inexplicably) and probably a lot more that I don't even want to think about. These things are constant reminders of the trauma I put my body through on a daily basis, but they also remind me how far I've come since, and how worse off I could have been now had I continued on that path.

20. EATING IN PUBLIC

This is a joy I couldn't live without. Right this moment, in fact, I am eating in public, something I would rarely have done throughout my eating disorder, as I would always feel as if people could tell when I was on a binge. I would feel totally embarrassed, wanting to go home and hide myself away so I could eat more in private. To me, eating in public is a statement. It's activism against eating disorders. It's letting the world know that you are allowed to eat, and that you don't give a shit what they think.

Plus, annoyingly, my family don't stock toasted teacakes at home...

21. A FUTURE

Everyone has a different vision for their future, and that is fine. Some want a family, some want 30 cats and some just want to travel around the world eating pizza. What recovery does is allow the clouds to lift, and for your ideal future to seem achievable and bright. It strengthens your body, health and mind – all needed for a future on this planet.

You only get one life (unless you believe in an afterlife) so don't let an eating disorder sap the joy from yours! You can do it; recovery is possible. Just look at us.

OUR FINAL 10 TAKEAWAY TIPS

Much like the sadness you feel when you reach the end of a good meal, when the pasta's all gone and you've licked the bowl clean, we've reached the end of our book, and it's time for us to say goodbye and to wish you all the luck in the world as you wade through the eternal amount of diet culture shit that you've recognized isn't doing your health any good. It's time to start living your lives free from guilt, free from deprivation and free from the endless quest of resisting gaining weight.

We hope you've learned that you're more than how much you weigh, and how high your follower count is. You owe it to yourself to go forward in search of happiness, and not in search of the latest fad diet.

Remember that it's never too late to get help with your relationship with food, and if this is something you're still battling with, we hope that this book has offered some respite in the meantime. We hope to be the reason you truly enjoy your next meal, and every meal after that, and we hope that you'll take these final tips and run with them speedily into the recovery you deserve.

Good luck, babes.

1. HAVE AN ATTITUDE

It's difficult functioning in a world where someone's always ready and waiting to ridicule you about what you eat, no matter what that is. You could eat steak and chips, and the vegans would pounce. Fancy just a bowl of carrot sticks and hummus one day, and you may be accused of having an eating disorder, yet eating two sandwiches in a row and you're headed for a heart attack, hun. Don't even think about eating in public if you're too fat or too thin, either! Prepare to get your photo taken secretly and uploaded to Subway Creatures Instagram if you do.

The point we are making here is that you're damned if you

do and damned if you don't. Whatever you do, and whatever you eat in this life, they're always be someone to tell you you're doing it wrong. We can't even take a shit nowadays without someone saying that if you push too hard you'll die.

So arm yourself with attitude, now you've learned how to eat everything. We've given you the science, now listen to your body and eat whatever the fuck and whenever the fuck you want from now on. You know that fruit and vegetables are important for your body. We told you that, but if one day you're really hungover and just want McDonald's, who are we to tell you no?

If anyone ever questions what you eat, politely tell them to suck a toe.

2. FUCK DIET CULTURE

This loops in with tip number one nicely. By reading this book, you will have learned that fad diets are dressed-up marketing schemes and that our quest for thinness comes from a culture in which we are taught to hate ourselves for profit. Okay. But how do you avoid all that? Especially in the age of the internet, Instagram #ads and fucking Bootea.

You unfollow. You delete everyone and everything that makes you feel like you need to diet in order to be a better person. A tidy newsfeed is a tidy mind. Read health articles with a pinch of salt, do your research and get involved with groups that make you feel like you are worthy – like the body positive movement for example.

Diet culture is always going to be around, but all we can hope is that if we treat ourselves with kindness and ignore the bullshit, our children will be able to do the same and live lives free from eating disorders.

3. SCREW THOSE WHO DON'T CARE ABOUT YOUR MENTAL HEALTH

Having an eating disorder is a sure way to realize who your real friends are. Some people that you confide in won't give a shit. Even if they have known you since birth. Honestly, it's true. But you know what? Fuck them, because there will be someone else out there who cares enough to nurture you through this rough time. It's just about finding them.

It can be very lonely when you listen to people who aren't good for your mental health, and the sooner you tell them to do one, the sooner you'll be able to get better.

4. TRY TO LOVE WHO YOU ARE RIGHT NOW

This is tough, because we too wake up some days and feel like the world is shit, everything is shit and we are shit. Try writing a book if you want to open up a world of insecurities, for example. But know that these things come in waves; today you might feel like you hate yourself, the way you look and the way you think, but tomorrow is a new day. Tomorrow you might wake up and cure cancer! Hey, you never know...

Please don't live your lives believing that if you could just lose another stone, you'll be able to taste happiness. Trust us, it doesn't work like that. You'll only want to lose another, then another, and then be miserable because your hair's falling out and your kidneys are failing. Success is not something that is earned through weight loss. Success, to us, is learning to be happy with what you have, what you've done and who you are right now.

Think of your kind heart, your quick tongue and your sass. Love your curly hair, the way your nose points a bit to the left and the narrowness of your eyes, because at the risk of sounding like your mum, these are what make you special...they're what make you you.

5. LISTEN TO SCIENCE

You know the drill by now. We're all about science here so choose to listen to experts over bloggers with no nutritional qualifications every time. But if there seems to have been a hiccup and a few false news stories fall through the net, be sure to check your sources. Is what you are reading based on a study? Who conducted the study? How many participants did the study have? Could it have any bias – for example was the person spouting the nonsense paid to do so?

The internet is a wonderful place, but it's also dangerous in that anyone can publish anything and state it as fact. If something sounds too good to be true…it probably is.

6. READ STUFF

Not just any stuff. For every post advocating the skin-saving properties of goji berries, there are articles that challenge the fat-phobic rhetoric and offer blameless solutions to problems. They are out there, it's just a case of finding them. Read books and recipes written by nutribabble-buster Ruby Tandoh, whose celebratory attitude to everything edible is delicious and infectious. The food writer Bee Wilson writes similarly thought-provoking pieces about food, food shame and the complexities of food choices. Her words are in praise of food and the eater while rejecting any rules or regulations moulded by industries to make us feel guilty or off-kilter with our bodies. The work of Linda Bacon and Lucy Aphramor on the Health At Every Size movement is a fantastic, informative tool for freeing you from body-conscious thoughts. The Angry Chef blog (as featured in this book) and Ben Goldacre's books are examples of content using evidence-based science to debunk pseudoscience in the media sphere. Botanist James Wong does a similar service in the field of plants – give him a follow on Twitter. Elsewhere, Instagram pages such as The Rooted Project (who also hold events in London) are a great, informative and balanced resource for making sense of nutrition news or information. Read feminist literature, including Germaine Greer, to understand how and why we've come to be so focused on the way we look, and learn of all the super women who dedicated their lives to women's freedom. The same goes for men too – learning the dark and oppressive root of gender roles can reduce the pressure to live up to something governed by a load of powerful people 10,000 years ago. It's totally and utterly bogus. Oh, and check out www.notplantbased.com...obviously.

7. BREATHE

Mindfulness and meditative practices can be challenging for some, given that they involve non-judgemental acceptance of all the ridiculous thoughts that chatter in your annoying head. However, if you stick with it and continue to practise, it's worth it. Trust me. Download a guided meditation app and work your way through the ten-minute sessions. If you can, carve out a portion of time each day to dedicate to mindfulness so you're not unduly distracted by bodily odour stench on a tube or the incessant ping of your emails.

If you can't get on with mindfulness meditation, at least take note of the guiding principles. At the very heart of all meditative practices, including yoga and Pilates, is an acute focus on the breath. Taking deep, measured breaths – in through the nose and out through the mouth – will deliver an extra supply of oxygen to your brain, both relaxing you and easing the emotional experience. Don't be tempted to stop after only a couple of breaths – do it for at least ten and concentrate on the sensation of your stomach filling up with air as you inhale. It's a useful way of bridging the gap between feeling sad or worried and having a full-blown panic attack. Remember, everything is going to be okay, as long as you don't forget to breathe.

8. TALK

To someone. Anyone. Over Skype, via WhatsApp or (I hate to say it) Instagram...if you must. Even if your choice of sounding board makes a wrong move or says something stupid, at least you have taken ownership and acceptance of your feelings by saying them out loud. They exist, they are real and they are worthy of attention. At other times, it might be nice to have a reminder that the world is so much more than simply what goes on in your head – and a meaningful relationship with another human is a life-affirming example of what happens when you grant yourself a break from your brain. Perhaps you can be of service to someone else by hearing their story; perhaps they also need someone to talk to, maybe they are even going through the same thing. If you are suffering with an eating disorder, UK charity Beat[1] has excellent resources, including daily phone support and online forums where you can share with others with similar experiences. The mental health charity MIND[2] offers a similar service, as does Mental Health Mates – an initiative set up by the journalist Bryony Gordon that organizes group walks for people struggling with mental health issues[3]. If you're really stuck, email us and we'll send you a card and a cupcake (or a touching email response).

9. JUMP OUT OF A PLANE

Or find an activity of a similarly risky/invigorating description. Mental health problems have a habit of restricting you to a comfortable mile radius and keeping you there. Feeling locked inside your head can create a gap between you and your external surroundings. The peaceful swooshing sound of an ocean wave or the pungent fragrance of freshly smashed basil goes largely unnoticed if all you can think about is how you can't wait to get back into bed and cry. One way of reconnecting with emotions other than sadness and anxiety is to create situations where physiology and bodily sensation take over. If you're not feeling bold enough (or rich enough) to jump out of a plane or walk on hot coals, try smaller things like going for a swim in a freezing cold swimming pool, eating really spicy food or taking a weird and wonderful dance class. Anything that takes you out of yourself and lets your body do its natural, incredible ting.

10. EAT

I know, I know, you haven't spent however much on a book for us to tell you what you already know. But stay with us...

The truth remains that in order to make peace with food, you must eat. This may be easier said than done, but we're not asking you to inhale an entire four-cheese pizza immediately. Start small, maybe with a square of chocolate. Allow it to melt on your tongue. Swallow the silken richness and revel in the feeling of pure, unadulterated pleasure. Maybe it's spreading a thin layer of butter on your toast rather than reaching for the lacklustre tub of low-fat margarine. Try taking a bite of roast chicken if you've been dodging meat, or ending a summer's day with a small scoop of gelato. Eat bread. Start with a thin slice of nutty rye bread before upgrading to crusty, warm sourdough, followed by supermarket (!) packaged bread. If the fear begins to bubble up, reread the dietary chapters of this book and be assured that nothing bad will come of it, only goodness.

In a world of nuclear weapons, endless types of cancers, food banks, race hatred and, er...Donald Trump, clutch with both hands one of the easiest, cheapest routes to momentary happiness: eating. You absolutely deserve it.

Given time, you will learn how to taste again. Meals and snacks will mostly become non-events, with the focus on a fleeting experience for your taste buds rather than how whatever you've just swallowed may present on your body. This, of course, is exactly as it should be. Any fear will expand – and even multiply – if left to fester for long enough. Eve's began as an attack on full-fat milk, then grew to encompass breakfast, and before she knew it she was terrified of pretty much any meal than wasn't a bowl of salad/apples. Our only route back to freedom and away from fear was through food – all foods. There are now no foods which we do not eat and guess what? Our predictions of world collapse and uncontrollable weight gain were wrong. So very, very wrong. What happened was an acceptance of a new, bigger body. We didn't suddenly develop a protruding gut and embark on impromptu pilgrimages to supermarkets to soothe our out-of-control desires to eat. We didn't develop type 2 diabetes, heart disease or cancer. And we didn't have constant IBS-type symptoms after eating bread – with or without gluten.

What did happen was our lives began...again. Best friends, boyfriends, families, concentration, career prospects, salaries, festivals, weddings, birthdays, beachside walks, drunk Uber rides that we can't fully remember, travelling, stimulating reads, thought-provoking podcasts, leather handbag purchases, different kinds of yoga, Twitter conversations with Nigella Lawson and Diana Henry, spa mini-breaks, the launch of a supper club initiative for people with eating disorders, a successful website, a book. Food is there too, of course, supplying the nourishment to keep our minds and bodies ticking over, allowing us to withstand all the wonderment (and sometimes shitness) that life has to offer, without us even having to think about it.

Your life needs you. Now go and live it.

ENDNOTES

DAIRY

1 https://books.google.co.uk/books?id=
   dxmNAgAAQBAJ&pg=PA142&a
   mp;lpg=PA142&dq=porridge+186
   0s&source=bl&ots=sljU9tc-
   pB&sig=qKKRtPRsZQ_DlrK_cyAfdz
   L8264&hl=en&sa=X&ved
   =0ªhUKEwiQh7-CtpbQAhWCMSYKHS_
   mBhs4ChDoAQg7MAY#v=onepage
   &q=porridge%201860s&f=false

2 http://www.healthyeating.org/Milk-Dairy/
   Health- Benefits-of- Milk/Article-Viewer/
   Article/1944/Is-Milk- Healthy-For-
   Breakfast.aspx

3 https://dairygood.org/content/2016/what-is-
   cheese?ref=www.nationaldairycouncil.org

4 https://en.wikipedia.org/wiki/Government_
   cheese

5 https://www.cancerresearchuk.org/about-
   cancer/causes-of-cancer/diet-and-cancer/
   food-controversies#food_controversies3

GLUTEN

1 https://www.statista.com/statistics/646593/
   gluten-free-food-sales-united-kingdom-uk/

2 https://www.bbc.co.uk/news/business-
   39488047

3 https://www.ncbi.nlm.nih.gov/pmc/articles/
   PMC3573730/

4 http://www.tim-spector.co.uk/wp-content/
   uploads/2016/03/Diet_Myth_press_release.
   pdf

DRINKS

1 https://www.cancer.org/latest-news/coffee-
   and-cancer-what-the-research-really-
   shows.html

2 https://www.ncbi.nlm.nih.gov/pubmed/
   19347842

3 http://www.eurekaselect.com/94052/article

4 https://www.drinkaware.co.uk/alcohol-
   facts/health-effects-of-alcohol/effects-on-
   the-body/is-alcohol-good-for-the-heart/

5 https://www.nhs.uk/news/food-and-
   diet/sip-red-wine-for-health/#what-
   interpretations-did-the-researchers-draw-
   from-these-results

6 http://www.bbc.com/future/story/
   20130920-what-causes-a-beer-belly

7 https://www.bmihealthcare.co.uk/health-
   matters/mens-health/the-science-of-the-
   beer-belly

8 http://hams.cc/mods/

9 https://www.ncbi.nlm.nih.gov/pmc/articles/
   PMC4989857/

10 https://www.ncbi.nlm.nih.gov/pmc/articles/
   PMC3888645/

11 http://psycnet.apa.org/record/2007-13443-
   001

12 http://www.maudsleyparents.org/
   whatismaudsley.html

13 https://www.ncbi.nlm.nih.gov/pmc/articles/
   PMC4870737/

14 http://www.talktofrank.com/drug/alcohol

15 https://www.drinkaware.co.uk/alcohol-
   facts/drinking-habits-and-behaviours/am-i-
   alcohol-dependent/

16 https://www.nhs.uk/live-well/alcohol-
   support/

EXERCISE

1 https://www.ncbi.nlm.nih.gov/pmc/articles/
   PMC4270305/

2 https://www.ncbi.nlm.nih.gov/
   pubmed/10735978

FRUIT AND VEGETABLES

1 https://www.bda.uk.com/foodfacts/
   FruitVeg.pdf

2 https://www.theguardian.com/society/2017/
   feb/23/five-day-10-portions-fruit-veg-cut-
   early-death

3 https://www.livescience.com/48853-
   spirulina-supplement-facts.html

SUGAR

1 http://behavioralscientist.org/no-sugar-isnt-new-heroin
2 https://www.ncbi.nlm.nih.gov/pubmed/3059850
3 https://www.researchgate.net/publication/221892901_Obesity_and_the_brain_How_convincing_is_the_addiction_model
4 https://www.ncbi.nlm.nih.gov/pmc/articles/PMC1892017/
5 https://www.ncbi.nlm.nih.gov/pmc/articles/PMC3151474/

DIETS DEBUNKED

1 http://foodnsport.com/about/
2 https://www.nhs.uk/Livewell/loseweight/Pages/the-truth-about-carbs.aspx
3 https://www.ncbi.nlm.nih.gov/pubmed/29466592
4 https://www.ncbi.nlm.nih.gov/pubmed/25614199
5 https://www.nhs.uk/news/food-and-diet/news-analysis-does-the-52-fast-diet-work/
6 https://www.ncbi.nlm.nih.gov/pubmed/23489753

FAT

1 https://www.ncbi.nlm.nih.gov/pmc/articles/PMC2386473/
2 https://www.nhs.uk/live-well/healthy-weight/
3 https://www.nhs.uk/live-well/eat-well/different-fats-nutrition/
4 https://www.bda.uk.com/foodfacts/TransFats.pdf

MIDNIGHT MUNCHIES

1 https://www.telegraph.co.uk/health-fitness/body/shouldnt-eat-late-night-according-science/
2 https://theconversation.com/health-check-food-comas-or-why-eating-sometimes-makes-you-sleepy-44355
3 https://www.mindful.org/jon-kabat-zinn-defining-mindfulness/
4 Horney, Karen: *The Neurotic Personality of Our Time*, Norton, New York, 1937

NEW FOOD RULES, ACCORDING TO THE EXPERTS

1 http://www.dailymail.co.uk/health/article-4107370/Want-lose-weight-Stop-eating-2pm-Study-shows-INCREDIBLY-early-dinner-beats-cravings-burns-fat.html
2 https://www.nhs.uk/news/food-and-diet/should-we-eat-breakfast-like-a-king-and-dinner-like-a-pauper/
3 https://www.nhs.uk/live-well/eat-well/remedies-for-bloating-and-wind/
4 https://blogs.scientificamerican.com/anthropology-in-practice/the-social-benefits-of-dinner-parties/
5 https://altarum.org/health-policy-blog/pass-the-peas-please-the-benefits-of-family-style-meals
6 https://www.sciencedirect.com/science/article/pii/S2352618115000657
7 https://www.ncbi.nlm.nih.gov/pubmed/30009930
8 https://www.ncbi.nlm.nih.gov/pubmed/14599286
9 https://www.nhs.uk/live-well/eat-well/starchy-foods-and-carbohydrates/
10 https://www.nhs.uk/live-well/eat-well/fish-and-shellfish-nutrition/
11 https://www.nhs.uk/live-well/eat-well/eggs-nutrition/

TAKEAWAYS

1 https://www.beateatingdisorders.org.uk/
2 https://www.mind.org.uk/
3 http://mentalhealthmates.co.uk/

All websites accessed on 22 November 2018

INDEX

ACKNOWLEDGMENTS

If the Not Plant Based journey has taught us anything, it's that when women help other women up, mind-blowing things start to happen. Thank goodness for our own expansive team of wonder women. Let's begin with one who believed in the "eat everything" message right from the simple days of two hundred followers – our agent, Hattie Grunewald. It's really down to you and your blind faith that any of this is a reality; thank you for never giving up, for always championing our cause and for spotting our embarrassing typos.

A huge thanks to Eleanor, Leanne, Clare, Megan, Karen and the rest of the incredible team at Octopus for making our dreams come true, and giving us the platform to elevate the issues we hold dear to the world. If one person reads this book and feels understood, supported and momentarily relaxed, our job is done. Thank you for your tireless persistence with our reams of nonsensical sentences and highly unnecessary swear words. But most of all, thank you for finding a place for this book – and the thousands of people that so desperately need it.

Thank you to all of our amazing contributors, who allowed us to pick their brains and steal their tasty recipes – Dan Doherty, Michael Zee, Nicola Millbank, Susie Orbach, Anthony Warner (the unmistakable Angry Chef), Ching He Huang, Grace Victory, Tome Levi, Hannah Lewin, Ryan Riley, Cassius Powell, The Hairy Bikers, Candice Brown, Angela Hartnett and, of course, the wonderful Ruby Tandoh. We hope we've done your work justice. For someone out there, your dish will be the first taste of freedom.

Thank you to the dietitians, doctors, psychologists and other scientists who put up with our incessant questions. Kimberley Wilson, Tome Levi, Nick Trott, Anjali Mahto, Carrie Ruxton, Frankie Phillips, Alan Levinovitz, Kirsten Crothers, Ursula Philpot, Professor Janet Treasure, Susan Hunter, Suzanne Barr, Ellen Mansfield, Oonagh Trehin, Rebecca Jennings and Renee McGregor. Renee – you are a rock, both professionally and personally.

Thank you to the awe-inspiring team at Beat for both your championing of us, and your endless dedication to the millions like us who have struggled. Eleanor O'Leary – you've always had our backs (even when we struggled to have our own) and continue to inspire us with your relentless ambition. Thanks to Alice Stanners and all the gorgeous girls at Rude Health, Catherine Humphreys at Bacchus, Holly Chapman at Papier and Shona at Space at 61, for letting us destroy her kitchen and decorate her tables with Jelly Babies. Thanks also to Kay Lockett for the cover photography.

Most of all, thank you to our army of loyal, bright and loving readers who drive us to gift you with the truthful, entertaining and anxiety-alleviating content you deserve. Without you, there would be nothing to read.

EVE'S ACKNOWLEDGMENTS

There are a number of women without whom my role in Not Plant Based would be non-existent – mainly because, let's be honest, I'd most likely be dead. Teena (why did I never learn your surname?), Kath Wetherill, Dr Steven Cooper and Charlotte Chiu – the real heroes – who dedicate their entire lives to fighting this beastly illness, giving thousands like me a second chance. It is not an exaggeration to deem your everyday efforts life-saving. Thank you for building me back up, bite by bite. Equally, Lucy Harding, Miriam Davidoff, Jess Goodwin, Lucy Wilkinson, Dee and the rest of my fellow patients – I would never have survived the most traumatic six weeks of my life without you. You were in my thoughts while writing every page of this book. I hope it brings you the comfort that you brought me in those weeks of unfathomable darkness.

Thanks to all the talented pals I've met along the way – Dave Chawner, Una Foye, Hannah Lewis, Anthony Warner, Natasha Devon and Daniella Isaacs.

Thanks for your tireless contribution to the fight – we'll get there one day, I'm sure of it.

Luci Daniels – the only medical professional to actively encourage my obsession with Haribo – for devoting her scarce and precious time to tell me her honest opinion of the low-carb/high-fat brigade. And for all the support she gave Mum when I was sick.

Thank you to the best boss I could have ever hoped for, Barney Calman, at the *Mail on Sunday*. This book would not have been possible without your compassionate support of my work and my cause. And thank you for introducing me to crisp cocktails. I learn my trade from the best in the business; and for that I am overwhelmingly privileged.

Now onto the glitterati of my mini world. Laura – WE WROTE A BOOK!!! I cannot begin to describe how grateful I am that you stumbled upon my BBC documentary and that, remarkably, I was the only "Eve Simmons" on Twitter. Thank you for putting up with my panic-stricken rants, and for being the most adoring comrade. Here's to changing the world, babes.

I cannot imagine how it must have felt to see your best friend seemingly slip away from you, but my girls faced the unimaginable with love, kindness, strength and unwavering support. Emma Powell, Hannah Ewens, Ali Laurie, Nico Stevens – my dream soul sisters. Claudia Thorne, whose vocal concerns prompted me to seek treatment. Let hers be a lesson – if you're worried about someone, tell them.

And to Anastasia Antoni and Grace Gabriel Stogdon – my best friends, who held my shaky hand on the day of my diagnosis, and still haven't let go.

My Sam Sam – thank you for sharing 99 per cent of my childhood meals with me, most of which involved me crying with laughter and you stealing my potatoes.

Thank you to the world's best dad who, despite his absence, was more present than ever at the time of writing this book – and beyond.

Behind every successful woman is another, similar-looking woman teaching her to chant the phrase, "I am a strong woman", before she is old enough to walk. Or is that just me? Thank you to the ultimate supermum, who is responsible for most of my endeavours. She bestowed me with confidence, motivation and self-belief that have propelled me to follow my dreams. And no, you wouldn't have done a better job if Dad were around. You have been, and always are, perfect.

Lastly, thank you to my soulmate, William Grice, who ate opposite me before, during and after, and never once left the table. And to all the wonderful boyfriends, girlfriends, partners, parents and best friends out there who continue to love us, regardless of what we do, or don't, eat.

LAURA'S ACKNOWLEDGMENTS

Firstly, I would like to thank my parents for being endlessly supportive, despite not really understanding how blogging works. Eating disorders are a difficult thing to understand for anyone who has never experienced one, and it's especially difficult to watch helplessly as your child goes through something so awful when you don't know what you can do to help. I'm incredibly grateful for their unwillingness to give up trying to protect their daughter, and to love her regardless.

Thank you to my partner Jed who has made me realize that the world isn't entirely awful. He has given me the confidence to enjoy my book's success, rather than focus on those everyday anxieties that are normally so overwhelming to me. Thank you for not judging me when I eat cold leftover Chinese for breakfast and for being supportive of my career, and of me, always. Thank you also to Jed's parents, who for some strange reason seem to be my biggest fans. They have always been so welcoming of me and are greatly interested in all my successes, so much so that they've hinted at buying their poor other son this book as his birthday present, which unfortunately for him falls on our publication date (get those sales numbers up!).

Although I've lost touch with lots of friends throughout the years, due to a number of different reasons, there are a few I want to thank for sticking around: Lucy Coldicott, Eilidh Houghton, Grace Strong, Natalie Kelleher, Amie Squire, Louise Jackson and Scarlett Kefford. Thank you for always having my back, even when I'm being an annoying little shit.

Thank you to Eve, who believed in the Not Plant Based idea when I approached her with it, even if I couldn't. Thank you for working tirelessly on a project because you knew how many people it could help and thank you for joining me in the daily meltdowns and weekly highs – I couldn't have done it without you.

Thank you to the Dawsons, who are legends by default because they are related to me, but also thank you for housing me when I first moved to London and got a scary corporate job. I'm really pleased we are now all so close and I look forward to our dinner parties together.

I would like to thank the teachers throughout my educational life who noticed my creativity and who encouraged me, despite my reserved nature. Thank you to the tutors in college who noticed that I was ill, and didn't blame me for flunking my usually high grades. Thank you to the tutor who even shipped me off to the doctor immediately when I told her I was struggling. Thank you to the girls in college who have contacted me since seeing my blog and related to my story, even though we didn't really talk back then, you have made me feel normal. Thank you also to Fiona Webster, who got me through my journalism diploma and who has been supportive of my career ever since.

Thank you to Monica Brown, who gave me my first journalistic internship, and who has been a mentor to me both in my personal and professional life. She made me feel like I had a voice that was worth sharing, and had all the time in the world for me when I was unsure about which direction I wanted to go in with my life. She is the reason I became a journalist.

Lastly, I'd like to thank that editor at my first paid journalistic job, who was totally unaccommodating of the blog Not Plant Based in the early stages. He thought it would become a "real problem". These words gave me the drive to carry on regardless and are in part be why this book exists.